MW00669257

PIVOT

PIVOT

*How Top Entrepreneurs Adapt
and Change Course to
Find Ultimate Success*

REMY ARTEAGA AND
JOANNE HYLAND

(With academic perspectives by
Dr. Gina O'Connor and
Dr. Lois Peters)

WILEY

Cover Design: Paul McCarthy
Cover Image: ©Getty Images / Paul Taylor

Copyright © 2014 by Remy Arteaga and Joanne Hyland. All rights reserved.

Published by John Wiley & Sons, Inc., Hoboken, New Jersey.

Published simultaneously in Canada.

No part of this publication may be reproduced, stored in a retrieval system, or transmitted in any form or by any means, electronic, mechanical, photocopying, recording, scanning, or otherwise, except as permitted under Section 107 or 108 of the 1976 United States Copyright Act, without either the prior written permission of the Publisher, or authorization through payment of the appropriate per-copy fee to the Copyright Clearance Center, Inc., 222 Rosewood Drive, Danvers, MA 01923, (978) 750-8400, fax (978) 646-8600, or on the Web at www.copyright.com. Requests to the Publisher for permission should be addressed to the Permissions Department, John Wiley & Sons, Inc., 111 River Street, Hoboken, NJ 07030, (201) 748-6011, fax (201) 748-6008, or online at http://www.wiley.com/go/permissions.

Limit of Liability/Disclaimer of Warranty: While the publisher and author have used their best efforts in preparing this book, they make no representations or warranties with respect to the accuracy or completeness of the contents of this book and specifically disclaim any implied warranties of merchantability or fitness for a particular purpose. No warranty may be created or extended by sales representatives or written sales materials. The advice and strategies contained herein may not be suitable for your situation. You should consult with a professional where appropriate. Neither the publisher nor author shall be liable for any loss of profit or any other commercial damages, including but not limited to special, incidental, consequential, or other damages.

For general information on our other products and services or for technical support, please contact our Customer Care Department within the United States at (800) 762-2974, outside the United States at (317) 572-3993 or fax (317) 572-4002.

Wiley publishes in a variety of print and electronic formats and by print-on-demand. Some material included with standard print versions of this book may not be included in e-books or in print-on-demand. If this book refers to media such as a CD or DVD that is not included in the version you purchased, you may download this material at http://booksupport.wiley.com. For more information about Wiley products, visit www.wiley.com.

Library of Congress Cataloging-in-Publication Data:
Arteaga, Remy, 1962-
  Pivot : how top entrepreneurs adapt and change course to find ultimate success / Remy Arteaga and Joanne Hyland.
       pages cm
  Includes bibliographical references and index.
  ISBN 978-1-118-55971-0 (cloth); ISBN 978-1-118-55997-0 (ebk);
ISBN 978-1-118-55984-0 (ebk)
  1. New products. 2. New business enterprises. 3. Creative ability in business. 4. Entrepreneurship. I. Hyland, Joanne, 1960- II. Title.
    HF5415.153.A77 2014
    658.4′063–dc23

                                                                2013020676

Printed in the United States of America

10 9 8 7 6 5 4 3 2 1

To all of those who have shared my dream of making a difference in our companies and the world, this book is for you—our collective wisdom of what innovation is and will be. I could not have written it without all the valuable learning experiences we have shared together for over 30 years. You are not just colleagues but friends, and I thank you. This book is also for Monique, my partner in business and in life, and Tara, our very much loved dog whom we almost lost in the final days of writing this book. Their love and support throughout the process have been unconditional; and, of course, I cannot forget Nikita, seizing every opportunity to be the center of attention. And for Dad, whom we did lose on July 31st, 2013. You are far better off where you are now. I know how proud you would have been to see the final product.

Joanne Hyland

To my beautiful wife, Barbi Bistrowitz, you inspire me every day with your smarts, and you have partnered with me on so many startups—this book could not have been written without your love and support. This book is also for my mom, Hilda, who instilled the entrepreneurship bug in me with crackers and cheese. I don't think I could have gotten through this book, much less this life, without my pets past and present; you will always have a space in my heart and mind. Not to be forgotten, to my dad, Pepe—this one's for you.

Remy Arteaga

CONTENTS

PART II PLANT = DISCOVERY—THE BUSINESS VISION   77

LIST OF TRADEMARKS

1. Facebook® is a registered trademark of Facebook, Inc.
2. Big XYZ™ is a trademark of Bisart LLC.
3. Learning Plan™ is a trademark of rInnovation Group.
4. The Pivot Startup™ is a trademark of Bisart LLC.
5. Bill Me Later® is a registered trademark of Bill Me Later Inc.
6. Gorilla® glass is a registered trademark of Corning Inc.
7. Lotus™ glass is a trademark of Corning Inc.
8. MotionSense® is a registered trademark of Moen Incorporated.
9. Swiffer® is a registered trademark of Procter & Gamble.
10. NetActive® is a registered trademark of NetActive Inc.
11. Genesis Pad™ is a trademark of Innovation Genesis LLC.
12. SIGMA WATERHEATER™ is a trademark of Grundfos.
13. PayWithMe™ is a trademark of PayWithMe LLC.
14. Trade Shades™ is a trademark of Cory Goodenough and Jonny Rio.
15. Stage-Gate® is a registered trademark of the Product Development Institute.
16. Google Trends™ is a trademark of Google, Inc.
17. MySpace™ is a trademark of Myspace LLC.
18. Friendster® is a registered trademark of Friendster, Inc.

ACKNOWLEDGMENTS

We would first like to acknowledge our academic contributing authors, Professors Gina O'Connor and Lois Peters, for their exceptional insights and commentaries in Chapters 5, 8, 13, and 16. We also appreciate their excellent feedback for guiding us in how to make each chapter clearer, more consistent, and have the right type of impact.

This book would not have been possible without the Rensselaer Polytechnic Institute (RPI) team's academic research and the two foundational books: *Radical Innovation: How Mature Companies Can Outsmart Upstarts* (Harvard Business School Press, 2000) and *Grabbing Lightning: Building a Capability for Breakthrough Innovation* (Jossey-Bass, 2008). These books provide the principles and inspiration for the Discovery, Incubation, and Acceleration (D-I-A) model being put into practice through our teaching, training, coaching, and consulting activities. Dr. Mark Rice has also been a source of inspiration from the beginning, starting at RPI, and then in collaboration with Babson College, while he was dean of the Business School.

We are similarly indebted to Jake Schonberger, Kyle Brody, Cory Goodenough, Jonny Rio, and Chase Darlington for letting us share their journeys through the startup process. The Pivot Startup methodology molds together ideas born of experience and research. The seed was first planted at General Motors, where a rising executive, Tim Costello, took the risk of recruiting a very brash young engineer, Remy, into the Methods team. Tim's insights on new product development and the results from the Methods team served as one of the inspirations for The Pivot Startup. Jacob Brix, a doctoral student from Denmark, also assisted with his keen insights on knowledge construction and innovation.

Special thanks to Jeff Hovis of Product Genesis. He contributed tools to make the Discovery and Incubation Toolkits even more robust. We have had a wonderful partnership over the years, become friends, and I (Joanne) look forward to many years to come. Over the past few years, we have developed another great partnership with the International Society for Professional Innovation Management (ISPIM), offering a good blend of academic theory with the practice, and a vehicle for getting the word out. Thank you, Iain and the rest of the ISPIM team, for sharing our passion about innovation.

For their direct contributions to this book, I would like to thank all my corporate colleagues and friends from Grundfos (Lars Spicker Olesen, Soren Bro, Jesper Ravn Lorenzen, Jesper Bagge Pedersen while at the Danish Technical University, Steve Pierson, and Arun Ramasamy); from Moen (Louise Quigley and Mike Pickett); and from NOVA Chemicals (Alan Schrob). As much as you have learned from us, we have learned from you.

Denmark became our incubator of sorts for progressing our thinking and tools. I would like to thank Hanne Arildsen for taking a chance in our early days and bringing our company and D-I-A model to Denmark while she worked at Danfoss, and I thank Stig Poulsen for carrying on the torch. Hanne and I met while I was teaching a segment on corporate venturing at MIT, thanks to Ken Morse. I extend thanks to Thomas Schafer and Rasmus von Gottberg (we also met at MIT) from Novozymes for seizing upon the importance of uncertainty reduction in new business development, and many others who made it work—Karolina, Helle, Marianne, Kristoffer, and Henriette, to name a few. Peter Bruun, Jacob Holst, and Peter Skat-Rordam at the Danish Technical University also believed in our model for new business creation, which we continue to teach today. We have worked together to evolve it to a world-class certificate program in entrepreneurial leadership. Lars Ib, at the Danish Business Institute, is also a believer and has made it an important module in his MBA curriculum. I thank Mads Prebensen for introducing me to Lars and bringing us to Grundfos. Henning Sandager, Thorbjorn Machholm, and Fei Chen (we met at Novozymes initially) have also played a key role in embedding the D-I-A mind-set in Grundfos through the leadership they provide. I also want to thank Allan Silfverberg and Martin Groth for being eager to learn and contribute great insights to our business based on their master's thesis. With these believers and our teaching at the Danish Technical University and the Business Institute, I am delighted we have had the opportunity to have such a great impact in a highly innovative country. There are many others, and you are in my thoughts.

It goes without saying that I have worked with a number of great companies in the United States and Canada in addition to Moen and NOVA Chemicals, such as Westinghouse with Joanna, Kate, Tom, Cenk, and John; Air Products with Ron, Martha, and Nancy; Kennametal with George; and Hewlett-Packard (HP) with Rich, to name a few. Each of you has added new dimensions to our thinking and twists on the D-I-A model. Finally, I would not even be writing this book without my Nortel Networks Corporation experiences. I want to thank my Business Ventures Group team and other colleagues who were a part of this venturing experiment. You were all important contributors to our success. I want to particularly thank Rene, Susan, and Garth for all you did to guide me in the years we were getting started; Jeff for our great partnership; and Pat for making us all more effective communicators. It was just not the right place and time for us to continue.

In 2001, if you had asked what we thought about systematizing what we do in an innovation tool platform, Gina and I would have said, no way. Well, here we are in 2013 doing it. Of course, we still have a few lingering questions and we are likely not completely there yet, but isn't that what learning is all about? So thank you all (those mentioned and in my thoughts) for being a part of the journey so far, and we hope you continue on this path with us.

I (Remy) am grateful to my students at RPI for having given me more than I ever gave them. Their enthusiasm, optimism, and intelligence energized me. I love them all and wish them only the very best as the move on to their careers. Some of the students at RPI took it upon themselves to challenge my thinking on entrepreneurship, including Arthur Ford, Ben Prager, Cory Goodenough, and Logan Shire. A special thank-you goes out to Sam Hagen of UpSmart.com for sitting through many meetings discussing startup methodologies. My time at RPI, as Entrepreneur in Residence and Program Director of the Severino Center for Technological Entrepreneurship, led to many of the insights in the book. The daily mentoring of university startups gave me the opportunity to observe the startup process over and over again. I am of course indebted to Dr. Gina O'Connor and Dr. Lois Peters for their guidance, mentoring, and support. They went from being my professors to becoming my friends—priceless.

The following experiences, in addition to many I could not fit here, helped form the tapestry of ideas in the book. First is my time as founder and COO at Extreme Interactive Media Inc.—my second startup. It was driven with a gunslinging approach to entrepreneurship, and due to extraordinary selflessness on the part of Al Isaacs, Barbi Bistrowitz, and "Freakboy" John Brodigan, we were able to successfully exit. Next, I had the chance to mentor some wonderful startups over the years, including PayWithMe, Vitalvio.com, Vulcan Technologies, Green Energy Efficiency Solutions (GEES), VirtuallyShow.com, and Synderela.com. Synderela LLC sticks in my mind, as it was the first fashion startup I ever mentored. The women at the startup, Nicole Petito, Susan Dimeo, and Yalenis Cepeda, spent countless of hours discussing ideas with me, and for that I am very grateful. Finally, my time as CEO of DualAlign.com taught me so many lessons about what to do and not to do with a startup. I am thankful to all the members of DualAlign LLC for their support and encouragement over the years.

INTRODUCTION: IS THERE A BETTER WAY?

It was Friday morning, July 20, 2012, when Remigio Arteaga (Remy, as he is known to his friends) and Joanne Hyland were meeting in Troy, New York, to discuss their new cloud innovation platforms. As the meeting entered its fourth hour, Remy began to think back to his third startup, Ironsilk—a web platform that enabled the delivery of premium content to members. It was launched in 2001, a year after Remy's second startup was acquired. Remy thought back to how excited he was then. Like so many startups, Ironsilk started with a detailed business plan covering everything from business model to five-year financial projections. Remy spent considerable time working on Ironsilk's business plan. Today, premium content can be found everywhere, but at the time it was an unproven business model. In fact, the debate on whether to restrict content to registered members was still a few years away.

Remy's idea was to have Ironsilk deliver premium content from video game websites to fans of such websites. In return for viewing free premium content, fans would opt in to receive third-party e-mail advertisements. By opting in for e-mail advertisements, fans' e-mails became a valuable asset that was then shared with third-party advertisers for a fee. This fee was then split between Ironsilk and the video game website owners. With the success of his previous venture and a strong business plan at his back, Remy put pedal to the metal and quickly developed and launched Ironsilk. Ironsilk grew quickly and in the first six months had roughly 500,000 members. You might think that this is the story of another great success—but not quite. There were a couple of key assumptions that Remy baked into the startup. One was the rate that advertisers were willing to pay. Another was the amount of work needed to manage the video game owners. Both assumptions proved to be wrong, and Ironsilk was closed within the year. Its demise could have been prevented, Remy thought.

At the same time, Joanne was finding it hard to concentrate. Earlier that day she had read an article about her former employer, Nortel Networks Corporation. The article was about the fall of the once multibillion-dollar multinational telecommunications firm. In 1996, prior to founding the rInnovation Group, a well-respected innovation-consulting firm, Joanne was the director, and eventually vice president, of the Business Ventures Group (BVG) within Nortel. Like so many internal venturing groups, BVG's mission was launched with good intentions. It was supposed to make a giant company like Nortel nimble and quick, so that it could compete with all those Internet startups. BVG had many of the same enlightened elements that you see in today's corporate venture groups, including an advisory board made up of internal executives, a structure that allowed for spin-outs and spin-ins, business assistance, access to equipment and office space, and financing. It even had incubator space separate from Nortel's space.

Not surprisingly, BVG began to struggle. It was very clear to Joanne early on that there were different expectations among Nortel's stakeholders about the alignment of investments with current versus future strategy, the right balance between spin-ins and spin-outs, the role of the advisory board, the time and investment required for market creation, when was the right time to spin out a venture and bring in venture capital, the requirement for more strategic skill sets to deal with the uncertainty and complexity, the need for streamlined processes, and so forth, although Joanne lacked the experience to describe them as clearly as she could today. On top of that, her team was working to establish a complete management system for innovation to overcome the management challenges, but mergers and acquisitions (M&A) activities started to take precedence over what had been Nortel's strong research and development (R&D) heritage, with its ability to leapfrog generations of technology. Joanne wondered where Nortel might be today if a different path had been chosen. In Chapter 2, she will elaborate upon her story of Nortel and this leading-edge approach to innovation.

INSPIRATION FOR THE BOOK

I (Remy) love startups. Some may think the word *love* is too strong, but if people can love their cars, then I can love startups. The process of starting with nothing and ending with a Google is nothing short of remarkable to almost everyone, including me. People find the stories of Apple, Google, Instagram, and Groupon inspirational. The triumph of determination, intellect, and hard work against insurmountable odds is part of the human DNA. How else did we make it from cave dwellers to space travelers, if not for our intellect and determination? It turns out there was another aspect of humanity that helped our earlier versions progress—creativity. Not the modern use of the word, the historical use. Historians are quick to point out that the result of creativity is tools. Humans are the only species on earth that use their creativity to improve and enlarge their tools. We don't need to limit tools to handheld objects; they can include things like writing and reading. The key point is that as humans we build upon the work of others. We refine, enlarge, and combine tools to make new tools. We learn from the past to improve the present. We take this notion for granted. Yet, when it comes to startups, entrepreneurs and their advisers seem to be constantly working on re-creating the wheel. They treat startups more like an art project then a business endeavor. They view the entrepreneur as an artist who is there to produce the next *Mona Lisa,* or in the case of startups, the next Facebook.

It was this type of thinking that started me down the road that eventually led to this book, because I knew that startups could and should be managed. In fact, I had even developed startup management methods to assist the entrepreneur in launching and managing a startup. Developing methods and processes is in my blood. My first job after graduating from college was at General Motors (GM). My job at GM was to develop new product development methods based on the latest research and best practices. To do this I had to synthesize information, detect subtle patterns, and connect the dots. This came naturally to me and I thoroughly enjoyed my job. Since then, I have been on a path to do the same thing with startup management. It took time—nearly two decades of being an entrepreneur, being around entrepreneurs, studying entrepreneurs, and studying innovation—for the stars to align. When I was presented with the opportunity to write the book, I immediately contacted Dr. Gina O'Connor about contributing to the book because of her outstanding research in studying corporate entrepreneurs. She suggested that I coauthor the book with Joanne, who is a world-class innovation consultant, and I agreed. Joanne has spent about as much time studying and working with corporate startups as I have spent working with startups, and our two methodologies are based on the same type of thinking.

The inspiration for this book comes down to our desire to change the way startups are managed, from a "go with your gut" approach to a more methods-based approach of managing the uncertainties that every startup faces.

HOW WE GOT HERE

Joanne and I met in 2004 at Rensselaer Polytechnic Institute (RPI), when Joanne was a guest lecturer at my MBA innovation class. I approached her after the class and asked her what it would take to launch a consulting business. I was passionate about how innovation methods could be applied to startups. I knew from firsthand experience that traditional management methods did not work.

As I mentioned earlier, my first experience with innovation came at GM, of all places. It was my first job after graduating with an electrical engineering degree from the University of Rochester. I was selected to be part of an internal group that served as a quasi think tank or consulting group for a division of GM. The mission of our group was to change the way GM did business—quite a lofty mission for a group of very young engineers (the oldest at the time this group launched was 26). But I was young and did not understand how big a mountain we had to climb. My job was to develop new product development methods based on customer needs and competitive analysis. This was the mid-1980s, well before books on competitive analysis, Quality Function Deployment (QFD), or six sigma became commonplace. There I was meeting with experienced engineers and scientists, telling them that their approach to new product development was wrong. Needless to say, they did not welcome me with open arms. Over time, though, many groups began to implement these new methods; unfortunately, most groups did not, and by now we all know what happened to GM.

I could see even then that applying traditional management techniques to the development of truly different new products did not work. Unknowingly, our group developed methods that had learning built into them. The discovery methods that we developed had many of the elements that author Frans Johansson wrote about in *The Medici Effect*,[1] a book on how people develop ideas. After GM, I went on to launch or be the CEO of seven startups. It was during this time that I came to appreciate fully the fact that traditional management techniques should not be applied to startups. I realized that the myths perpetuated by the media, of entrepreneurs succeeding because of natural-born talent, persistence, and sheer will were just that—myths. We've all heard these myths and we want to believe them, because they are great stories. The stories of Steve Jobs, Bill Gates, or Mark Zuckerberg all making it big on one idea and their gut instincts make us all believe that if we can just come up with that one idea we too can create the next Facebook. But reality is more complicated than that.

Over the past couple of years, I have worked as an entrepreneur in residence and program director of the Entrepreneurship Center at

RPI. During this time I have mentored more than 100 student and faculty startup teams. I have seen how strong the desire to put the pedal to metal is. Eric Reis in his book *The Lean Startup*[2] writes about how entrepreneurs are taught to just do it. I couldn't agree more. In my career, I have had that same desire to just build it. Ironsilk was a classic case of moving too quickly, of being too focused and of executing too well. Focus on executing a plan gets rewarded in mature firms like GE and IBM, but will kill most startups. Why? The answer is that most entrepreneurs are focused on the wrong things. Instead of focusing on testing the underlying assumptions that their startup is based on, they are focused on executing business plans that are filled with untested assumptions. In my experience, I find that entrepreneurs do this in an attempt to fit traditional management techniques to a startup environment. I too have found myself following the advice of seasoned corporate executives who never launched a successful startup in their lives. These well-meaning corporate advisers attempt to mold the startup in the image of their corporate experience, only to find that it doesn't work. The famed psychologist Abraham Maslow once wrote, "If you only have a hammer, you tend to see every problem as a nail."[3] To these well-meaning advisers, a traditional management technique is their hammer. They are unaware that focus and execution on a plan are great for a mature business with little uncertainty, but fail miserably in an uncertain environment. Later in this book we will discuss how every startup is faced with numerous uncertainties based on assumptions. We will delve into how to identify these uncertainties and ultimately how to reduce the level of uncertainty surrounding your new venture.

Let's revisit the Ironsilk story. After 18 months of working around the clock, I learned that advertisers were willing to pay less than I expected and that Ironsilk's partners took up more face-to-face time than I expected. Naturally, I wanted to modify Ironsilk (i.e., pivot). Unfortunately, by this time we had exhausted all our funds and patience. I had failed. I remember asking my wife and partner, Barbi, if we could have figured this out sooner. At the time I wasn't sure. I was a few years away from putting the pieces together. I sometimes forget my successes, but I never forget a failure. I never forgot

Ironsilk. I promised myself that I would never put myself in that position again, so, with my wife's blessing, I went back to school to get my MBA. It was at RPI that I met Dr. Gina O'Connor, who is now the associate dean of the MBA program at RPI, and Dr. Lois Peters, an associate professor at RPI. During one of their first joint lectures on breakthrough innovation, a lightbulb went off in my head. During this lecture, everything seemed to connect—my experience at GM, my startup experience, and innovation theory. It all made sense, and I knew my future lay in adapting innovation concepts to startup management. I have spent the past eight years doing just that and in the process developed an approach to entrepreneurship.

What follows is Joanne's road to this point.

I (Joanne) have always been a fairly independent thinker and driven by what is new or different as well as representing the underdog. Even on my first day of school, I wanted to take the bus and meet my mother there, a good example of this early independence. In my formative years, I was very involved in sports as a player, as a referee or umpire, and as a coach. I believe these roles provided me with the skills to assess what is fair, encourage the development of teams, and become an inspiring leader. It wasn't always easy being independent since I did not fit in easily to any group, especially during those challenging years of high school. At the time, I experimented in many ways to test the limits of what was possible. However, this helped me to build more emotional intelligence and develop increasing sensitivity to the resource and organization issues dominant in more established companies. Once I embarked on my career, I went from one series of firsts to another—from introducing a new calling card format in response to unprecedented long distance fraud, leading a team of close to a thousand people across Canada to introduce a new signaling technology and database for 800 service, negotiating and being the marketing chair of a multilateral international alliance for the financial industry, bringing the Netscape business opportunity to Canada through our membership in Bellcore, building the internal venturing program at Nortel, and so forth. Of course, I did not do this on my own and it was only made possible by all the talented people I worked with.

Based on my 18 years in industry, combined with my personal ambitions to make a difference in this world, I embraced the RPI model for innovation because I saw it as the right path forward for companies. The road has not been easy, because change in companies takes time and is fraught with organizational resistance, especially considering that while we have come a long way in what we have learned about how to build a systematic capability for innovation, we still have further to go. In my time working with companies and teaching today, I am firmly convinced that we have cracked the code or the principles for how to make innovation work as the basis for propelling companies into the future and as a key source of country competitiveness. When I left for Nortel in 1996, my New Business Opportunities team gave me a plaque (still in my office today) that says, *"Excellence can be attained if you . . . Care more than others think is wise, Risk more than others think is safe, Dream more than others think is practical, and Expect more than others think is possible."* For me, this is what innovation is all about, and it requires courage. It is accomplished through passionate people, within the right culture and support structure that enables them to conceive of opportunities, experiment with them in the market to reduce uncertainty, and then proceed to the commercialization process.

THE BOOK IS NOT . . .

I (Remy) often get asked if I've ever read *The Lean Startup* by Eric Reis. The answer is yes. In fact it was one of the two required texts for one of my startup classes, the other being the *Steve Jobs* biography by Walter Isaacson.[4] Bear with me as I delve into some business-speak here, as it is needed to fully understand how this book differs from Eric's book.

There are decades of books and academic research on innovation. You might think after all these years that people would have a clear definition for innovation, and you would be wrong. One only needs to Google the phrase "what is innovation" to see how many definitions there are. However, there does appear to be a general consensus that innovation is not an invention or idea (see the first sidebar, "What Is Innovation?"). In order for an invention or idea to be of value, it must move through the innovation process and be commercialized. I use the word *commercialized* in the broadest sense to mean that an idea or invention has been transformed into some product, process, or service that people are using. Creating a prototype is also not enough since it is not in commercial use. Joanne and our academic contributors view innovation as an emerging discipline in more established companies with an enabling process, and not as an outcome. If you think of innovation as a discipline, then the failure to commercialize doesn't mean innovation hasn't occurred. I agree; however, I want to emphasize that for the startup, the startup process is the innovation process. It evolves to a discipline only once it becomes a systematic capability in the startup ecosystem. This takes us away from innovation as an outcome and suggests that we need to think about the future of innovation as a discipline in the startup world as well.

WHAT IS INNOVATION?

What is innovation? Former Prime Minister Tony Blair defined innovation as the exploitation of new ideas.[5] Yet other definitions exist, including "development of new customers' value through solutions"[6] and the commercializing of an invention or idea. In 1998 Brian Cumming, a supervisor at the Ford Motor Company, wrote an insightful article on innovation that appeared in the *European Journal of Innovation Management*.[7] He reviewed close to 30 years of innovation definitions, and came up with this one: "the first successful application of a product or process." Upon closer examination, all of these definitions can be filtered into two parts. Part A is the invention, idea, or concept. Part B is the implementation, commercialization, or value addition. From a business perspective there is another part that must be considered when analyzing innovation, and that is the management process. Innovation can be viewed as sitting atop a three-legged table. One leg is the invention, the second leg is commercialization, and the third leg is the innovation management process. Take away any one of those legs, and your ability to innovate is greatly hindered.

If innovation can be so easily defined, then why is there "a plethora of definitions for innovation types"?[8] In some cases it has to do with not understanding that innovation is made up of the three parts just mentioned, which leads some scholars to confuse an innovation with an invention. But another more plausible reason is that invention and commercialization are multidimensional, and this leads to many ways to invent and commercialize a product, process, or service. Each of these ways can lead to a different classification of innovation. In a paper that analyzed radical innovation, the author wrote that "there has . . . emerged a problem. In the literature there are varying definitions . . . to the range of innovation types. In some of the literature the denominations have been mainly the same but with different definitions. In other literature the definitions have been roughly the same but with different denominations. This has been confusing to many academics."[9]

With so many varying definitions, it is no wonder that so few firms truly understand what is meant by innovation. Even fewer firms can articulate the difference between different types of innovation like breakthrough and disruptive innovation. Can a breakthrough innovation be a disruptive innovation? Does it matter? Yes, if your company aims to build up a capability in innovation. You need to understand where an innovation type fits on the continuum of uncertainty and focus on the Pivot or Incubation as the missing link.

Another area that has gotten a great deal of attention is the type of innovation. One will often hear terms like disruptive, discontinuous, breakthrough, game-changing, radical, evolutionary, incremental, and more in any innovation discussion. We believe that innovation lies on a continuum from incremental (small changes) to break-through (very large changes).

This book does not deal with incremental changes. In the corporate environment, incremental changes are handled by traditional management techniques such as a phase gate process. In the noncorporate environment, small business owners who open up a restaurant or store handle incremental changes. As an innovation becomes more of a breakthrough, the level of uncertainty dramatically increases. One can tell when the level of uncertainty is high by the number of assumptions that the new business plan is based on. For example, opening up a State Farm insurance office has some degree of uncertainty centered mainly on the organization and market, but such a level is nothing when compared to what the entrepreneur deals with. In addition to technical uncertainty, the entrepreneur deals with organization, market, and resource uncertainties. The goal, then, for any entrepreneurship method is to help the entrepreneur manage and reduce the uncertainties.

There also appears to be a general consensus by innovation specialists that there are phases that ideas and inventions go through to be transformed into a product, service, or solution. We believe those phases to be Discovery, Incubation, and Acceleration, or, as featured in this book, Plant, Pivot, and Propel. These three phases make up the innovation process and discipline described in Chapter 2. Plant is where ideas come to light and a business vision is seeded. It is the phase where the entrepreneur or corporate entrepreneur decides on what business opportunity he or she will proceed with (see the second sidebar, on nonprofits and social ventures). Notice that we use the word *business*, not *product*. Unlike the inventor, the entrepreneur is concerned with innovating, which means that entrepreneur is concerned with developing a business. The same holds true for the corporate entrepreneur, yet within the company. Therefore, before moving on to the Pivot or Incubation phase, both entrepreneur types must have a business or opportunity concept. It is during the Pivot phase that the entrepreneur begins to incubate the concept by going through a validated learning process that reduces the uncertainty.

xxx INTRODUCTION: IS THERE A BETTER WAY?

SOCIAL STARTUPS AND NONPROFITS

We are often asked if our methods apply to social startups and nonprofits. The answer is an overwhelming yes. Before I explain why, I would like to define how I use the term *social startups*, as I have seen many valid definitions that vary somewhat from the one we use here. A social startup is a new business that is designed to achieve a good for society while obtaining modest profits and maximizing good. The biggest difference between a social startup and the standard business venture is that the social startup is driven by a social outcome like reducing poverty, while the business venture is driven by profits. However, unlike a nonprofit organization, a social startup must be sustainable on its own revenues, whereas nonprofits can achieve sustainability through revenues and donations or grants. In other words, the social startup needs to make a profit, but instead of distributing the profits to its members or shareholders, the profits get reinvested in the startup for the purpose of maximizing good. A nonprofit, in contrast, is dependent on donations or grants and does not need to make a profit. In either case, both social startups and nonprofits experience the same types of uncertainties as a standard business venture, including technical, market, resource, and organization uncertainties.

Now back to *The Lean Startup*. We believe that *The Lean Startup* deals primarily with Incubation, while this book deals with all three phases. Also, *The Lean Startup* appears to us to deal mainly with lower levels of uncertainty and not with breakthrough-type innovations. In fact, applying any type of lean methodology to breakthrough innovations will most certainly result in failure. We do owe Eric Reis our thanks for spreading the concept of validated learning to such a wide audience. Eric, along with others, is part of a movement that has been dissatisfied with the "pedal to the metal" approach to entrepreneurship. This movement recognizes that learning methodologies have a real-world impact on the probability of success. Joanne Hyland,

Dr. Gina O'Connor, and Dr. Lois Peters have been preaching the value of validated learning since 2001. According to the book *Technology Ventures*,[10] the concepts of validated learning date back to the early 1980s, when Tom Peters and Robert Waterman wrote about "Ready, Fire, Aim" in their best-selling book *In Search of Excellence*.[11] In *Technology Ventures* the authors put forth their own validated learning model of Act—Review and learn—Fix and adjust. In a 1995 paper entitled "Critical Assumption Planning,"[12] Sykes and Dunham wrote, "Corporate managers of existing businesses are judged against meeting plan. In growing new businesses, however, strict adherence to 'the plan' can lead to business failure. To manage business development risk, venture managers must learn to deal with uncertainty. Whereas managers of mature businesses practice the ethic of predictability, venture managers must follow a learning ethic." Sykes and Dunham were right on target!

HOW THE BOOK IS ORGANIZED

The book is organized into chapters that cover individual startups and corporate startups separately. While there is certainly agreement on the management concepts between the individual entrepreneur and the corporate entrepreneur, each has enough of its own challenges and methodologies that we felt it was important to deliver separate chapters focused on each.

The book is divided into four parts: Part One, "The Tale of Two Entrepreneurial Worlds"; Part Two, "Plant = Discovery—The Business Vision"; Part Three, "Pivot = Incubation—The Missing Link"; and Part Four, "Propel = Acceleration—The Business Ramp-Up."

"The Tale of Two Entrepreneurial Worlds" covers the foundational concepts of the book. This part makes the case for why traditional management techniques fail in a startup environment. It covers fundamental concepts like innovation, uncertainty, and assumptions. The goal is not to make you an expert in this field, as there are many other books that do this; instead, we want the reader to feel comfortable with innovation concepts. We also discuss the differences and similarities between the entrepreneur and the corporate entrepreneur.

"Plant" is considered the first phase of innovation. It is the Discovery phase where ideas are generated and opportunities identified. In this part, we cover how to define a business or opportunity concept, and we touch on the Open Innovation imperative. We introduce the Big XYZ framework, a unique approach to stating a business concept, and discuss how to identify the problem, define the startup's vision, and determine the addressable market. In addition, we cover how to identify the best market opportunity for a technology or platform. From the corporate perspective, we cover how to conceptualize an opportunity and communicate its organizational value. We also highlight the importance of the business vision for keeping the game in play.

"Pivot" is the second phase of innovation and includes all Incubation activities. It covers our market-learning framework for the corporate entrepreneur known as the Learning Plan. We also delve into our market-learning framework for entrepreneurs known as The Pivot Startup methodology. We cover issues like identifying uncertainties and creating experiments that convert assumptions into knowledge. This is the phase where startups often pivot, if they haven't already run out of money. We cover methods that empower entrepreneurs to get answers quickly, so they can get to the pivot point with plenty of time and money to spare. On the corporate side, teams work through learning loops as they experiment and evaluate learning outcomes in terms of staying the course or pivoting.

"Propel" is the last phase of innovation, when a startup is ready to grow quickly and scale. Move from Pivot to Propel too quickly and you risk failure. Move too slowly and you risk missing the opportunity. We cover methods that help the corporate startup integrate with product development processes and transition into business units smoothly and effectively.

Let's move now to Chapter 1 and challenge this "pedal to the metal" mind-set.

NOTES

1. Frans Johansson, *The Medici Effect* (Boston: Harvard Business School Press, 2006).
2. Eric Reis, *The Lean Startup* (New York: Crown, 2011).
3. Abraham Maslow, *The Psychology of Science* (New York: Harper & Row, 1966).
4. Walter Isaacson, *Steve Jobs* (New York: Simon & Schuster, 2011).
5. UK Department of Trade and Industry (DTI), "The Innovation Report," December 2003.
6. "Innovation," *Wikipedia*, http://en.wikipedia.org/w/index.php?title=Innovation&oldid=519961810.
7. Brian S. Cumming, "Innovation Overview and Future Challenges," *European Journal of Innovation Management* 1, issue 1 (1999): 21–29.
8. Rosanna Garcia and Roger Calantone, "A Critical Look at Technological Innovation Typology and Innovativeness Terminology," *Journal of Product Innovation Management* 19, issue 2 (March 2002): 110–132.
9. Dan Olofsson, "Radical Product Innovations," *IDP*, January 15, 2003.
10. Thomas Byers, Richard Dorf, and Andrew Nelson, *Technology Ventures: From Ideas to Enterprise* (New York: McGraw-Hill, 2010).
11. Thomas J. Peters and Robert H. Waterman Jr., *In Search of Excellence* (New York: Harper & Row, 1982).
12. Hollister B. Sykes and David Dunham, "Critical Assumption Planning: A Practical Tool for Managing Business Development Risk," *Journal of Business Venturing* 10 (1995): 413–424.

PART ONE

THE TALE OF TWO ENTREPRENEURIAL WORLDS

CHAPTER 1

PEDAL TO THE METAL

While I was launching my startups, I often heard that nine out of ten startups fail. I have seen this statistic challenged, but it is clear to anyone involved with startups that the odds are stacked against the entrepreneur. It has been shown time and time again that entrepreneurs launch startups that have high degrees of uncertainty. With higher degrees of uncertainties come greater risks. With greater risks come greater rewards, along with a greater chance to fail. So, as an entrepreneur you might be tempted to conclude that high failure rates are something you must live with. I disagree and contend that with the proper management techniques you can increase your chances to succeed. Before you start deploying traditional management techniques, let me share a little history on these techniques.

A LITTLE HISTORY

Traditional management techniques are based on a 1930s movement focused on helping large corporations manage their firms. Many believe that Peter Drucker, an icon in the world of management, started this movement. Drucker was a fascinating person with a rich history. His view of the world was most definitely shaped by his father, who used to have gatherings that included guests like Sigmund Freud and Joseph Schumpeter. Drucker evolved a strong interest in human behavior, which eventually led to a desire to understand how humans engage in business. This interest led him to write a number of very important management books, at a time when only a handful of books on the subject existed. Go into any bookstore and walk over to the business section and you will find numerous books by Drucker. Do a search on management on Amazon.com and Drucker's books will appear. His contribution to management practices and theory is what led to him being "known widely as the father of management."[1]

It's interesting to note that business schools weren't always regarded so highly as today. In fact, when Drucker first began his study of management in the 1930s and 1940s, business schools were poorly regarded.[2] What changed? One theory is that the rise of business schools was driven by the rise of business consulting. In his book *The Lords of Strategy*,[3] author Walter Kiechel III writes about the rise of business consulting from its modest roots in the 1930s to the current multibillion-dollar industry. Kiechel discusses how the Boston Consulting Group (BCG) revolutionized the consulting business by introducing frameworks that helped large firms gain competitive advantages. These effective frameworks helped consulting firms like BCG bill millions of dollars.

TRADITIONAL MANAGEMENT TOOLS FAIL ENTREPRENEURS

Unfortunately, the traditional management frameworks developed by consulting firms fail entrepreneurs. Why? One reason that some experts have put forth is that these management frameworks, theories, and principles were developed for and tested on big corporations like General Electric (GE), not startups, and that the vast majority of the literature and case studies were on large, successful firms. This rings true to me, as a search for entrepreneurship on the *Harvard Business Review* website returns only 40 books, whereas a search for strategy returns 444 books and innovation 224 books. While consulting firms' focus was on corporations, successful startups like Microsoft and Apple were thought to have succeeded on the sheer

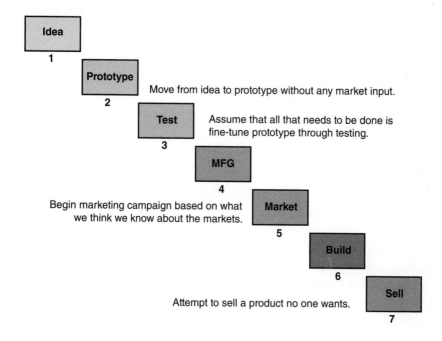

FIGURE 1.1 Traditional Product Development

will and talents of their celebrity founders. Movies on Steve Jobs and Bill Gates further perpetuated the myth that entrepreneurs were born rather than made and that one should not constrain these artistlike entrepreneurs with a structured approach. In the face of overwhelming media hype, entrepreneurs around the world absorbed these myths into their DNA.

In the early 1990s, I set off to start my first business, which was a digital prepress operation. Like so many other entrepreneurs, I bought into the myth of Jobs and Gates, who at the time were the equivalent of Mark Zuckerberg and Larry Page today. I did so by doing what I saw in the movies—I proceeded to deploy traditional management techniques. The steps I took are consistent with a traditional new product development framework (see Figure 1.1):

1. Come up with idea.
2. Develop prototype.
3. Test prototype until it works.

4. Prepare for manufacturing.
5. Prepare for market.
6. Build.
7. Sell.

I also picked up every business plan book I could find at the bookstore—no Amazon back then. In addition, I spoke to successful business professionals and I looked to my experience at General Motors (GM). I succeeded; however, I didn't realize it at the time, but the steps work rather well when a firm is trying to produce a new iteration of a current product, yet they fail miserably when applied to more breakthrough-type innovation opportunities. It wasn't until my third startup, Ironsilk, that I came to realize that this traditional approach does not work with game-changing, disruptive, or discontinuous types of innovation.

The steps are an overview of the traditional new product development method, and they are by no means comprehensive. There are many tools that big firms use to bring new products to market, including phase gate, surveys, and focus groups, that when applied to startups fail to deliver results. Why? It comes down to the level of uncertainty that surrounds new product development. "New" in most new product development teams means incrementally new. When I was working at General Motors, most of the new product development centered on marketable incremental improvements to existing products. These incrementally improved products have low levels of uncertainties, as the firm has built up a great deal of knowledge in bringing this type of product to market. In most cases the firm will already have resources and capabilities tailored to test, manufacture, market, sell, and support the incrementally improved product. The customers, distribution channels, and partnerships are all essentially the same. That's why the firm is able to focus and execute on the plan. What happens when a firm has no past experience to fall back on? How does it determine the criteria to be used in a phase gate process when it doesn't have the experience to know what's important? In these cases the startup needs to focus on learning about the technical, market, resource, and organization factors that will drive the business.

WHY STARTUPS FAIL

The topic of startup failure is both complex and important. It's complex because we are dealing with decades of misconceptions as to what startups do, how they do it, and how they succeed. It's important because startups create lots and lots of jobs.

The importance of startup failure has led to millions, if not billions, of dollars invested in trying to get an answer to the question "Why do startups fail?" The effort is driven by the fact that job growth is fueled by startups. A look at the often-referenced statistics from U.S. Census Bureau's 2007 *Survey of Small Business Owners* reveals that in 2005 small businesses with fewer than five employees accounted for only 163,000 net jobs created. By comparison, firms with five employees or more created over 2.3 million net jobs. The Kaufman Foundation while examining the same statistics delivered good news and bad news. The good news was that recently launched startups created over three million jobs; the bad news was that existing startups lost over one million jobs. The reason for the lost jobs was startup failure. How much failure? Well, the failure rate of startups is open to interpretation. I've seen failure rates vary from 25 to 93 percent depending on who is doing the reporting. According to a *Wall Street Journal* article, Shikhar Ghosh of the Harvard Business School performed a study that showed that 75 percent of venture capital (VC)-backed firms failed. Yet, the same article points out that the National Venture Capital Association estimates that only 25 percent of VC-backed startups fail.[4] The difference in the stats is due to how one defines failure. If you use the most common definition of failure, that investors in a startup are not getting a return on their investment, then according to Ghosh the failure rate is 75 percent. Now, he was researching venture-backed startups, but what about bootstrapped startups that fund themselves through family, friends, savings, credit cards, and mortgages? The numbers can only get worse, as venture-backed startups are considered the most promising startups. What about corporate startups? Are the failure rates any different within the secure walls of a corporation? We will be discussing this further in the chapters to come.

If we could figure out why startups fail, then we might be able to figure out how to help them succeed. There is no lack of theories as to why they fail. Some experts point to the lack of experienced teams, others believe it has to do with the inherent risk associated with breakthrough innovation, and some believe it has to do with the low barriers to entry. Some recent studies have suggested that startups self-implode by prematurely scaling. I agree with all of them. Startups fail for a variety of reasons, because they are launching high-impact business opportunities with high levels of technical, market, resource, and organization uncertainty. Later in the book we will go into greater depth on uncertainties, but for now let us touch upon a way to think about them. The opposite of uncertainty is certainty. When you accidentally knock a glass off the kitchen table, you know for certain that the glass will fall to the floor. This is certainty. You don't know whether the glass will shatter, crack, or remain intact. This unknown outcome to knocking a glass off the table is considered uncertainty. If the outcome can lead to a loss, then this possibility is considered a risk. When a startup begins with an idea, the number of unknowns and guesses is very large; therefore the degree of uncertainty is high. Since the startup is investing time, money, and reputations, some of the possible outcomes can lead to losses in those areas; therefore the startup is taking risks. If the startup is unaware of the risks and uncertainties, then the likelihood of guessing everything right from day one is probably around the same as the likelihood of winning a major lottery. If the startup is aware of the risks and uncertainties but does not know how to manage them, then it will most likely fail. The key to improving a startup's chances of success lies in the startup's ability to manage uncertainties and correctly determine what risks to assess.

ORIGINS OF THE PIVOT METHODOLOGY

Most entrepreneurs will tell you that they had to pivot or change course at least once on the path to success. Groupon stemmed from a do-good website called The Point. PayPal started as cryptography-based libraries for Palm Pilot devices. Hotmail started as browser-readable database software. TiVo started as a home server network. YouTube started as a video-dating platform. Twitter first launched as Odeo, a platform to subscribe to podcasts.[5] These startups were hugely successful; unfortunately, as we have discussed, the vast majority of startups fail. Some of these successful startups got lucky stumbling upon a new path, and some experimented with a new path. In all cases, they changed from the path they initially felt was best to a new path to success.

The question for the startups that failed or for the startups that were one pivot away from failure is: "Could you have avoided or reduced all the wasted resources and time that it took to launch your product or service only to fail at attracting enough customers to succeed?" There is now a general consensus among thought leaders in the field of entrepreneurship and innovation that the answer to this question is a resounding *yes*. I must admit that the corporate startup professionals got there before the individual startup professionals did. A reason for this could be that corporations might have been looking into how to innovate for a very long time and therefore funding a great deal of the effort that went into examining all aspects of innovation. In contrast, movies and books have painted a picture of startup success based on determination, intellect, and hard work against insurmountable odds, and this has led startups astray. This picture was intoxicating to technology geeks like me who grew up watching *Star Trek* and *Star Wars*. So, instead of managing startups, entrepreneurs used a seat-of-the-pants, gut-check approach to launching startups that led to one slow failure after another.

There is an effort afoot by experienced startup professionals to question the pedal to the metal mind-set by changing the way startups are managed to a more structured approach based on learning, knowledge construction, and the reduction of uncertainty. Experienced professionals like me have put forth methodologies centered on validated learning loops, which have been used to construct market experiments aimed at getting better answers quicker than before. As I will go into more detail in Chapter 4, this concept first appeared in the mid-1980s. My love for startups drove me to work on this for the past eight years, bringing my experience as an entrepreneur, professional, and mentor together with the latest academic research on best startup practices to work on The Pivot Startup methodology. I believe that the path to success is paved with learning better and quicker than the competition.

My coauthor, Joanne Hyland, has also been teaching the principles of validated learning since she launched her consulting firm in 2001. In Chapters 2 and 3, she will set the stage for why innovation is about bringing discipline to chaos and will introduce the corporate entrepreneur.

NOTES

1. Leigh Buchanan, "The Wisdom of Peter Drucker from A to Z," Inc.com, 2009, www.inc.com/articles/2009/11/drucker.html.
2. "Remembering Drucker," *The Economist*, November 19, 2009, www .economist.com/node/14903040?story_id=14903040.
3. Walter Kiechel III, *The Lords of Strategy* (Boston: Harvard Business School Press, 2010).
4. Deborah Gage, "The Venture Capital Secret: 3 out of 4 Start-Ups Fail," *Wall Street Journal*, September 19, 2012, http://online.wsj.com/article/SB100008723 963904437202045780049804764291 90.html.
5. "Best Pivots in Internet History," Ranker.com, February 13, 2013, www.ranker .com/list/best-pivots-in-internet-history/ready-to-startup.

CHAPTER 2

INNOVATION IS BRINGING DISCIPLINE TO CHAOS

PLANT = DISCOVERY; PIVOT = INCUBATION;
PROPEL = ACCELERATION

Two very well known companies had very different outcomes—Kodak and IBM.

Kodak invented the digital camera yet struggled to commercialize it due to the dominance of its film business and the power of its distribution channels. Clearly, digital photography displaced the film business, which had been a very profitable one for many years. In the end, Kodak is selling off its intellectual property and is bankrupt.

In contrast, IBM asked why it was missing emerging business opportunities in 1999 and set a direction to fix it. It has moved into whole new platforms of growth in blade computing, bioinformatics, cloud-based services, and cyber security, among others. It even sold off its personal computer business since it was not a part of its vision of the future or its strategic intent. IBM is a success story recognized by *Fortune* magazine, *Forbes*, and others for its growth, profitability, and contributions to innovation.

Companies that pursue and correctly execute upon more game-changing strategies have consistently outperformed competitors focused on sustaining existing business areas. This is due to their ability to reshape markets and industries. Kodak came up with the invention but could not commercialize it. IBM came up with many inventions and did successfully commercialize them. There are very few companies that have been able to sustain this type of growth and renewal process over many years. I, along with many others, have wondered over the years why this is so.

I began to realize in the mid-1990s that approaches to next-generation and new business area innovation were often ad hoc and unsystematic. As people move on, the learning is lost. There is no organizational system in place to capture the learning and develop the competencies as well as establish the leadership principles and managerial practices that are required for sustained success. In addition, companies have repeatedly tried to apply product development approaches to uncertain new business opportunities and have failed. There is a high cost associated with this failure—there is a potential for higher return, yet riskier opportunities do not make it to market, careers are damaged, and companies lose their competitive advantage or even meet their demise.

Well-intentioned leaders do not understand why these higher-uncertainty types of innovation have to be managed so dramatically differently from product development, or, even if they do grasp this fundamental principle, they do not know how to go about it. Therefore, investment in these types of opportunities creates organizational havoc if not implemented effectively. In fact, left unattended, it can seriously harm an organization and set individuals up for failure. Many companies have poured millions of dollars into higher-uncertainty innovation opportunities that do not succeed. Most of the failure results from the managerial resource and organization processes surrounding the project, rather than an inability to overcome technology hurdles or to understand markets. Then, in frustration, companies retreat from these speculative investments.

In viewing these significant potential costs, it appears more prudent not to do this at all than to do it ineffectively; however, this must be balanced against the long-term risks of doing nothing.

Introduction to the D-I-A Model[1]

In the previous chapter, we started to make the case for why traditional management techniques fail the entrepreneur; now we build on this from the corporate perspective. Since 1995, Rensselaer Polytechnic Institute (RPI) has conducted an ongoing academic longitudinal study of Fortune 1000 and other companies. The research team has identified seven management challenges that must be overcome and new competencies that companies must have to be successful. These challenges are the foundation of a new management framework that transforms the pursuit of these higher-uncertainty opportunities from an unpredictable model to a management discipline and structure that guide companies through the uncertainty to reduce the risk and improve the return of innovation investments. The seven challenges are:

1. Capturing promising, game-changing ideas and converting them from the reservoir of technical or operational knowledge into compelling business opportunities.
2. Managing Incubation projects in a chaotic environment with no predetermined end point.
3. Learning about unfamiliar markets or creating new markets by using market probes to learn quickly and inexpensively through incremental steps and failure by design to redirect or pivot.
4. Building the business model through a value chain or network experimentation process to uncover the most appropriate market entry strategy.
5. Bridging resource and competency gaps by pursuing a resource acquisition strategy and developing an entrepreneurial mind-set.
6. Accelerating the transition from Discovery to Incubation to Acceleration to operations status by understanding when to transition through a systematic uncertainty-reduction process.
7. Acknowledging the importance of individuals in driving strategic innovation, supported by an innovation focal point.

Very few companies have people in place with the right competencies to carry this out. Companies do not typically train individuals on how to deal with ambiguity, manage multiple dimensions of uncertainty, recognize opportunities, develop business concepts, manage complex stakeholder relationships, engage in market learning, and develop other competencies that are unique to the highly uncertain terrain of strategic innovation. Often, companies underestimate what it takes to be successful at commercializing these higher-uncertainty projects. Leaders make unreasonable requests of individuals who are not equipped with the necessary skills. Leaders themselves do not know what to do and are silently hoping that someone will come up with the right solution. When the moment of truth arrives, the individuals do not meet or even understand expectations that were inappropriately set in the first place. Inadvertently, they were set up for failure.

This is where the Discovery, Incubation, and Acceleration (D-I-A) model comes in. Without this approach, the cycle of failure will only continue to repeat itself. The D-I-A model has been developed to facilitate the learning and decision-making processes. The objective is to ensure that the right questions are asked and appropriate methods are utilized for seeking answers to these questions based on the maturity of an opportunity and the uncertainty it faces. The D-I-A model is not linear and must be orchestrated as a dynamic learning system. During Discovery, the focus is on the attractiveness of the technology or business model options to the market and the company, leading to the development of the business concept. During Incubation, the focus is on engaging the market through experimentation and the organization as the strategy emerges, leading to clarifying the market entry strategy and development of the business proposal. During Acceleration, the focus is on growing the business to make it reliable and scalable. It is also about making it profitable and working through multiple iterations of the business plan.

We will come back to these D-I-A building blocks in Figure 2.1 throughout the book, under the umbrella of the Plant, Pivot, and Propel framework.

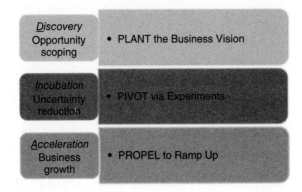

FIGURE 2.1   D-I-A Building Blocks
Source: rInnovation Group

If Only I Had Known Then What I Know Now...

I have learned through my own innovation journey that a simple, linear process is not the solution to ensure that strategic innovation initiatives are successfully implemented in companies. There must be far greater emphasis on the people, their mind-sets, and their ability to adopt a discipline for innovation. In the end, it is about change management. This must be embraced at all levels within the company to ensure that everyone understands the expectations and they become comfortable in their roles. If the CEO does not make strategic innovation a priority, then it will not happen.

While leading the internal venturing activities at Nortel Networks, our team attempted to establish a complete management system for innovation to overcome the management challenges cited earlier, only to lose our strategic relevance. Mergers and acquisitions (M&A) activities started to take precedence over what had been Nortel's strong research and development (R&D) heritage, with its ability to leapfrog generations of technology. At the time, our strategic innovation model was considered leading-edge by RPI, *Fast Company*, and the Corporate Strategy Board, among others. I left Nortel in 2000 acknowledging that what I valued, which was a balanced internal and external investment strategy for growth, was not shared at the highest levels in the company. Unfortunately, Nortel no longer exists, and its patent portfolio alone was sold in 2011 for $4.5 billion. Ironically, one of the venture spin-outs in my group's portfolio, Bill Me Later, was purchased by eBay in 2008 for $945 million, which at the time was greater than Nortel's market capitalization. This was about 10 years after we placed our initial investment. This validated for me the importance of why I am so committed to educating innovation practitioners and helping companies to build a capability for strategic innovation. I often wonder where our team and company would be today if Nortel had only persisted with its plan to incubate and assimilate our new technology ventures.

In contrast with my Nortel experiences, a few companies have been successful with their game-changing strategies. Let's return to the successes of IBM. It has been able to transform itself from a stodgy mainframe computer company to a vibrant technology and consulting company, consistently achieving double-digit growth. IBM was able to achieve this only once it understood that business success was not about a process or funding approach to growth but rather a change management approach, referred to as the Emerging Business Opportunities (EBO) system. In addition, IBM knew that this strategy could transform the company only if led by the CEO, Lou Gerstner at the time. Corning is another company that has focused on its core competency in glass to move from lightbulbs to television tubes to durable glass dinnerware to fiber optics, and when that industry imploded, to display technologies such as Gorilla glass and the environmentally friendly Lotus glass. After the telecom crash, Corning experienced a near-death experience and implemented its Four Rings of Defense to better respond to market cycles. Corning adopted a strategy of consolidating and strengthening R&D, with R&D cuts being its last line of defense. Both these companies were part of the RPI research and did not make significant headway in building their management systems for innovation and growth until their CEOs asked why they were missing emerging business opportunities (IBM in 1999) or how they could weather market downturns more effectively and protect their R&D investments (Corning after the telecom crash).

Which group of companies do you want to be part of—Nortel and Kodak, once highly successful companies that lost their way, or IBM and Corning? It is unfortunate that Nortel and Kodak did not have the leadership insights of IBM or the R&D mind-set of Corning. Perhaps they would still be thriving companies today. This is why I am passionate about a holistic, systemic model for innovation, including innovation as the driver of a company's strategic ambitions for tomorrow, not its current strategy for today. I also see the importance of a systematic approach to build a sustainable capability and help work around the failure of innovation leadership.

After 12 years of guiding companies in their own innovation pursuits and another 15 before that of figuring it out in concert with others, I am firmly convinced that the D-I-A model works and more people would benefit by making it available to a wider group of practitioners.

Of course, the insights in this book will not answer all of your questions or completely set the story straight in your minds and hearts. Yet, it will go a long way toward providing a clear innovation landscape and some essential practical tools for telling your story and paving the way for a more informed innovation community of practice. Let's work together to orchestrate innovation today for a prosperous tomorrow. The first place to start is with a common language and shared mind-set.

INNOVATION DEFINED IN THE CORPORATE SETTING

Let's expand on our definition of innovation in the Introduction. Innovation is so seriously misunderstood in companies that it is essential to be clear on what it is and what it is not. In reviewing this chapter, my colleagues have suggested that there is too much detail on or coverage of definitions. I have decided to leave in these details. Based on our training workshops, our discussions on this topic are numerous and extensive. Getting to a common understanding of innovation is critical to cracking the code of what a well-recognized discipline should be. I will leave it to you to delve into the details or skip over them, though I would highly recommend you give some additional thought to what follows!

Beyond Invention and Creativity

An invention is a new object, process, or technique. Companies that invest heavily in R&D reap the benefits of invention: many patents and many published papers. But that is where it ends unless they also know how to innovate. Innovation is the introduction of something new to the marketplace. All of the rest of the work to develop an invention into a marketable offering and a business platform comprises innovation. Inventions are the inputs to innovation. Inventions, on their own, might never come to market. Think of the lightbulb without the advent of a system for the distribution of electricity or even the facsimile or fax machine without widespread adoption.

Creativity is vital to generating new ideas and shaping business opportunities. Yet, as with inventions, the ideas become the inputs to innovation, and the creative process enables a learning environment. This learning environment is critical to success, and creativity needs to be infused throughout the company. We often see companies focusing on idea generation as part of a discovery process, yet they miss out on the opportunity-shaping part, and then what? It doesn't happen.

There is much work involved in innovation beyond the initial Discovery covered through invention and idea-generation activities. This work is called Incubation and Acceleration, which along with an elaborated Discovery are the three major building blocks of corporate entrepreneurship as introduced previously. The startup operating model of invention + commercialization also requires further elaboration. Therefore, the definition of innovation, which applies equally to the corporate and startup worlds, is:

Conceptualization (Invention + Opportunity) + Experimentation

   + Commercialization

This is consistent with our three building blocks of Discovery = Plant, Incubation = Pivot, and Acceleration = Propel. With this as our generic definition, we build upon this to incorporate the focus on innovation management and an emerging discipline.

Emerging Management Discipline

What goes around comes around, or history repeats itself. I was having a conversation the other day about the decline and fall of the Roman Empire and the topic of innovation came up. We were discussing what happened to this very advanced civilization. Innovation and the Roman Empire could certainly be a very interesting book on its own, and I am certain others have written about it. Being neither a scholar of innovation nor of history, I will leave that part to others. What I will give you is my perspective as a "conceptual practitioner," which is how my colleagues at the Danish Technical University (DTU) refer to me. It essentially means that I translate innovation theory or concepts into practice. I am certain you think I am digressing, but let me elaborate a little more to make my point.

I decided to do a little more research and went to see the origin of the word *innovation* on *Wikipedia* to see what others are saying. The word *innovation* derives from the Latin word *innovates*, which is the noun form of *innovare*, "to renew or change," stemming from *in* "into" + *novus* "new." So the word *innovation* has been around since Roman times, and its great civilization practiced a form of disciplined or systematic innovation for many years, which fell into neglect. There are many reasons why the Roman civilization disappeared, but the neglect of innovation stemmed from a lack of research as the foundation to progress, and from complacency with the status quo. The Roman institutions lost their ability to grow and renew themselves. The status quo was so comfortable that they did not see the cliff. As with many other great discoveries from this era that were lost for centuries, this disciplined approach to innovation remains an uncommon practice within established companies, especially when aiming for higher-uncertainty innovation opportunities. Of course, these are my opinions based on assimilating what my colleagues have read[2] and what we discussed. I also see in my encounters that many scholars and practitioners of innovation still view innovation as an *emerging* management discipline.

Based on the preceding, our inspiration, and input from others such as Teresa Amabile (a creativity scholar at Harvard University), innovation broadly defined is the management discipline with the objective of transforming creative ideas into market successes. Of course, not all ideas that go through the innovation process will be successful in the marketplace and many will fail along the way. Failure needs to be designed into the innovation process, especially when we are faced with higher uncertainty. Yet, for those innovation opportunities that do rightfully find their places in the market, success is our ambition. Creativity and innovative thinking are companywide responsibilities, yet innovation is a discipline not any different from engineering, finance, marketing, and so forth that needs to be learned. In Figure 2.2, innovation is broadly defined to cover this ambition for success. It also covers the reality that not all innovation pursuits will be successful—they "*could* bring value."

Innovation practices are consistent with any other discipline, yet they are the ones that are most unfamiliar to most people. How many times have you been in a room where the discussion about innovation is all over the map? This is a symptom of innovation as a buzzword rather than a true, albeit still emerging, management discipline. How many times have you heard your CEO say, "I want everyone in our company to do innovation," and then the CEO has walked away? What this really means is that he or she wants everyone to be innovative in their thinking. Yet, just as much as we would not expect everyone to be in engineering or marketing roles, why then

> "Innovation is the discipline to transform creative ideas into opportunities that could bring value to the market and the company."
>
> Applies to all forms of innovation in a company:
> technology-based, business model, process, products, services...

FIGURE 2.2   Innovation Broadly Defined
Source: rInnovation Group

do we expect everyone to do innovation? I see three reasons: The first is that innovation is not commonly taught in schools; second, it is difficult to teach since it is based on experiential learning; and third, a common language is missing so we can understand each other. Let's start with definitions.

Innovation Definitions

Innovation is not well understood in companies. The term *innovation* alone has multiple definitions, depending on a person's role and experiences. Through studying and working in and with companies pursuing leading-edge innovation strategies, I have learned that as much as we struggle with getting definitions right, this is not what is most important. Rather, it is about understanding the level of uncertainty faced by innovation teams. It requires applying the right innovation practices to reduce this uncertainty and integrating with product development once it makes sense. This requires acknowledging that there are different management practices for product development and higher-uncertainty innovation initiatives.

Innovation refers to doing something new, rather than doing the same thing better. The latter is called improvement. We also are not talking about incremental innovation, which offers small changes or new varieties of products to known customer segments and is easily managed by a phase-gate-like process approach. This type of approach comes after technical, market, resource, and organization (TMRO) uncertainties are reduced in the front end of the innovation life cycle. Of course, we ultimately want to come up with a product or solution that can be developed and launched through a more conventional phase gate process. The challenge is that we often have only business concepts or undeveloped ideas, and do not even know what that product or solution will be. Therefore, the first step is to adopt a more entrepreneurial mind-set and invest in options so we can turn these concepts into products, with the objective of significant growth through a family of products and/or solutions over time. To do this, we all need to be on the same page first with respect to the type and nature of innovation we are dealing with.

This same page can come in a variety of ways. Each company will develop its own terminology. For *type of innovation*, most companies have only two buckets—(1) incremental and (2) breakthrough or radical, which is more commonly used outside the United States (still the lingering radicalism of the 1960s in the U.S. psyche!). While our original definition started with incremental and radical, we now have a third bucket—evolutionary. Since up to 90 percent (or more) of company investments are in incremental innovation, it is a dramatic step change to go from this to higher-uncertainty breakthrough innovation. In reality, for the remaining 10 percent, most companies invest more in next-generation evolutionary opportunities rather than true breakthroughs. This is likely a symptom of our more risk-averse times, but at least with three buckets, companies feel more comfortable stepping out. Therefore, I highly recommend that a company defines three buckets as follows: one for today's more incremental improvements, a second for around-the-corner next-generation innovation or platform, and a third for the longer-term, more breakthrough innovation.

Now to the *nature of innovation*. Innovation takes many forms. Historically, technology-based innovation was considered the primary form. In recent years, especially enabled via the Internet, innovation has expanded to encompass business model innovation (e.g., Apple, Amazon). We also see innovation in the form of services, processes, and even organizational transformation, to name a few. It is also important to understand the nature of innovation because this provides another measure of the level of uncertainty a company faces. Some companies might be better able to address a business model or process innovation than a technological one, or vice versa, based on the competencies they have and the ones they do not have.

Building on the type and nature of innovation, we have finally settled on a continuum for our definition of innovation based on degrees of uncertainty across technical, market, resource (people, money, and competencies), and organization (gaining and maintaining legitimacy) considerations. I will describe the continuum once we have elaborated on these uncertainties later.

Common Language and Mind-Set

Getting to the tricky and most important part, how do we develop this common language and more entrepreneurial mind-set? Unfortunately, there is no magic solution. It takes time, effort, and ongoing communication to get everyone singing from the same song sheet. Culture change takes time. With a common language, it is much easier to build alignment since roles and expectations are much clearer, the playing field is better defined, and a sense of organizational purpose emerges. By creating an environment for the right people, processes, and tools, the cultural change takes place. In my earlier years, I thought if I focused on culture change, it would just happen, always knowing it would take time. Now I realize that change is difficult for many and it requires time for people to come along. People need the means to change their norms of behavior, which requires a supportive leadership, different governance mechanisms, the right performance measures, and processes and tools to enable innovation, among other management system elements. This is why IBM was successful once it realized that a process or funding approach alone was insufficient. It embraced change management as the more comprehensive approach, which provided the right environment for change to happen.

Now back to the D-I-A model or approach. It is important that we do not call it simply a process. Of course, there is a process underlying the model, yet it is designed to be an enabler to learning, not the control point. This is why I now emphasize the discipline and the mind-set in our company workshops. The D-I-A approach does not provide answers. It is designed to guide the learning, which brings about answers and shifts mind-sets. Change is the outcome. I have had a few telling moments with teams when it became clear that, rather than embracing uncertainty through the D-I-A model, they were using it as a gated process to *eradicate* uncertainty! I am certain you are still struggling with this mind-set versus process differentiation since process is so ingrained in the corporate DNA. We will come back to this throughout the chapters. I understand that some of you are skeptical for now.

Navigating the Culture Divide

One last point regarding this common language and mind-set. There are lurking cultural challenges in the innovation world. We affectionately (all right, sometimes not quite so) refer to this as the great cultural divide, as described in Figure 2.3. There are many cultures operating in companies. The two that we pay the most attention to are operational excellence and innovation. Operational excellence is the enemy of innovation with its risk aversion, execution orientation, and short-term focus. In contrast, innovation is longer-term in perspective and experimentation oriented; it is all about uncertainty and more entrepreneurial by design. The key is to learn how to navigate these two cultures. They need to coexist. The operational excellence world is critical to today's business, and the innovation world is critical to tomorrow's business.

Before moving to uncertainty, there is one other culture worth mentioning—customer intimacy. Now, this is a tricky one. It is definitely good business practice to listen to our customers, especially when the market uncertainty is low. But what if the market uncertainty is high, the time horizon is longer, and what you pursue

	Core Business Focus		Innovation Focus
Strategy and Type of Innovation	Current Strategy; Incremental Innovation to Extend Existing Business Areas	[----------]	Strategic or Innovation Intent and Opportunism; beyond Incremental innovation for Growth and Renewal
Culture	Operational Excellence; Customer Intimacy and Execution skills	[----------]	Cultivation; Employee Intimacy and New Business Creation Skills
Risk Profile	Risk averse with Focus on System Efficiency and Operations	[----------]	Uncertainty Reduction and Risk Mitigation through Iterative Learning and Strategic Partnerships
Investment Timing and Revenue Focus	Products, Services, and Solutions in Shorter Term Driven by Traditional Key Performance Indicators	[----------]	New Business Investments over Long Term with Portfolio Management to Pursue Options

FIGURE 2.3 The Great Cultural Divide Defined
Source: rInnovation Group

could even disrupt this customer relationship? Do you want to be another Kodak? Clearly, not. With innovation, we want to listen to the market and watch the trends. We want to be close to the market, but not necessarily close to customers. They can become your blind spot, as Kodak learned too late by listening to its distribution channels. In many cases, existing customers are not the ones you will be doing business with tomorrow. Innovator beware.

IT'S *ALL* ABOUT UNCERTAINTY

What opened my eyes about the importance of uncertainty? I struggled during the Nortel years to understand why people did not get it. We had a good system for managing ideas and developing opportunities, a talented team, a governance model that our CFO said was "too good to be true," yet something was missing. It was difficult to make the case for why we needed to do things differently from our divisions and we lacked legitimacy. We were seen as a black hole rather than an engine for the future. If only I had known then what I know now...we were facing very high levels of resource and organization uncertainty.

Uncertainty versus Risk

In companies, the words *risk* and *uncertainty* are most often used interchangeably and yet they are very different. This distinction is crucial for innovation, as we introduced in Chapter 1. We need to understand what we are dealing with so we can set an idea or business opportunity on its proper course. Clearly, investing in innovation is a risk for the business, but we are focusing on project uncertainty in this book.

With risk, the possible outcomes are known. A probability of occurrence can be assigned to each one. Investments are hedged accordingly to minimize risk. With uncertainty (and ambiguity), however, the possible outcomes are not known, and therefore assigning a likelihood of occurrence cannot yet be done. The only way to manage projects is through iterative learning to learn in increments, then decide, learn more, and decide again to reduce uncertainty.

Why is making this distinction so important? Because innovation is *all* about uncertainty. When the uncertainty is low, then we are in the world of product development and risk management. Before that, when the uncertainty is high, we are in the world of innovation and uncertainty management. Let's get back to our D-I-A model. Discovery and Incubation focus on uncertainty reduction, whereas Acceleration is part of risk management.

Uncertainty Types: Technical, Market, Resource, Organization

My experiences with uncertainty were subsequently validated by the RPI research and one of its most important insights. While companies spent time addressing technical and market issues, they were not managing resource and organization issues. After tracking the time lines of many projects, a trend emerged. It was these resource and organization uncertainties that were getting in the way of success, not the technical and market areas where the focus was. This set us on the course to design a model to manage four uncertainties, not two. This revelation has been one of my most defining moments, both professionally and personally.

From this moment forward, I encourage you to think about these four uncertainties together, yet with special emphasis on the resource and organization ones. The TMRO uncertainties broadly defined are as follows:

- *Technical*—Understanding technology drivers, value, and economic feasibility.
- *Market*—Learning about market drivers, value creation, and business viability.
- *Resource*—Accessing money and project-specific people and capabilities internally and externally.
- *Organization*—Gaining and maintaining organizational legitimacy for projects aligned with business units yet on a longer time horizon, or projects where there is not a clear organizational home.

And we are just getting started with uncertainty. . . .

Innovation Continuum and Uncertainty

Let's go back to the definition of innovation. We have flipped it completely around so that it is uncertainty that drives how we think about innovation based on a continuum from high to low levels of technical, market, resource, and organization (TMRO) uncertainty. Instead of a definition that varies from company to company, we have defined the type of innovation and characteristics of innovation under these uncertainty levels, as shown in Table 2.1. This provides us with an organizing framework for knowing when we are dealing with evolutionary and breakthrough innovation or simply incremental innovation or product development.

The ABCs of Innovation Uncertainty

A few years ago I was reflecting on a question: How would I describe the ABCs of innovation uncertainty? The most important

TABLE 2.1 Innovation and Uncertainty Levels

TMRO Uncertainty Level	High	Medium	Low
Type of Innovation	Breakthrough	Evolutionary	Incremental
Market Timing (Industry-Specific)	Long Term: 5+ Years	Medium Term: 2 to 5 Years	Short Term: 0 to 2 Years
Discovery Focus	Future and/or Technology Voice and Opportunity Recognition	Market Voice and Opportunity Recognition	Customer Voice, Idea Generation, and Market Research
Market Focus	New Markets and Customers	Adjacent Markets and New Application Areas	Existing Customers
Process and Tools	D-I-A Model for Opportunity Scoping and Uncertainty Reduction	D-I-A Model for Opportunity Scoping and Uncertainty Reduction	Phase Gate Process for Product Development (PD)
Transition Readiness	D-I-A Transition Points and Interface Management	D-I-A Transition Points and Interface Management	Prioritized in PD Phase Gate Process

Source: rInnovation Group

thought was that if we stick with what we know, we will never be successful at innovation. Innovation is about asking questions and finding answers through learning, because it is fraught with uncertainty. We often treat assumptions as facts to our detriment, so the first ABC became *admit* what you don't know so you can make the uncertainties explicit. My next thought was that this is not about serendipity, and yes, chaos needs to thrive but it also requires a systematic approach to move ideas forward. The second ABC became *bring* discipline to chaos to reduce uncertainties. Finally, I had learned the hard way that it takes people time to understand why innovation is different. They might get it in their heads but often they don't feel it in their stomachs and they underestimate what it takes. The third ABC became *communicate*, communicate, and communicate more to legitimize uncertainties. While communicating about the activities undertaken to reduce uncertainties is important, it is even more fundamental to get people to understand that uncertainties exist and that it is acceptable within the culture to acknowledge them. I recently added "or risk failing because of them" to reinforce their importance. They are summarized in Figure 2.4.

To wrap up this chapter, remember the importance of having a common language for innovation; thinking in terms of uncertainty, not risk; and being willing to admit what you don't know. This will go a long way to bringing some discipline or order to the inevitable chaos.

Admit what you don't know to find uncertainties.

Bring discipline to chaos to reduce them.

Communicate, communicate, and communicate more to legitimize them.

Or risk failing because of them!

FIGURE 2.4   Innovation ABCs

You might also want to consider a fourth ABC: D—*do* it! This came from one of my students at DTU, Jesper Bagge Pedersen. He said in our coaching sessions that I always encouraged this.

In the next chapter, I describe what it means to be a corporate entrepreneur.

NOTES

1. Richard Leifer, Christopher M. McDermott, Gina Colarelli O'Connor, Lois S. Peters, Mark Rice, and Robert W. Veryzer, *Radical Innovation: How Mature Companies Can Outsmart Upstarts* (Boston: Harvard Business School Press, 2000; Gina C. O'Connor, Richard Leifer, Albert S. Paulson, and Lois S. Peters, *Grabbing Lightning: Building a Capability for Breakthrough Innovation* (San Francisco: Jossey-Bass, 2008); and teaching, training, and coaching experiences.

2. Edward Gibbon, *The History of the Decline and Fall of the Roman Empire* (London: Strahan and Cadell, 1776–1789, republished in 2010).

CHAPTER 3

THE CORPORATE ENTREPRENEUR

So you want to be a corporate entrepreneur. To better understand what this means, we need the perspectives from the academic and business sides to see what we mean by corporate entrepreneurship.

AN EXAMINATION OF THE DEFINITION

Our definition of corporate entrepreneurship (CE) is: Corporate entrepreneurship is the creation of new businesses within and outside the company, which leverage current competencies and evolve new ones through innovation for the purposes of growth and corporate renewal.

Academic thought and business practices have evolved significantly in the past 20 to 30 years. Terms such as intrapreneurship,[1] corporate venturing,[2] and corporate entrepreneurship[3] have been used to describe a company's entrepreneurial pursuits. Today, the term *corporate entrepreneurship* has evolved as the label of choice when referring to organizational efforts to leverage current competencies and evolve new ones through innovation in new product market spaces. It extends beyond technology-based innovation to new business models, processes, and so on. New business model innovation is often the driver in service industries, with information technology as the enabler. In addition, CE is becoming recognized as a set of activities that promotes organizational learning, leading to the creation of new skills, competencies, and valuable firm-specific knowledge.[4] Its financial value to the firm, in terms of growth and profitability, has been empirically demonstrated for medium-sized and large firms, even given the risks and uncertainties inherent in the process.[5] In fact, the financial value to the firm of embedding a CE capability grows over time, as the capability matures.[6]

Clearly, ongoing discussions continue with respect to the definitions. We have chosen to adopt the term *corporate entrepreneurship*. While corporate venturing is more commonly referred to in the business world, it is considered only one form of CE. We have also chosen to expand upon the original definitions and build upon recent developments in the external world of innovation and corporate entrepreneurship to incorporate the elements of open innovation. In addition, other terms such as new business development, game changer, new business creation, and strategic innovation are also utilized, with the common denominator being the focus on an innovation discipline to manage higher levels of project uncertainty.

Now back to the corporate entrepreneur. Any of you who are one understand that it is not always easy being different, yet this difference is necessary for innovation success. Most of us have come up through the existing business, and it is difficult to step out.

Conceptually, the idea of a corporate entrepreneur or intrapreneur makes sense, especially if we look to draw parallels from the startup world. Yet, in practice, it is virtually impossible to be successful without a CE capability to support people in these roles.

I remember when, as director of new business opportunities, I brought back from a Bell Communications Research (Bellcore) meeting the idea of investing in the Internet (based on Netscape's Mosaic browser) to our telecommunications company board in 1994. At the time, we had a long distance division (where I came from) and a data division. Obviously, there was no clear fit for this business opportunity, and we did not invest. Our team was recommending we do so, but it was too different. Furthermore, the board did not see its potential or, more importantly, its threat.

As corporate entrepreneurs, we are seen either for our potential or as a threat, because we are different and challenge the status quo. In traditional product development teams, people from different functions come together to offer their expertise. For innovation teams, we are looking for cross-functional individuals—people who are capable of working across multiple functions or disciplines that make up a more holistic business approach.

Clearly, there are entrepreneurial types in companies. In speaking with chief technology officers and others during research by Rensselaer Polytechnic Institute (RPI) about desirable qualities for corporate entrepreneurs, these characteristics emerged. Corporate entrepreneurs have superior technical capabilities, are inquisitive, and are not afraid to be different. They are extremely curious and assertive, yet are often perceived as aggressive. They are risk takers, entrepreneurial, and passionate. They are broadly educated and integrative. They embrace change and uncertainty, and are goal-oriented.

Finally, and worth emphasizing, they are business and market savvy, excellent networkers, effective communicators, and comfortable working in ambiguous environments. Why are these last points worth emphasizing? Because this sets them up well for addressing resource and organization issues that, as mentioned previously, get in the way of success!

If this describes you, then read on. My goal is to make your life easier. If you understand the system you are working in, it can help you navigate the cultural divide. If this does not describe you, then read on anyway. At the very least, you will have better appreciation for the mavericks in your company and a sense of what to do to help your company build a management system that supports them.

AN IN-DEPTH LOOK AT CORPORATE ENTREPRENEURSHIP MODELS

Let's delve a little more into six models of corporate entrepreneurship.[7] Professor Gina O'Connor developed this framework, and these models form the structure of a course she developed on corporate entrepreneurship. It is always important to know how we got to where we are now and to see what companies have implemented to support their corporate entrepreneurs. I have chosen to go into a fair amount of depth in this section because we do need to learn from the past to engineer ourselves for success. We have learned a lot about what works and what is missing. We are not completely there yet, but, once again, if only I had known then what I am sharing with you now ...

The first three models, Intrapreneurship, Arm's-Length Approaches, and Internal Venturing, have been around for many years and have evolved through time as more has been learned about the phenomenon of innovation. The next three models, New Business Creation, Open Innovation, and Innovation Function, have really come to light in the past five to 10 years as more was learned about what is required to institutionalize corporate entrepreneurship. Each model provides valuable learning as to what constitutes a mature innovation system. The latter three models draw upon the learning of the three earlier models and are increasingly being introduced in companies as enablers to the development and implementation of an innovation strategy.

Model One: Intrapreneurship

I want to spend a little more time describing the Intrapreneurship model since intrapreneur is another term that is widely used in companies and often used interchangeably with corporate entrepreneur.

Intrapreneurship is the term used to describe independent entrepreneurial behavior on the part of individuals in an established company. Intrapreneuring captures the essence of championing behavior. However, it is undertaken solely by individuals in an informal way: They are granted no specific authority or mandate for innovation from senior leadership. They operate on their own.

In 1985, Gifford Pinchot wrote the book *Intrapreneuring: Why You Don't Have to Leave the Corporation to Become an Entrepreneur,* in which he prescribed that corporate entrepreneurs learn to seek out senior sponsors for protection, break rules as needed, and get the new business created within the firm in spite of the resistance they face. Pinchot defined intrapreneurs as: "Any of the dreamers who do. Those who take hands-on responsibility for creating innovation of any kind within an organization. The intrapreneur may be the creator or the inventor but is always the dreamer who figures out how to turn an idea into a profitable reality." He contrasted this with an entrepreneur, who is "someone who fills the role of intrapreneurs outside the organization."[8]

Intrapreneuring became a mantra to those in companies with new business creation ambitions. Dow Chemical, 3M, DuPont, Apple, and others are examples of where intrapreneurs in these companies made the intrapreneurial honor roll. In addition, case studies were written to contrast Dow Chemical's nonsupportive versus 3M's supportive culture. While Pinchot's model is an important contributor to corporate entrepreneurship, it is one of exception rather than one of organizational capability. It depends on champions, on exceptional individuals. And we know that there are many breakthrough ideas that lie fallow because the idea generator and the opportunity recognizer are not always endowed with champion-like or maverick-like personalities.[9]

Model Two: Arm's-Length Approaches—Corporate Venture Capital and External Corporate Incubators

Corporate venture capital (CVC) is the term used to describe the investment of corporate funds directly in external startup companies.[10] It can also include company investments in venture capital funds as limited partners. It does not encompass corporate venturing, which represents the funding of internal ventures. CVC is a revolving door. Companies come and go with varying degrees of success. Success is also difficult to define given the range of investment objectives. Companies such as Intel, Unilever, Pfizer, Johnson & Johnson, and Visa have been recognized for the effectiveness of their programs, especially Intel's ecosystem approach. The CVC investment philosophy is typically driven by a combination of strategic and financial objectives. The strategic objectives are linked to improving a company's own businesses, whereas the financial objectives are focused on generating attractive returns. CVC programs' strategic aims are about seeking new directions, providing a window on new technologies and markets, supporting existing businesses, developing new products, and, to a significantly lesser degree, improving manufacturing processes. CVC is a good complement to realizing the goals of an innovation strategy, especially in identifying strategic partnerships and competency-based acquisitions.

Another arm's-length model is the external corporate incubator set up outside a parent company, similar to the well-known Xerox PARC and Monsanto's life sciences incubator. These incubators are independent from the parent company, with their own culture, investment dollars, and decision-making authority. They house the parent company's projects but also incubate projects from other sources. It is viewed as a badge of honor to be independent from the parent company and disassociated from the bureaucratic ways that would limit the innovation potential of these projects—that is, an opportunity to break free from a nonentrepreneurial culture. When they started, they were expected to provide new platforms of business for the parent company, similar to a portfolio of skunk works (special status, underground) projects. The reintroduction of those businesses into the mainstream was a complete failure. These incubators have experienced varying degrees of success from an external, entrepreneurial perspective. However, they do not represent an effective corporate entrepreneurship model due to their distance from the parent company and, therefore, their inability to take the parent into new directions that would become fundamental to its core.

Model Three: Internal Venturing—Spin-Ins and Spin-Outs

New ventures divisions are formed to incubate, inside the company, projects that do not fit the current business models or organizational structures of the firm. Nortel Networks' Business Ventures Group (the group I led) and Lucent Technologies' New Ventures Group are examples of this model.

The purpose is to capture the creative ideas of those in the company with entrepreneurial talent and drive and develop those opportunities into businesses that would either be spun in to the company (core to business) or spun out (noncore to business) as stand-alone ventures. Regardless of the commercialization path, these projects are provided with the same level of incubation services. Most are focused on transforming R&D investments into business value. Often, there is also an element of transforming the culture to be more entrepreneurial. Executives expect to see a mix of spin-in and spin-out investments, and place a greater weight on spin-ins. Spin-in investments are ventures that move to an existing division or business area after being incubated in a corporate or R&D function. In contrast to spin-ins, spin-outs are stand-alone businesses that are set up outside the company with equity distributed among the parent, employees, and new investors.

The greatest challenge that all of these venturing models have faced over the history of their development and use is survival. Given the learning curve required to develop a structure, management system, and pipeline of promising projects, the time required to deliver credible results is longer than most senior leadership teams' patience levels. Since the ventures take time to achieve large-scale growth, managerial patience wears thin and these internal venturing programs are shut down. When companies decide again to grow organically, they cannot draw on the experiences of these venture groups because the people frequently leave the company. The cycle of learning starts again and the time line to results remains the same, patience wears thin, and these groups are shut down once again. If only companies could manage through these times and recognize innovation as a permanent part of their makeup, companies would then be in a far better position to capitalize on their innovation portfolios when favorable business conditions improved the company's ability to absorb and exploit innovation.

Based on my experiences at Nortel and my passionate commitment to make innovation work inside companies, this is why I see the emerging models as a solution to the organizational dilemma of sustaining the current development path and innovating for new growth.

Model Four: New Business Creation—Inside Corporate/R&D or Established Divisions

A new business creation (NBC) group can be formed inside a corporate/R&D function or within a division. Corporate New Ventures at Procter & Gamble is an example of this. Regardless of the organizational placement, this group is the CE innovation focal point for building new competencies to pursue higher-uncertainty innovation opportunities. The group's role is to facilitate the definition of strategic intent, develop an investment portfolio of major innovation investments, provide a natural home for innovative individuals, act as a knowledge management resource, facilitate learning and decision making, nurture internal stakeholder relationships, and manage external partnership opportunities to access technology and know-how, as part of an open innovation model.

The NBC group plays a prominent role in education and expectations management since the world of new business creation is dramatically different from the world of operations. As such, a common language around new business creation and innovation needs to be developed. New capabilities are required for discovery and incubation, new skill sets are necessary for new business creation and business building, and new roles need to be defined to move from a hierarchical structure to a governance model. A strategic communications approach is essential to help establish and build organizational legitimacy.

The linkage to strategy and senior management is critical. Unlike the internal venturing model, there is a much tighter linkage with the firm's growth and corporate renewal strategy. In fact, all investments are considered in light of these objectives, and only nonstrategic investments would be spun off after market learning confirms that a given investment does not fit with the company's strategic intent.

Of course, companies use other approaches in attempts to pursue new business creation activities, such as phase gate processes, skunk works, and CEO special projects. However, experience has proven that these approaches are not effective in building a sustainable capability for higher-uncertainty innovation projects.

For new product development (NPD), these projects follow a phase gate, which is not designed for higher-uncertainty innovation projects. The NPD process is effective for dealing with incremental innovation opportunities and line extensions. Uncertainty reduction in the NBC front end prepares these projects for NPD. If introduced into the NPD process too early, the innovation potential of these projects will be lost.

A skunk-works approach is another model companies have tried. Skunk works are relatively small work groups, physically separated from mainstream operations so as not to be subjected to the burdensome rules, overhead, or bureaucratic pressures of the corporation. The skunk-works approach is designed to develop a particular product and is not used as a systematic process for developing a pipeline of innovation opportunities. The same can be said for CEO and other sponsored special or strategic projects that come and go, as with an ad hoc approach.

Model Five: Open Innovation Hybrid Approach

In his landmark book *Open Innovation: The New Imperative for Creating and Profiting from Technology,*[11] Henry Chesbrough defined open innovation as a new paradigm that rebuts the standard closed innovation paradigm, which holds that successful innovation requires control and instead assumes that firms can and should use external as well as internal ideas, and internal and external paths to market, as they look to advance their technology. He later elaborated it as "The use of purposive inflows and outflows of knowledge to accelerate internal innovation, and expand the markets for external use of innovation, respectively."[12] The open innovation paradigm also incorporates the point that internal ideas can be taken to market through external channels, outside a company's current businesses, to generate additional value.[13] The concept may not be new and has, in fact, been practiced to some degree for many years. The emphasis, however, on sharing information rather than considering it the sole source of competitive advantage has drawn immense attention from R&D communities of established companies since his original book was published, and is affecting the ways in which R&D is managed in a major way. Companies are exploring new sources of ideas, new partnership forms, and shared business models, and perhaps to some extent are considering open innovation as an answer to the pressures on R&D groups to consistently produce breakthrough ideas. Open innovation approaches include in-licensing, strategic partnerships, competency-based acquisitions, joint ventures, and new organizational intermediaries to broker external ideas with companies.

As mentioned previously, this is why we evolved our definition of corporate entrepreneurship to include the bringing together of outside and inside sources of innovation opportunities—the hybrid model.

Model Six: An Innovation Function—Institutionalizing Corporate Entrepreneurship

Innovation is in a management discipline that people need to learn. In the fourth model, New Business Creation, the elements of the management system required to institutionalize corporate entrepreneurship are starting to emerge. In this sixth model, innovation is taken one step further and viewed as an innovation function—a critical organizational competence on equal footing with engineering, marketing, operations, finance, and other disciplines. During difficult business cycles, these functions or departments are not shut down. Of course, there could be some downsizing and recasting of priorities, but these departments do not disappear entirely. All well-managed companies do need to take into account their organizational capacity to pursue new opportunities, but innovation should not be the first place to cut. In fact, there is supporting evidence that those companies that invest in innovation in down cycles are much better positioned when favorable business conditions return.

Given the learning that has taken place over time, this is the most developed model for CE and one that should be around for years to come. The Emerging Business Opportunities (EBO) group at IBM is the best representation of how this model has been applied and a key contributor to RPI's research. All the models leading up to the Innovation Function have influenced the development of this leading-edge model and require corporate venture capital, new business creation, and open innovation. Previous models were difficult to sustain because they were too loosely coupled with the company and/or the strategy to be effective. With innovation as an integral part of the strategy, companies can now effectively institutionalize corporate entrepreneurship. This is done by formulating an innovation strategy where corporate entrepreneurship is on par with operational excellence and new product development, distinguishing between invention and innovation as described previously and setting appropriate expectations to ensure corporate entrepreneurship programs do last. Tables 3.1 and 3.2 summarize the similarities and differences among these six models.

TABLE 3.1   Early Corporate Entrepreneurship Models

Dimension	Intrapreneurship	Arm's-Length Approaches	Internal Venturing
Objectives	An individual's drive to make a difference.	Corporate venture capital (CVC): Strategic fit, financial return, or hybrid. Corporate incubator (CI): Setting up new businesses and ROI.	Incubate inside the company ventures that do not fit with current business models and structures.
Measures of success	Start a business. Become part of intrapreneurship honor roll.	CVC: New business areas and products and ROI. CI: Financial returns and shareholder value.	Cultural transformation to a more entrepreneurial environment. Profitable growth.
Tightness of link to corporate strategy	None, happens in spite of organization.	CVC: Tight, provide new directions and window on technology. CI: Loose, no formal tie to strategy.	Loose, pursuing areas that are not core.
Tightness of link to ongoing businesses	Arbitrary, depends on what is uncovered.	CVC: Tight, often require business unit or R&D sponsors CI: Loose, build value out of incubator businesses.	Loose, find fit only if businesses are stretching beyond core.

Source: Professor Gina O'Connor, RPI

TABLE 3.2   Emerging Corporate Entrepreneurship Models

Dimension	New Business Creation	Open Innovation Hybrid	Innovation Function
Objectives	Growth and corporate renewal.	Accelerate internal innovation and expand markets for external use of innovation.	Growth and corporate renewal.
Measures of success	Creation of new business units. Favorable portfolio returns over the long run.	New partnerships and business models that lead to successful businesses.	Sustainability of CE efforts. Innovation integral to corporate strategy.
Tightness of link to corporate strategy	Reciprocal influence on strategic intent and portfolio investments.	Moderate to highly coupled, depending on how much open innovation is part of strategy.	Tightly coupled, with influence on strategic plans, strategic intent, opportunistic bets, and acquisition strategy.
Tightness of link to ongoing businesses	High for aligned opportunities. Moderate for multi-aligned opportunities. Low for unaligned or whitespace opportunities.	Loose, as most partnerships and investments will be in areas beyond the core.	High for aligned opportunities. Moderate for multi-aligned opportunities. Low for unaligned or whitespace opportunities.

Source: Professor Gina O'Connor, RPI

A BRIEF LOOK AT ACADEMIC RESEARCH

Academic research reinforces the failings of previous approaches, including the cultural limitations described earlier, and reinforces the need for a more evolved corporate entrepreneurship approach. Let me summarize a few key insights from this research.

Large, established companies are capable of creating and commercializing new products that offer incremental benefits to the market, but they struggle to move beyond incremental improvements. While the pursuit of higher-uncertainty innovation, defined as any innovation beyond incremental improvements, is an important path to growth, there is plenty of evidence to suggest that the dominance of the core business and an operational excellence culture can impede a company's success. Processes and other activities, focused on efficiency to gain economies of scale and scope, stop an innovation opportunity before it even has a chance to get started.

This is because what makes a company profitable in well-established markets reduces an organization's ability to cope with uncertainty in any manner other than to ignore it or elect not to engage in opportunities that introduce it. A company requires the ability to engage in situational learning to reduce these uncertainties in technical, market, resource, and organization areas. Each opportunity will raise a number of new and often different uncertainties. Many companies view this type of learning as inefficient, and therefore of little or no value, especially within the context of a rigid, efficient organizational machine.[14]

Finally, some scholars believe large, established firms are incapable of meeting the demands of current stakeholders while simultaneously planning for future disruptive technologies.[15] Other scholars, however, argue that organizations can develop appropriate management systems for higher–uncertainty innovation initiatives but simply have not.[16]

Companies face increasing challenges to stay ahead or at least be competitive in a global world. In fact, as we have seen with Kodak and Nortel, companies literally disappear if they are not able to innovate and successfully commercialize their opportunities. For these reasons, academics are calling for new models of innovation enabled through CE-related management systems. Companies are responding to this call and attempting to build new capabilities for managing higher–uncertainty innovation opportunities.[17]

A LOOK AT CORPORATE CULTURE

In living in the world of corporate entrepreneurship, we experience, just about every day, conflicts between the entrepreneurial systems required for learning, cultivation, and innovation competency development and the efficient systems in place for operational excellence and customer intimacy. Senior leaders with ongoing operations have limited freedom to operate based on the existing strategy, culture, mind-set, skill sets, customer expectations, business model, processes, infrastructure, timing, and so on. I think you get the point. Companies are set up to preserve the status quo. Unfortunately, due to these constraints or handcuffs, innovation opportunities cannot achieve their full potential as they become "incrementalized" in business segments or units.

At the individual level, we see the tyranny or dominance of roles, power, status, and prestige. We also see personalities with a low tolerance for ambiguity and lacking skills in project leadership and communications. How many times have you been in a situation where you are afraid of not having the answer since having answers is the currency in your company? Part of our coaching is about changing the culture so it is valued not to know but to come up with a plan to find the answers. Think about what that would look like in your company when knowledge is the source of power, status, and prestige.

At the department or business level, the tyrannies are of current markets, customers, business models, and business theories. How many times have you been told to listen to your customers or make your opportunity work with an existing business model when you know it is wrong to do so? I see this all the time with programs like "customer first." We make the distinction between listening to the market indicators versus customers focused on what they need now. Of course, customers can also be forward-looking, but, in these discussions, it needs to be clear that it is not about business as usual.

At the organizational level, we see tyrannies of the current strategy where hurdles are too high and the scope is too narrow, of the current organization structure where connections are too loose and separations are too sharp, of current process mechanisms where the controls are too tight, and of leadership where the outlook is too operational and success is too focused on the present. How many times have you been in a meeting with a big elephant in the room and no one points it out? I was with a company a few months ago that uses a photo of an elephant in a meeting room (a big

African elephant at that) to make the point about everyone avoiding the real issues. In case you have need of the photo, it is available through search.

Another part of the cultural dilemma is that projects fail because of the uncertainty, not the team, yet often people are seen as the failures. Innovation projects are all about uncertainty, and therefore are unpredictable, where making the case for support cannot be based on traditional metrics, and consequently expectations are not aligned. The scale or size and scope of a fledgling business are insignificant compared with the core business areas and so are not viewed to be of equal value. I remember realizing that no matter what we did in our portfolio, our success would be considered rounding errors in the revenue growth of Nortel. So why be associated with it? Innovation is perceived as a career time-out rather than a career-building opportunity, and careers can atrophy or diminish in their perceived organizational value.

Finally, there is a recognition discount or lack of recognition for successes since it is difficult to trace back contributions in the early stages of innovation. Now that we know how to deal with opportunities and build a capability for innovation, admittedly, the innovation career path is the last frontier, but the RPI team is working on it, along with its colleagues.[18]

What is required for success is that companies be ambidextrous in their management. Each major objective requires different activities to be successful. Successful organizations excel at operations, new product development, and strategic innovation simultaneously. One of the questions I am most often asked, which is also one of the greatest organizational challenges, is how to preserve resources for the important (strategic innovation) in the face of urgent (ongoing operations) organizational needs. Per the cultural divide described in Figure 2.3 in the preceding chapter, part of the solution is to create an environment so that cultures can coexist. This is not easy, and to do this effectively requires an understanding of each culture's purpose, where the operational excellence culture serves today's business objectives and the innovation culture plants the seeds to fulfill tomorrow's business vision. Figure 3.1 tells an interesting story of how this does not quite go as planned!

FIGURE 3.1   The Golden Egg
Source: Tom Fishburne, Marketoonist

PERSONAL EXPERIENCES

So based on all the aforementioned organizational hurdles, why would anyone in their right mind want to be a corporate entrepreneur? For the challenge and the opportunity to make a difference, of course. People take great pride in being a part of a larger company and want to see it grow and prosper through new opportunities. I remember in my time at Nortel that we had outstanding employee satisfaction scores, and 100 percent of my team members loved their jobs.

Anything straightforward is not challenging enough. I want to make a difference in this world, and besides, it is fun and rewarding. It has its up sides and down sides, but what doesn't? After my experiences at Nortel, I wrote a chapter in 2001 about "Using VC (Venture Capital) Experience to Create Business Value"[19] and came up with the following to define what corporate entrepreneurship meant to me: "Corporate entrepreneurship is...the convergence of passion, commitment, and masochism with chaos, change, and uncertainty to inspire the dreams and create the wealth of future generations. Yes, there is the roller-coaster effect."

Over the past 20 years, I have reflected upon insights from early days of scouting for new opportunities and have adapted the venture capital principles to the realities of corporate life. The RPI research has become our foundation and provides the guideposts, and I continue to learn from each and every workshop, meeting, and teaching engagement. I have captured these in my top 10 insights:

1. There needs to be a reason to believe or an organizational purpose, driven by a clearly articulated and prioritized innovation intent.
2. Seed funding is essential to minimize resource competition and free up time to focus on innovation opportunities.
3. Discovery is more than technical and business model insights. It is about recognizing opportunities and articulating their value in a compelling way.
4. Incubation is about engaging the market early to test business concepts and reduce their uncertainty. Companies need to resist the urge to jump from Discovery to Acceleration.
5. Failures as well as successes are to be valued to feed the learning cycle.
6. Metrics must be clearly articulated in terms that define innovation success.
7. The right people need to be on board, taking into account the evolving objectives.
8. People need the right environment for creativity and innovation to thrive and for culture change to emerge.
9. A learning network or innovation community of practice should be nurtured to share experiences and transfer know-how.
10. Senior leadership must be committed for the long run and be available to open doors and remove resource and organizational roadblocks.

Of course, I could go on and on, but let's start with these, and we will cover them throughout the book. I am sharing this list with you so perhaps you can accelerate your learning and be more effective in your professional and even personal life. It is amazing how having a better appreciation for resource and organizational issues carries through to all types of relationships. I hope this inspires you to see a promising path forward and that it can be done, once we know the way. It also sets the stage for the chapters that follow, which provide you with more practical guidance on the how-to of this equation.

Let me digress somewhat. I remember our first training and coaching workshop in 2006 with Novozymes, a biotech company headquartered in Denmark with a strong focus on enzymes production. Professor Gina O'Connor, associate dean at RPI, my esteemed colleague and cherished friend, and I facilitated our training and coaching workshop. We received mixed feedback on the workshop—some thought it was what they had been waiting for, but others thought we went through too much material too quickly, and still others thought it was too slow and there was nothing new. I remember arriving in Paris for a weekend off quite disturbed by the feedback, and our follow-ups met with limited success.

Then about nine months later, I received a call from Thomas Schäfer, our primary contact. He said that during the training session, all he was thinking about was how theoretical this whole D-I-A model was—that Novozymes was a well-managed company and that the stories we told would never happen there, especially around the resource and organization issues we had seen in other companies. He then said, "Guess what, they did. Once we started pursuing our new business development opportunities, all of what you suggested could happen, did, and then some. It is time for you to come back and teach us how to do this well." We worked together over the next three years. They took our uncertainty management model to heart and even renamed it MTOR for Market, Technical, Organization, and Resource, a much catchier acronym than our TMRO, at least for them. Yet, did you know that mTOR is a bad protein, implicated in many types of diseases? Maybe they found their inspiration from that since we do want to find answers to uncertainties, as we do to diseases! Another company came up with ToMoRrOw. In the end, what is most important is that companies make it their own.

So, as the story goes, the rest is history. Novozymes is still a well-managed company, but now there is room to discuss and resolve uncertainties before they get in the way of success.

Moen, a global company providing kitchen and bath fixtures headquartered in the United States, has found another part of our model to be of great value—the Discovery, Incubation, and Acceleration or D-I-A building blocks. It is not that the uncertainties are unimportant, but for a consumer products company like Moen, the uncertainties are lower compared with a biotech company like Novozymes. Moen was looking to move beyond sustaining innovation and knew it needed a way to conduct small tests in the market to do this, rather than jumping straight to product development.

Per Insight 7, as Moen's innovation objectives evolved, so did its team. Margie Rowe played a significant role in bringing our approach to Moen and really embraced the importance of Insight 1, the need for a reason to believe to direct innovation activities. Each member of the innovation core team, from Todd Loschelder to Judy Riley to Jack Suvak to Tim O'Brien, played a key role in moving the ball down the field, and Mike Pickett, who holds the overall responsibility for innovation, kept the corporate commitment strong per Insight 10. The team did a superb job of defining its strategic intent. When Louise Quigley came along, Moen dedicated time to learning how to use the D-I-A model for systematic uncertainty reduction. She worked with her extended team to ensure Incubation got the attention it deserved. With her core team, they have embraced Moen's guiding principles for success per Insight 8. These were adapted to Moen's environment based on the guiding principles in Figure 3.2. This has created room for Moen to nurture opportunities that have the potential to take the company beyond the sustaining innovation activities in the business units.

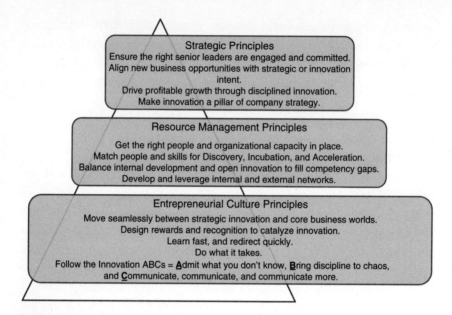

FIGURE 3.2   Guiding Principles for Success
Source: rInnovation Group, inspired by work with Kodak

By embracing these principles and the D-I-A methodology, Moen introduced in late 2012 MotionSense, not simply one of its most innovative products in years, but also one that is a market success. How many times have you dreamed of turning one of your opportunities into a market success? We will get back to this story in Chapter 10 and other insights in Chapters 9 and 10 discussed in April 2013, with Louise and Mike.

It is time now to get into more detail about the innovation journey based on these four uncertainties and three building blocks described in Table 3.3. These will be covered in Part Two: Plant = Discovery, Part Three: Pivot = Incubation, and Part Four: Propel = Acceleration.

Before that, it's time to pass it over to Remy so he can tell you the stories from the world of the entrepreneur in Chapter 4 and to Gina and Lois to frame our perspectives in Chapter 5.

TABLE 3.3 Innovation Business Opportunity Evolution

D=PLANT I=PIVOT A=PROPEL	*Discovery* Conceptualization Output = Opportunity Concept	*Incubation* Experimentation Output = Concept Proposal	*Acceleration* Commercial- ization Output = Business Plan
Technical Uncertainty Understanding technology drivers, value, and economic feasibility	Technical Feasibility and Capabilities, IP Landscape Scoping	Technology Prototypes, Simulation, IP Strategy and Plan Execution, Product or Solution Specifications	Product Development Plan
Market Uncertainty Learning about market drivers, value creation, and business viability	Application Possibilities, Value Proposition, Business Potential, Business Model Options	Early Adopter Experience, Market Learning, Business Model, and Market Entry Strategy	Market Development and Sales Plan
Resource Uncertainty Accessing money, people, and capabilities internally and externally	Availability of Funding and Right People, Competency Gaps Identification for Partnering Options	Innovation Talent and Partnership Development	Business Area Team Composition and Partnerships Aligned for Business Commercialization
Organization Uncertainty Gaining and maintaining organizational legitimacy	Capacity for Innovation, Fit with Strategic Intent, and Senior Level Commitment	Structure and Process to Support D-I-A Mindset and Effectively Transition Concepts or Projects	Organizational Commitment, Transition, and Final Home

Source: rInnovation Group

NOTES

1. Gifford Pinchot, *Intrapreneuring: Why You Don't Have to Leave the Corporation to Become an Entrepreneur* (New York: Harper & Row, 1985).

2. Zenas Block and Ian MacMillan, *Corporate Venturing: Creating New Businesses within the Firm* (Boston: Harvard Business School Press, 1993).

3. Peter Drucker, *Innovation and Entrepreneurship* (New York: Harper & Row, 1985).

4. S. A. Zahra, A. P. Nielsen, and W. C. Bogner, "Corporate Entrepreneurship, Knowledge and Competence Development," *Entrepreneurship Theory and Practice* 23, no. 3 (1999): 169–190.

5. S. A. Zahra, "Predictors and Financial Outcomes of Corporate Entrepreneurship—An Exploratory Study," *Journal of Business Venturing* 6, no. 4 (1991): 259–285; Hee-Jae Cho and Vladimir Pucik, "Relationship between Innovativeness, Quality and Growth, Profitability, and Market Value," *Strategic Management Journal* 26, no. 6 (2005), 55–75; and R. G. Leifer, D. R. Kasthurirangan, and R. Mahsud, "R&D Investment and Innovativeness: Their Contributions to Organizational Success," paper presented at the Strategic Management Society Annual Meeting, Austria, 2006.

6. S. A. Zahra and J. G. Covin, "Contextual Influences on the Entrepreneurship-Performance Relationship: A Longitudinal Study," *Journal of Business Venturing* 10, no. 1 (1995), 43–59.

7. Gina Colarelli O'Connor and Joanne Hyland, "Corporate Entrepreneurship: Models, Infrastructure and Critical Success Factors," report prepared for the Danish Enterprise and Construction Authority (DECA) by the rInnovation Group, 2008.

8. Pinchot, *Intrapreneuring*.

9. Richard Leifer, Christopher M. McDermott, Gina Colarelli O'Connor, Lois S. Peters, Mark Rice, and Robert W. Veryzer, *Radical Innovation: How Mature Companies Can Outsmart Upstarts* (Boston: Harvard Business School Press, 2000).

10. Henry Chesbrough, "Making Sense of Corporate Venture Capital," *Harvard Business Review* 4, no. 11 (March 2002).

11. Henry Chesbrough, *Open Innovation: The New Imperative for Creating and Profiting from Technology* (Boston: Harvard Business School Press, 2003).

12. Henry Chesbrough, Wim Van Haverbeke, and Joel West, eds., *Open Innovation: Researching a New Paradigm* (New York: Oxford University Press, 2006).

13. Henry Chesbrough, "Managing Open Innovation," *Research Technology Management* 47, no. 1 (2004): 23–26.

14. Kathleen M. Eisenhardt and Jeffrey A. Martin, "Dynamic Capabilities: What Are They?," *Strategic Management Journal* 21, issue 10–11 (2000): 1105–1121; Rajesh Chandy and Gerard Tellis, "The Incumbent's Curse? Incumbency, Size, and Radical Product Innovation," *Journal of Marketing* 64, no. 3 (2000): 1–17; Leifer et al., *Radical Innovation*; and Mark P. Rice, Gina Colarelli O'Connor, and Ronald Pierantozzi, "Implementing a Learning Plan to Counter Project Uncertainties," *Sloan Management Review* 49, no. 2 (Winter 2008): 54–62.

15. Clayton Christensen, *The Innovator's Dilemma: When New Technologies Cause Great Firms to Fail* (Boston: Harvard Business School Press, 1997).

16. Gautam Ahuja and Curba Morris Lampert, "Entrepreneurship in the Large Corporation: A Longitudinal Study of How Established Firms Create Breakthrough Inventions," *Strategic Management Journal* 22 (2001): 521–543; Clayton Christensen and Michael E. Raynor, *The Innovator's Solution* (Boston: Harvard Business School Press, 2003); C. W. L. Hill and F. T. Rothaermel, "The Performance of Incumbent Firms in the Face of Radical Technological Innovation," *Academy of Management Review* 28 (2003): 257–274; Mariann Jelinek and Claudia Bird Schoonhoven, *The Innovation Marathon* (San Francisco: Jossey-Bass, 1993); Leifer et al., *Radical Innovation*; Joseph G. Morone, *Winning in High Tech Markets* (Boston: Harvard Business School Press, 1993); and Gina C. O'Connor, Richard Leifer, Albert S. Paulson, and Lois S. Peters, *Grabbing Lightning: Building a Capability for Breakthrough Innovation* (San Francisco: Jossey-Bass, 2008).

17. Julian Birkinshaw and Susan A. Hill, "Corporate Venturing Units: Vehicles for Strategic Success in New Europe," *Organizational Dynamics* 34, no. 3 (2005): 247–257.

18. Gina Colarelli O'Connor, Andrew Corbett, and Ron Pierantozzi, "Create Three Distinct Careers Paths for Innovators," *Harvard Business Review*, December 2009.

19. E.J. Kelly Editor, *From the Trenches: Strategies from Industry Leaders on the New E-Conomy* (New York: John Wiley & Sons, 2001).

Additional Notes

Sources of inspiration for the CE models in this chapter and the other chapters are as follows.

Model One: IMD 145: Internal Entrepreneurship at the Dow Chemical Company.

Model One: Harvard Business School HBS9-395-017: 3M Optical Systems: Managing Corporate Entrepreneurship.

Model Two: Babson College BAB049-C99A-P: Xerox New Enterprises.

Model Three: Babson College BAB057: Nortel Networks Business Ventures Group: One Corporation's Take on Corporate Entrepreneurship.

Model Three: Harvard Business School HBS9-300-085: Lucent Technologies New Ventures Group.

Model Four: Harvard Business School HBS9-897-088: Corporate New Ventures at Procter & Gamble.

Model Six: Harvard Business School HBS9-304-075: Emerging Business Opportunities at IBM (A), (B), and (C).

CHAPTER 4

SO, YOU WANT TO BE AN ENTREPRENEUR?

In the previous chapter, we highlighted some key traits of the corporate entrepreneur (CE), including superior technical capabilities, inquisitiveness, curiosity, assertiveness, risk taking, and passion. One can apply these same characteristics when attempting to describe an individual entrepreneur. Although the CE and entrepreneur share some qualities, there are differences. For example, why does an individual entrepreneur choose a path to lower median lifetime earnings than what could be earned by working for larger corporations?[1] When a person makes a choice to be an entrepreneur, the individual does so generally against the advice of friends, colleagues, and family. Why doesn't the entrepreneur take a job at a big organization and earn more money? Why do entrepreneurs choose to spend their savings, mortgage their homes, and borrow from family just to launch a startup that is likely to fail? Some would call this type of behavior irrational and a bit insane. Many have called this type of repeated behavior over the years a phenomenon.

There are many definitions of an entrepreneur in cyberspace. For example, *Merriam-Webster's Collegiate Dictionary* defines entrepreneur as "one who organizes, manages, and assumes the risks of a business or enterprise." I find this definition to be rather sterile and lacking insight. John Burgstone and Bill Murphy Jr. in their book, *Breakthrough Entrepreneurship*, discussed the concept that an entrepreneur is one who pursues "opportunity without regard to resources currently controlled."[2] This definition offers a little more insight. However, it depicts the entrepreneur as person focused solely on opportunity without regard for resources. This implies that the entrepreneur lacks the resources to pursue the opportunity. It leads to a view of the entrepreneur as starting off poor. As we will see in the next section, although there are statistics out there that depict entrepreneurs as starting off poor, one needs to consider the stories of Bill Gates, Steve Jobs, Paul Allen, and Mark Zuckerberg to see how misleading such statistics can be.

In this chapter, I acknowledge that an entrepreneur is more complex than a mere definition can hope to capture. I will move beyond the definition and examine the entrepreneur from many different angles, from looking at celebrity entrepreneurs to a discussion of whether entrepreneurs are born or made.

SWINGING FOR THE FENCES

Bill Gates and Paul Allen founded Microsoft in 1975. Bill Gates grew up in an affluent family in Seattle, Washington. Bill's mother served on several corporate boards, including the board of a bank founded by her grandfather, First Interstate Bank in Seattle. His father was a prominent Seattle attorney. Bill went to an exclusive private high school that happened to invest in a time-sharing terminal with a direct link to a mainframe computer. Most colleges didn't have this capability in 1968! Bill was far from poor. What about Paul Allen? It turns out he went to the same exclusive private school that Bill went to. His father was the associate director of the University of Washington libraries. Paul Allen definitely was not poor.

Now, what about Steve Jobs? Paul and Clara Jobs adopted Steve shortly after his birth in 1955. Paul was a mechanic and carpenter and Clara an accountant. Steve did not have the same affluent upbringing that Gates did, but he was far from poor. And how about Mark Zuckerberg? He was born in 1984 to Karen and Edward Zuckerberg. His mother was a psychiatrist and his father a dentist. He received private tutoring lessons in computer programming. Again and again the evidence suggests that the most successful entrepreneurs did not come from poor beginnings.

How about the definition of an entrepreneur as a person who swings for the fences and succeeds? This notion of an entrepreneur acting as irrational risk taker was prominent when I first started my career in the mid-1980s. Is there any evidence to back this notion? While surfing the Internet, I found several swing-for-the-fences startup stories; however, the founders of *failed* startups write them. In one story, Eran Hammer, the founder of a microblogging platform, Nouncer, wrote that he "started with an idea and hunt for logo."[3] On his website, Eran wrote that the idea was to "build a powerful platform for others to run microblogging services through." Interestingly enough, the idea began with a wishful-thinking question Eran first asked himself as he was "sitting down to write the first line of code. . . . What will happen if I build a microblogging service and it's an overnight success with a million users?"[4]

Eran admitted that this question influenced his work "more than any other factor." The reliance on this question in the summer of 2006 indicates that Eran assumed at the very beginning that his service would grow virally and that this question, better yet this untested assumption, drove the startup. One year later, in July 2007, Eran was on target to develop his first product, Nouncer. Less than a year later, in April 2008, he wrote, "My most exciting professional adventure to date has reached its conclusion last month when I decided to pull the plug on Nouncer, my attempt at building a microblogging web service."[5] Eran had spent two years on writing code and spent half the money he raised from family, and what did he have to show for it? According to his website, "it was all good" and "an amazing adventure." In addition, he learned many lessons. One of the lessons he points to has to do with launching his startup in New York City. Eran wrote that "the point of a business is to sell products, and if the target market is elsewhere, the best talent and resources are not going to make a difference." As we will discuss later in this book, all assumptions are important, including the location of your startup. Eran assumed New York City would be the right place, and he encountered several problems with that assumption. Eran's story is a classic story of swinging for the fences. He had an idea based on many assumptions; he worked tirelessly on the technical assumptions, but did not seem to spend a great deal of time on the market, resource, and organization assumptions. Like so many other entrepreneurs, Eran had swung and missed.

How do these risk takers compare to successful entrepreneurs like Bill Gates? The story of Gates and Allen developing a BASIC computer program after seeing the cover of the January 1975 issue of *Popular Electronics* magazine that featured a story on the world's first minicomputer is well documented. But is it true? Truth is often not as sexy as fiction. According to an article on Biography.com, Allen and Gates did get the idea to write a program, but before doing so, they called the company that was making the minicomputer, Micro Instrumentation Telemetry Systems (MITS). Gates and Allen "wanted to know if MITS was interested in someone developing such software."[6] As it turned out, the prototype MITS had sent off to *Popular Electronics* was never made due to a strike at the shipping company and the feature was based on photos that MITS supplied. The magazine story generated great interest in the minicomputer from the public, which probably led to Gates and Allen being invited to come to MITS to demo the BASIC software that would enhance the minicomputer's functionality. It was only after receiving the invitation that Gates and Allen got busy writing code. MITS was impressed with their work and offered to buy the program. At the time of the offer, Gates was still in his sophomore year at Harvard. It would be another 12 months before he decided to drop out of school to pursue the startup, Microsoft, full-time. So far this story does not sound like an entrepreneur who was swinging for the fences. It sounds more like a couple of entrepreneurs who tested out their assumptions about a potential customer, MITS, before coding.

In addition to testing assumptions, Gates and Allen had some help in the form of Gates's mom. In fact, Microsoft might never have reached the heights that it did if not for an introduction Bill's mom, Mary, made in 1980 between her son and the United Way's CEO, John Opel. Mary had served on the United Way's executive committee with John Akers and John Opel.[7] Akers and Opel both subsequently served as CEO of IBM. Opel served as CEO from

1981 to 1985 and Akers from 1985 to 1993.[8] It was during Opel's reign as CEO that IBM went on to sell its personal computers with an operating system developed by Microsoft (MS-DOS), and Microsoft soared.[9]

Gates and Allen are not alone. Mark Zuckerberg developed and tested Facebook while he was at Harvard, risking little. Steve Jobs and his partner Steve Wozniak cobbled together a prototype and received orders before committing to any real use of resources. Time and time again, we find successful entrepreneurs testing the market before they commit resources.

THE ACADEMIC SIDE

There is a current effort among domestic and international universities to instill entrepreneurial spirit into students. This effort may stem from the United States' renewed interest in innovation, which was highlighted during President Obama's State of the Union address given on January 25, 2011. On that day the President said, "The first step in winning the future is encouraging American innovation." As *Time* magazine noted, the President used the word *innovate* or *innovation* 11 times during that speech. These were not empty words. There is evidence that the White House believes that in order for the United States to maintain its position in the world it must produce innovation-driven opportunities that create both value and jobs. One such piece of evidence came in October 2011 when the National Science Foundation launched its Innovation Corps (I-Corps), a program to improve the United States' ability to commercialize university-based technologies. Another came just a few days after the State of the Union address, when the President stated, "Entrepreneurs embody the promise of America."

This newfound interest in entrepreneurship is not all that new. Universities have been intrigued by entrepreneurship for a very long time. In the 1920s, some academics viewed entrepreneurs as business fortune-tellers who could predict the future. In the 1930s, the view shifted to entrepreneurs as system innovators who come up with new combinations. Fast-forward to the early 1970s, and we see academia's view of entrepreneurs as more sophisticated fortune-tellers who can arbitrage market imperfections. By the late 1970s, the view had shifted to entrepreneurs as outworking and outwitting the competitors. The 1980s saw yet another shift to entrepreneurs as creating new businesses.[10]

There has also been a long-standing debate among academics and practitioners as to whether entrepreneurs are made or born. Some, like Tripod founder Bo Peabody, believe that entrepreneurs are born. He states in his book *Lucky or Smart?*, "One is an entrepreneur. Those who decide to become entrepreneurs are making the first in a long line of bad business decisions."[11] Bo rode the first Internet wave in the late 1990s and became a very wealthy man by age 26. He has a right to his opinion, but he is basing it on a very small sample size of one. Maybe he was a natural; maybe he was lucky—probably a little of both. On the other side of the debate, we have the author of *Entrepreneurs Are Made Not Born*, Lloyd Shefsky, a professor of entrepreneurship at Northwestern University's Kellogg School of Management. After interviewing more than 200 successful entrepreneurs, Shefsky concluded that successful entrepreneurs are made not born.[12] After interviewing entrepreneurs and venture capitalists (VCs), a 2005 study conducted at Brigham Young University concluded that entrepreneurs tend to side with the "born" concept, while VCs are split. The study was not black and white; instead it was looking at shades of gray, finding that entrepreneurs believe they are born with "75% of the factors that contribute to entrepreneurial success," whereas VCs believe entrepreneurs are born with "only 44% of the traits necessary for success."[13]

This "made or born" debate is just one niche of the overall "nature versus nurture" debate. Scientists have long been arguing one side or the other. In a recent article, Daniel L. Everett, best known for his study of the Amazon Basin's Pirahã people, writes, "Human reasoning is the core of human flexibility. And it is this flexibility, not hard-wiring, that is the truly distinctive advantage and characteristic of human beings." Everett is in good company when it comes to the concept that nature is nurtured.[14] Jesse Prinz's *Beyond Human Nature*[15] and Philip Lieberman's *The Unpredictable Species*[16] both confront the "entrepreneur is made" view and seem to side with the Brigham Young University study. In other words, trying to pick one side of the "made or born" argument is misguided; instead entrepreneurs are first born, then made.

What I told you at the end of Chapter 1 about the effort by practitioners and academics to challenge the pedal to the metal approach to entrepreneurship can be seen in business books, university programs, and government programs that promote a more learning-based approach. In fact, one of the unique characteristics of the I-Corps program is that it is based on a validation-learning model of entrepreneurship. This model parallels the scientific-method approach that scientists have been using for hundreds of years. Where does this scientific approach have its roots? To get an answer I examined corporate innovation management theory. What I found was that over the years there has been more attention paid to the corporate side of the innovation equation than to entrepreneurship. The reason is quite simply that corporations have had the funds to pay for the attention, while entrepreneurs have not. I don't mean to suggest, of course, that there was no effort to examine entrepreneurship. As I said in the beginning of this chapter, there was plenty of interest. But what is interesting here is that the amount of effort spent on corporate innovation dwarfs that spent on entrepreneurship.

In 1995, Ian MacMillan, director of Wharton's Entrepreneurial Research Center, and Rita McGrath co-authored a paper for the *Harvard Business Review* titled "Discovery-Driven Planning." The paper starts off by highlighting two well-known corporate flops in the 1990s—Walt Disney's entrance into Europe and FedEx's Zapmail. Both flops had led to huge losses, from $600 million to more than $1 billion. The authors pose the question: "Why do such efforts [into unknown territories] often defeat even experienced, smart companies?"[17] I remember hearing about these failures around the time when I was launching my first Internet startup. I didn't give them much thought then, but these authors did and their conclusions were ahead of their time. As I read the paper, I was impressed with the insight these two authors had. This was well before Clayton Christensen's book on disruptive innovations and Gina O'Connor's book on radical innovation. The authors correctly noted that there is a "difference between planning for a new venture [corporate startup] and planning for a more conventional line of business." In a conventional business, a firm's incremental new product development processes are based on the knowledge gained through past experiences. However, when you are dealing with "new alliances, new markets, new products, new technologies," then the startup is dealing with assumptions, not knowledge.

It is "sheer folly" to treat a corporate startup like you treat a mature business. A corporate startup has to "envision what is unknown, uncertain and not yet obvious to the competition." Unlike ongoing businesses, corporate startups "are undertaken with a high ratio of assumptions to knowledge." The authors propose that corporate startups focus on systematically converting assumptions into knowledge by using their methodology. Otherwise, these startups will likely miss assumptions that can derail their business. On the surface, this may seem like an obvious conclusion, but I constantly encounter entrepreneurs who resist or refuse to put in the effort to reduce the assumptions. I often encounter entrepreneurs who are so focused on building a prototype that they do not want to get slowed down by running business experiments. Instead, they are so confident of knowing what they think they know that they put the pedal to the metal, only to end up with a failed startup.

Prior to the 1995 "Discovery-Driven Planning" paper, in 1985 authors Zenas Block and Ian MacMillan suggested that startups need to consider and test underlying assumptions rather than focus on financial statements.[18] In 1995, Hollister Sykes and David Dunham wrote a paper entitled "Critical Assumption Planning."[19] The paper takes the concept of testing assumptions one step further by introducing the concept of a "learning loop." The authors state that the "primary activity in a new venture must be learning from testing the assumptions and responding to what is learned." Absolutely! It's amazing that it took another 15 years for this notion to take hold in the entrepreneurship world. The idea that startups should implement "a process of discovery—proposing and testing a series of hypotheses about what the market needs and how best to deliver it" is not new. What is new is the implementation of these concepts to entrepreneurship. I'm not saying that this is the first time that the concept of a learning loop appeared in a business context, but I am saying that it occurred well before the current movement toward validated learning appeared.

PERSONAL EXPERIENCES

It was the summer of 1965 when a tall, handsome man with blond hair and blue eyes wove his station wagon in and out of foot traffic looking for a place to park the car. Startled by the thousands of people surrounding the family's car, his three-year-old son was starting to cry in the backseat. Pepe gazed over to his beautiful wife, who sat patiently at his side. He wondered, not for the first time, how lucky he was to have her in his life. Pepe was worried about his family. He and his wife, Hilda, had made a decision to move to New York from Lima, Peru, and he was scared. He didn't know the language and had gathered what little he knew about the American culture from Abbott and Costello, Martin and Lewis, and Humphrey Bogart movies. At times Pepe felt like the uncertainty he faced was going to drown him. So he decided to take a break from all his worries and visit his son's favorite market, La Parada in Lima. In 1965, La Parada market was the place families would go to buy in bulk. Pepe finally found a spot and quickly parked the station wagon. He ran around to the other side of the car, opened the door for Hilda, and put his son on his shoulders. He navigated around the crowds and walked over to the fruit section where they sold bananas. His son laughed as he stared at what seemed to be an unending sea of bananas. I should say *I* laughed, and I never forgot that moment. Why? Certainly there were other memorable events that came after, including the trip to Miami, then to Brooklyn, and finally to Queens, New York. Maybe I picked up on my father's concerns. Maybe it was the beginning of living with years of uncertainty about every basic need from food to electricity. I like to think that it has something to do with my entrepreneurial spirit. The market was filled with entrepreneurs trying to sell their goods. Some of those entrepreneurs would go on to build supermarket chains. Others would fail. Did this environment influence me? Is this why the memory remains while so many others have faded? I choose to believe that it did influence me.

Unlike most people, I am comfortable with the uncertainty that goes along with being an entrepreneur. Uncertainty is what surrounded my family's lives. It is what I considered normal. When I was growing up in Queens, New York, we didn't know whether there would be heat, electricity, or food on any given day. At the age of 10, I would go with my parents to the mortgage company, Green Point Bank, where they would plead with the manager, coincidentally named Mr. Green, not to foreclose on the house. I think that my story is probably typical of many first-generation immigrants. It may be why so many immigrants turn out to be entrepreneurs.

My first startup was launched in the early 1990s with an idea and a handshake. At the time, I was consulting on the implementation of new desktop prepress technologies. One of my clients asked if I would be willing to partner with him on launching a separate business that could take people's desktop files and print collateral material like brochures and flyers. Today, I can do that by going to expresscopy.com and uploading a file. Back then there was no Internet as we now know it. People were saving files to floppy disks. Taking a file and generating a final high-quality printed piece was a big deal. So, we went all-in and six months later the startup was profitable. What about the handshake deal to be 50/50 partners? Well, the offer on the table was 90/10 with me getting maybe 10 percent! I was young and principled, so rather than signing the deal at 10 percent, I decided to walk away empty-handed and a little smarter for my troubles.

Soon after my first startup, my wife and I decided to create an incubator for Internet startups. We didn't call it an incubator, because we didn't know what an incubator was. Instead, we described it as an umbrella for creative people with Internet-based ideas. We called ourselves NY Metro and we were off to the races. We did several soft launches to test the market—the equivalent of doing market experiments today. We launched several sites, including City Magazine, Singles, Wrestling News, and Cyber Sitcom websites. We met some amazing people. This was the beginning of the dot-com bubble, and I was lucky enough to live in one of the main centers for dot-com startups, New York City. I would regularly have meetings in cafés around Fifth Avenue and 23rd Street—the original Silicon

Alley. I connected with Ted Leonsis, current co-CEO of Groupon, then an AOL executive, who recommended that I focus on one idea. I remember seeing John F. Kennedy Jr. at the table next to me at a café I frequented. The founder of MySpace, Brad Greenspan, who was running a startup named eUniverse, made a bid to acquire one of my websites. It was an exciting time, where eyeballs were king and the new economy was taking off. We ended up focusing on one of the soft launches that was doing well and managed to get a group of Oklahoma City angels to invest.

I would like to take a moment to give a brief explanation of startup funding. The term *angels* or *angel investors* or *business angels* is used to describe wealthy people who like to invest their own money in startups. Venture capitalists (VCs), in contrast, manage a fund for investments in startups. I find angel investors easier to deal with than venture capitalists, as the angels I have dealt with invested in the person and team more than the opportunity. Angels generally have more favorable terms in their agreements with startups. On the downside, angels generally invest smaller amounts (up to $1 million), while venture capitalists like to invest much larger amounts, preferably starting at $5 million. However, there are VCs that invest smaller amounts and angels that invest larger amounts.

Back to my story: In 1999, we sold the company to Snowball.com. It was during the negotiations with Snowball that I met Mark Jung, then CEO, who spoke about viral growth. I had never heard that word used in that context before, and it would become one of the most important concepts for Internet startups to understand. This experience had a profound impact on the way I viewed startups. It was during this time that I came to understand the process of fund-raising and deal negotiations. I became an amateur lawyer, drafting hundreds of agreements with advertisers, producers, writers, and firms. Although my first startup was a quick success, this second startup allowed me to reap the rewards of years of working seven days a week. I learned that you must have a passion for launching a startup and that the startup team is a fragile thing. You must love your fellow startup team members, because you are going to face tough times and bumps that will challenge these friendships. This second startup experience taught me the value of market testing, although I would not come to fully appreciate this for another eight years.

After selling my second startup, I went on to launch a few more startups in a soft launch mode. However, in March 2000 the dot-com bubble burst and by 2001 the launching of a site with only 500,000 visitors was not highly valued. Major Internet firms folded one after the other, including Boo.com, Freeinternet.com, and Pets.com. It was a time of introspection and thought as to what worked and did not work. I decided to get my MBA degree by going to school full-time while working on my next startup—a medical device startup out of Albany, New York. It was tough juggling a full-time class workload and launching a startup. This startup was the first one that I did not found; instead I was hired to be the CEO. I was able to recruit fellow MBA students to be part of the startup. We had great chemistry, and for the first time in my career I participated in a business plan competition. We won the competition and were able to raise funds from local angels. However, we decided not to move forward after it became clear that it would take years and substantial investment to bring the device to the market. Instead, the founders focused on selling the intellectual property (IP). Shortly after leaving the medical device startup, I was hired as a CEO of a software technology startup. This was a fantastic experience. It was with this startup that I honed my licensing deal skills, including drafting, negotiating, and closing numerous license agreements. It also reinforced my view on startup teams, the importance of market testing, and the importance of good advisers.

During the final fifth year at the software technology startup, I began as an adjunct professor and entrepreneur in residence at Rensselaer Polytechnic Institute (RPI) in Troy, New York. I started working with startups on a new startup management methodology, The Pivot Startup. I was able to take the lessons learned and combine them with the research on innovation to form a methodology for managing startups. As mentioned in the Introduction, it was my work here that led to my conversation with my friend Marty, which eventually led to this book being written. In my second year at RPI, I became the program director of the Entrepreneurship

Center. This role provided me the opportunity to reach out to more entrepreneurially minded students and faculty to provide them with the knowledge and capabilities to launch Pivot startups that are focused on reducing the uncertainty and increasing the learning.

Over the years I have been fortunate to be part of successful startups and have felt the sting of unsuccessful launches. I have also seen hundreds of other startups being led astray by business advisers who meant well but had no business giving advice. These advisers tried to fit corporate management techniques into a startup environment and sealed the fates of these unfortunate startups. I can't say for sure whether these startups would have succeeded without such advice, but what I can say and do know is that there are proven startup methodologies that will improve any startup's chance for success.

NOTES

1. Manju Puri and David Robinson, "Who Are Entrepreneurs and Why Do They Behave That Way?," Duke University and National Bureau of Economic Research (NBER), 2006.
2. John Burgstone and Bill Murphy Jr., *Breakthrough Entrepreneurship* (San Francisco: Farallon Publishing, 2012).
3. "The Last AnNounce(r)ment," Hueniverse.com, April 25, 2008, http://hueniverse.com/2008/04/the-last-announcerment/.
4. Ibid.
5. Ibid.
6. "Bill Gates.biography," Biography.com, www.biography.com/people/bill-gates-9307520?page=2.
7. Tim Ferriss, "Do You Really Know Bill Gates? The Myth of Entrepreneur as Risk-Taker," Fourhourworkweek.com, September 13, 2009, www.fourhourworkweek.com/blog/2009/09/13/bill-gates-risk-taker/.
8. "John R. Opel," IBM.com, www-03.ibm.com/ibm/history/exhibits/chairmen/chairmen_7.html.
9. "A History of Windows—Highlights from the First 25 years—1975–1981: Microsoft Boots Up," Microsoft.com, http://windows.microsoft.com/en-us/windows/history.
10. Murray Low and Ian MacMillan, "Entrepreneurship: Past Research and Future Challenges," *Journal of Management* 14, no. 2 (1988).

11. Bo Peabody, *Lucky or Smart? Secrets to an Entrepreneurial Life* (Charleston, SC: BookSurge, 2008).
12. Lloyd Shevsky, *Entrepreneurs Are Made Not Born* (New York: Glencoe/ McGraw-Hill, 1996).
13. Ervin Black, Greg Burton, Anne Traynor, and David Wood, "Are Entrepreneurs Born or Made? Views of Entrepreneurs and Venture Capitalists," Brigham Young University, March 2005.
14. "Where Nature and Nurture Clash: Pioneering a New Theory of Language," NYDailyNews.com, February 11, 2013, www.nydailynews.com/blogs/page views/2013/01/where-nature-and-nurture-clash-pioneering-a-new-theory-of-language.
15. Jesse Prinz, *Beyond Human Nature* (New York: Allen Lane/Penguin, 2012).
16. Philip Lieberman, *The Unpredictable Species* (Princeton, NJ: Princeton University Press, 2013).
17. Ian MacMillan and Rita McGrath, "Discovery-Driven Planning," *Harvard Business Review*, July 1995.
18. Zenas Block and I. C. MacMillan, "Milestones for Successful Venture Planning," *Harvard Business Review*, September/October 1985.
19. Hollister B. Sykes and David Dunham, "Critical Assumption Planning: A Practical Tool for Managing Business Development Risk," *Journal of Business Venturing* 10 (1995): 413–424.

CHAPTER 5

ENTREPRENEUR AND CORPORATE ENTREPRENEUR: FRAMING THE PERSPECTIVES

In Chapters 5, 8, 13, and 16, we, Professors Gina O'Connor, and Lois Peters, will offer our commentary on the various insights and perspectives provided by Remy and Joanne on the entrepreneur and corporate entrepreneur, respectively.

Let's start with some general thoughts and questions, not necessarily associated with a chapter, yet important for framing these two perspectives.

Are corporate entrepreneurship or individual startups riskier? Which have the higher likelihood of failure?

In the corporate entrepreneurship (CE) world, what prevents pivots?

There is an escalation of commitment through increasing sunk costs, from people taking an overly optimistic stance, and from the planning fallacy of thinking things will take a shorter time than can be reasonably expected. There is a system missing to support CE, with too much reliance on the passion model, a lone champion, and an intrapreneur, as described in the intrapreneurship model in Chapter 3. Commitment is to today's strategy versus an emergent one. Without the right learning mind-set, experiments are conducted that are inherently biased or too narrow. There is a tension between the need to focus and the need for flexibility required of experimentation, and this creates barriers to exploration.

This is an interesting observation because in many ways these are the same factors that derail success of startups, such as the passion model, focus, the immediate business strategy, and so forth. People believe these attributes drive the success of startups, but they do not.

So, what helps a corporate firm develop startups?

There is a requirement to embrace a portfolio approach and clearly define a strategic intent. There needs to be an information-rich environment, with easily accessible networkers and brokers to help develop it. In the startup world, venture capitalists (VCs) will replace founders if they do not work out and use boards to bring subject matter expertise and networks. Large firms, or more established companies, attempt to emulate this with advisory boards, but there is little consideration early on about replacing a team member. In fact, even when companies defund projects, they let champions go on and on and don't really stop those projects; the projects just go underground until the air is clear again.

Both of these corporate-related challenges—of defunding and never really stopping projects—are either blocking or apathy measures. The outcome is that corporations do not proactively work to leverage learning and move forward. Project churn and redirection are treated as failure, rather than as a norm of the learning process. With coaching, champions can play a pivotal role to help uncover assumptions and keep biases to a lower level. Ideally, they should provide easier access to resources and help with leveraging networks. In addition, a robust system can also provide a safety net to mitigate resource and organization uncertainties so the corporate entrepreneur can fail and still go on. For startups, resource and organization uncertainties are also prevalent, though they might look different. On the resource side, the focus is on sources of capital and labor, and organization issues are compounded by how a startup fits in its ecosystem.

COMPARING ENTREPRENEURS

Chapters 3 and 4 compare corporate entrepreneurs and entrepreneurs, and give us some background and context for each. We'd like to compare entrepreneurs on three dimensions:

1. The differences in the types of people who choose each career path option.
2. The differences in the contexts in which they are operating.
3. How well we understand the two processes, comparing starting up a new venture outside a company environment and our level of sophistication when starting up a new venture inside a company environment.

Differences between Entrepreneurs and Corporate Entrepreneurs

Table 5.1 compares points that Remy and Joanne have made regarding the characteristics of individual entrepreneurs and corporate entrepreneurs. Corporate entrepreneurs face not only the challenge of navigating unclaimed or undiscovered territory in the marketplace, but also the challenge of convincing the company's leadership how important it is to invest in this initiative. They love the challenge and want what they perceive as best for their companies. Otherwise, face it—they would get bored with their jobs! They're smart, they're multidisciplinary, and they understand political diplomacy. They want to accomplish something. These are not people who consider their jobs just a nine-to-five activity. Much of their self-identity is associated with making change happen in their company. Entrepreneurs, in turn, take uncertainty as a given. It doesn't bother them in the least. They know who to go to for just about any problem and are great at mitigating risk. They don't care about owning resources per se; their networks are their most important resource.

It's so interesting to observe how much more independent entrepreneurs are than corporate entrepreneurs. The latter love being part of a larger organization, and view their companies as

TABLE 5.1   Comparing Types of Entrepreneurs

Entrepreneurs (Chapter 4)	Corporate Entrepreneurs (Chapter 3)
Love the challenge of making a difference. Comfortable with uncertainty and very optimistic.	Love the challenge; want to make a difference to the market and to their companies. Sometimes perceived as threats or as aggressive because they challenge the status quo and push for opportunities. Embrace change and uncertainty and are goal-oriented.
Opportunity seekers, with or without resources under their control. Described as persistent, creative, and courageous leaders, who can motivate and manage a team.	Cross-functional individuals who see opportunities at the interfaces. Capable of working across multiple functions to develop a holistic business opportunity. Broadly educated and integrative. Possess superior technical capabilities, and are inquisitive, curious, assertive. Risk takers, passionate. Business and market savvy; excellent networkers and effective communicators; able to address resource and organization uncertainties.
Both born and made.	Both born and made. Not everyone is good at this (Insight 7).
Good entrepreneurs are capable of leveraging the startup ecosystem they launch in.	Good corporate entrepreneurs manage political battles as they move forward with business concepts.

full of smart, capable people who can be leveraged as resources. The company's name also enables the corporate entrepreneur to tap external networks easily. Entrepreneurs, on the other hand, view everyone in the world this way, and they act like it. They are very head strong about their idea and, as Remy indicates, frequently benefit from helpful coaching about learning to pivot since they can become very committed to their idea. Their startup ecosystem may help them mature into professional entrepreneurs, and they recycle into new and potentially more promising opportunities each time.

Differences in the Operating Contexts

Table 5.2 compares the work environments of the two types of entrepreneurs.

Individual startups do better in communities that support that culture. That is why technology parks, technology clusters around

TABLE 5.2 Comparing Entrepreneurs' Work Environments

Entrepreneurs (Chapter 4)	Corporate Entrepreneurs (Chapter 3)
Silicon Alley (New York) and other startup communities. Remy met famous CEOs and had a great support infrastructure. Advent of regional clusters, accelerator programs such as TechStars and Entrepreneurs' Organization chapters.	Watch out for isolation from strategic intent and for corporate tyrannies associated with dominant culture of operational excellence and short-term biases or perspectives. Corporate silos can be a really big hurdle.
Variability in the munificence of the investment community. Besides the up-and-down availability of capital, there are the fads for different kinds of investment opportunities (e.g., dot-com bubble and bust).	Organizational appetite for innovation waxes and wanes.
Choose advisers wisely; don't listen to them all. Sometimes VCs can help access relevant advisers, but can you trust their motivations?	Can't choose them. Seek out key sponsors but have to convince everyone in the company who could shut you down.
Importance of the team. However, finding the right people can be difficult—limited to the founder's network. Issue of not having a broad-enough pool to draw on.	Not as proactively managed. How do we get the right people on the team since everyone is assigned a role already? Need to draft people or else draw from a pool. Should we create an innovators' pool? Broad pool is theoretically available, but many who would be a great help don't want to get involved, or if they do, they don't want to be involved for the duration.
Importance of experience, learning, and development from one venture to the next. Failures viewed as strengthening and learning experiences, almost like a badge of honor. Serial entrepreneurs are often heroes in the United States.	Learning based on experience rarely occurs. People don't get recycled from one corporate entrepreneur project to the next. Failed projects are interpreted as failed careers. Here, political capital is burned when you are associated with a failed project.
More likely to focus on less capital-intensive opportunities, market niches, or nascent markets.	Need market promise through size, robustness of application opportunities, and rate of growth or ability to dominate a sector.

universities, military labs, and corporate research and development (R&D) centers have grown up. Beyond these physical parks and incubators, the startup community is taking hold. We are seeing the emergence of experienced startup professionals, that is, serial entrepreneurs, who anchor these communities and are willing to give back, pay forward, and invest in developing inexperienced entrepreneurs. It becomes a culture that feeds on itself. Boulder, Colorado, is one center that has gained attention with the recent publication of Brad Feld's book *Startup Communities: Building an Entrepreneurial Ecosystem in Your City*.[1]

The same principle holds true for corporate startups. They also do better in communities that support a startup culture. Alas, the supportive culture is much rarer in a corporation. On balance, companies seem reticent to acknowledge that there is a startup professional and a need to develop a sustainable innovation function. It's emerging, it's dawning, and it is going to be the next step in the evolution of a sophisticated management discipline. Books like *Grabbing Lightning: Building a Capability for Breakthrough Innovation*[2] will help, we hope.

Progress in Understanding and Effectively Executing the Two Different Types of Entrepreneurship

How far have we come? How much have we improved?

Remy refers to "experienced startup professionals" in Chapter 1, and to the National Science Foundation's I-Corps program in Chapter 4. We love this idea because it shows that entrepreneurship is becoming viewed as a profession and that new business creation is becoming a discipline, with a set of principles that can be learned, transferred, and improved upon. We see it happening: Mark Zuckerberg learned from Apple's CEO, Steve Jobs, and Netscape's CFO, Peter Currie; the Instagram guys learned from Zuckerberg, and so it goes. Brad Feld describes a similar situation in Boulder, Colorado, in which he founded the Boulder chapter of the Young Entrepreneurs' Organization in 1996 in the hope of connecting the entrepreneur community with the investor community, and the rest is history. Many startups were founded, grown, and acquired by other growing companies, and the founders have then started their next companies *and* become resources to the next generation of CEOs.

So within industries, there are serial entrepreneurs and their progeny. Surround them with start-up communities that Feld describes and the numerous entrepreneurship programs in colleges and universities these days, and we have knowledge transfer—knowledge about how to be an entrepreneur.

It's lagging in the corporate world. Joanne describes the transition of people at Moen, each of whom had an important influence in building the capability for innovation. When Louise Quigley found her way into that role, Moen then developed a repeatable approach to uncertainty reduction. She hadn't had much experience, nor had she been trained in the norms and conventions of the company. That was a blessing to help further a new mind-set. We have the emergence of the role of chief innovation officer and some new job titles indicative of innovation roles, but these are largely short-term assignments or not full-time assignments. They may be associated with being in a leadership training program or on a special project. Even IBM's Emerging Business Opportunities (EBO) program, so widely lauded as a professionalized management system for innovation, has been redirected away from new business creation and toward globalization of some of IBM's key strategic initiatives. Personnel who were EBO leaders are off on other projects or have left the company. The learning associated with a management system for innovation has been duly recorded but is not practiced at this time.

Of course, we know that a company's capacity for innovation will change over time and that the portfolio might be scaled back to adjust to strategic priorities, but it is not appropriate to abandon it entirely. Companies that do so have suffered financially or met their demise. The problem is that the implication of cutting off innovation activities doesn't raises its ugly head until a number of years later and people do not make the link back to innovation capacity. And when Louise decides it's time to move on at Moen, who will fill her shoes? This is why innovation is still an emerging discipline, and why we are making a call for companies to wake up and learn how to be ambidextrous—manage the present well and allow room for the future.

NOTES

1. Brad Feld, *Startup Communities: Building an Entrepreneurial Ecosystem in Your City* (Hoboken, NJ: John Wiley & Sons, 2012).
2. Gina C. O'Connor, Richard Leifer, Albert S. Paulson, and Lois S. Peters, *Grabbing Lightning: Building a Capability for Breakthrough Innovation* (San Francisco: Jossey-Bass, 2008).

PART TWO

PLANT = DISCOVERY—THE BUSINESS VISION

CHAPTER 6

DISCOVERY–
ATTRACTIVENESS
OF THE BUSINESS
OPPORTUNITY[1]

Let's go back to Insight 7 from Chapter 3 (that not everyone is good at this, you need the right people on board), and tell the story of Dylan and Frank.

Both were highly skilled analysts on my Nortel Business Ventures Group (BVG) team. They were early in their careers, ambitious, and diamonds in the rough that I knew would require my coaching to help them uncover their potential. They were part of the initial core team, and we developed our approach to innovation together. Dylan is an engineer, with an MBA, and Frank has his MBA, with a finance specialization. Their role was to screen and evaluate the ideas that were being submitted from Nortel employees to determine where we wanted to place our investment dollars. In the first few months, there was pent-up demand. A few teams came forward that had already been working on business opportunities, so we had to evaluate the merits of their proposals. We invested in two of these within our first few months, which took considerable time. We also had made a request for proposals from Nortel employees, so we also had to screen their submissions, most of which were simply raw, underdeveloped ideas, not investment opportunities. With the involvement of others on the team, Dylan and Frank screened out a few hundred ideas in the first year.

After about a year and a half of investing in promising Nortel technologies and business models, I received a call from our president of advanced technology, Gedas Sakus. A very disgruntled employee was not pleased that Frank had rejected his idea, and I was asked to look into it. So I spoke with Frank and he explained all the reasons for his rejection of the idea. On the surface, he applied very sound logic on the basis of appropriate assumptions, and yet my instincts told me I was missing something. I decided to ask a little more to get impressions from others on our team and was wondering why Dylan had not run into a similar situation.

What emerged reinforced Insight 3 that there is a lot more to Discovery than evaluating ideas and Insight 7 that not everyone is suited for certain innovation roles. Discovery is about the world of possibilities, not probabilities, where divergent thinking is required to conceive of how ideas can be shaped into opportunities. Frank, with his finance background, lives in the world of probabilities that can be factored into an economic model. He would shut down ideas, often prematurely, before the innovation group could get a better sense of their potential, because possibilities cannot be modeled. Dylan's background, in contrast, makes him more suited to the world of possibilities, and he also has the right mind-set for Discovery. In fact, Dylan is one of the best people I have ever seen, along with Hans Brink Hansen at Grundfos and Jamie Nielsen at NOVA Chemicals, for building upon ideas to shape them into opportunities and articulating their value in a way they can be understood.

Once I realized the skill sets required for Discovery were about opportunity elaboration and connecting the dots, not about evaluation, Dylan became our point person for Discovery and Frank's activities were redirected to the evaluation of business opportunities once they were more developed. And guess what? I never heard from Gedas again—at least not on that issue!

I know what you are thinking. Of course, many ideas do need to be screened out early and there are always going to be people not happy that their idea was not chosen, yet even delivering this message requires a finesse that not many people have. The bottom line is that Discovery is much more suited to people with the mind-set of asking questions to look for possibilities, rather than those who look for the reasons why something will not work. This requires working together with the idea originator to shape the opportunity, compared with asking the idea originator to convince me of why I should pay attention to the idea. Often, those with the ideas lack the skills to make the compelling case, which is where the opportunity recognizers, the Dylans, versus the idea evaluators, the Franks, come in. Both are talented, yet one is more suited to Discovery than the other. Think of the two legal systems in the world: one where you are innocent until proven guilty and the other where you are guilty until proven innocent. Which one do you think offers the best potential for a fair hearing? Which mind-set would you rather be facing when coming forward with an early idea? I know which one I would choose. Do you?

Now let's see how this carries through to Discovery, where we Plant a business vision of what *could be*, not what will be, since we do not know yet... with far too much uncertainty!

DISCOVERY PRINCIPLES[2]

Discovery is about the conceptualization of business opportunities that may have a major impact in the marketplace through the delivery of either new performance benefits or greatly improved performance over what already exists. We are often asked which is better—technology push, where the technology drives the innovation, or market pull, based on a clear market need. The answer is that it is not an either–or situation; rather, it requires that the technical and market considerations be addressed in parallel. Often for opportunities fraught with uncertainty, the potential of the technology or the market potential is not clear. The market needs to learn from the technology, and the technology needs to evolve based on what is learned from the market. For this reason, a serial product development or phase gate process does not work, because it does not support this type of iterative learning approach. Once the product is defined, it is developed and then field–tested prior to a full market launch. Discovery is the starting point to define the business concept that will be iteratively tested during Incubation to arrive at a definable product.

Discovery requires unique skills to uncover technical insights, recognize opportunities, and articulate their value. The technical insights come from understanding the underlying science, demonstrating or making assumptions regarding the feasibility of the technology or business model, as well as the evaluation of emerging or competing technologies and a company's intellectual property (IP) position. Opportunity recognition requires skills in external and internal scouting to clarify the potential of opportunities. For opportunity articulation, networking with potential market collaborators or early market adopters is required to identify sources of perceived value and clarify strategic possibilities for the company. This needs to be communicated in a language senior leaders can understand, which is less about the technology and more about the business potential. An important element of describing this business potential is in identifying a list of potential applications to begin investigating to reinforce that there are many strategic options.

Therefore, the four objectives for moving from Discovery to Incubation are to:

1. Focus on application possibilities that are most promising from a market perspective.
2. Develop clear value propositions for various stakeholders in the market and within the company.
3. Identify potential business model options as well as technology prototype requirements for testing during Incubation.
4. Provide a resource plan for moving forward (team, money, need for partnerships), including making the case for why this opportunity is ready for Incubation.

It is worth emphasizing that the most promising opportunity from a market perspective does not mean the biggest. We are looking for markets that can benefit the most from the innovation. This is a common mistake in most companies, which tend to be

TABLE 6.1   Discovery Focus Areas

Plant	*Discovery* Conceptualization Output = Opportunity Concept
Technical Uncertainty Understanding technology drivers, value, and economic feasibility	Technical Feasibility and Capabilities, IP Landscape Scoping
Market Uncertainty Learning about market drivers, value creation, and business viability	Application Possibilities, Value Proposition, Business Potential, Business Model Options
Resource Uncertainty Accessing money, people, and capabilities internally and externally	Availability of Funding and Right People, Competency Gaps Identification for Partnering Options
Organization Uncertainty Gaining and maintaining organizational legitimacy	Capacity for Innovation, Fit with Strategic Intent, and Senior Level Commitment

Source: rInnovation Group

concerned about what the market can do for them in terms of revenue generation, rather than what they can provide the market in terms of benefits.

See Table 6.1 for the Discovery Focus Areas from Table 3.3, Innovation Business Opportunity Evolution, in Chapter 3.

DISCOVERY AND OPEN INNOVATION

Prior to the breaking up of AT&T in 1984, and early in my telecommunications career, the closed corporate labs, such as Bell Labs, were the ones driving the model for innovation. What I mean by *closed* is that the source of inventions was internal—research and development (R&D) took place inside these labs, performed by the people working there. They did not look outside for inventions. The belief was that we have the best people working here, so why even look outside?

This is not to suggest that these inventions did not spur the growth of other companies. There were cross-licensing agreements that made these discoveries available to outside parties. In fact, many game-changing inventions came from these labs, such as the transistor, the laser, information theory, and C and C++ programming languages, to name a few. They certainly became the catalysts for the information and communications revolution and the early seeds of Silicon Valley. Other labs, such as those at Westinghouse, General Electric, Kodak, DuPont, British Telecom, Bayer, Merck, and so forth, provided the foundation for our twentieth-century infrastructure and our improved way of life. With the rapid adoption of technology, the world is becoming a much smaller place and all great ideas do not exist within the confines of a corporate research and development lab (they never did, yet it was the prevailing model for innovation of the times).

Interestingly, these monolithic, closed labs are actually a twentieth-century phenomenon, brought on by the two world wars, and they most certainly created many inventions and provided homes for inventors to bring their inventions to life. Now, the model for innovation has evolved to resemble how it was before then (forward or back to the past—history does repeat itself) to combine *Invention* activities from internally focused research and *Discovery* activities within and outside of the company. *Invention* is the creation of something from the laboratories that was previously unknown. *Discovery*, in contrast, is becoming aware of something known in other venues, but not known to the company or a group within the company. The most common model is where outside technologies are brought into a company to improve its Discovery capabilities. Of course, scientists have collaborated within and outside the company as a professional practice, but outside collaboration on a business level did not exist during the closed lab era, unless it was within the Bell family, for example.

The Open Innovation model combines these Invention and Discovery activities to shorten the time to understand a technology's or business model's market value and accelerate commercialization. Procter & Gamble's Connect + Develop open innovation approach is an excellent example, which brought Swiffer cleaning tools to the world through a partnership with a Japanese company.[3] Therefore, Discovery does not equal Invention. Invention is to create something new, whereas one can discover phenomena in the world that are used in other capacities, whether they are existing or new. In addition, Discovery does not equal R&D, as described in the story of Dylan and Frank; technical people often come up with the ideas, but need guidance to articulate their potential business and market value.

Today, the business outcomes of Discovery work depend on this Open Innovation model. While open innovation is not a new phenomenon, it is more widely embraced by the business community. Companies are now realizing that there needs to be a healthy balance between leveraging internal and external expertise to develop innovation opportunities.

DISCOVERY PROGRESSION: CAPTURING INNOVATION OPPORTUNITIES[4]

Ideas are only the beginning of the journey to create business value. While idea generation within the context of strategic intent, themes, or innovation portfolios and platforms is essential, the realizable value is in translating these ideas into business opportunities. An opportunity is defined as a match between a need in the marketplace (hidden or explicit) and a product or service offering that fills that need. Increasing the flow of good ideas requires directed idea generation based on strategic drivers and enablers such as think tanks, connection to external sources, and forecasting based on technology and market trends. It is not about serendipitous idea generation. Of course, accidental discoveries do happen, but these are rare. Most often a good idea comes through hard work, rather than a flash of insight, as in the famous quote from Thomas Edison: "Genius is 1 percent inspiration and 99 percent perspiration."

Opportunity Recognition

Going back to the story of Dylan and Frank: As we learned in our early years at Nortel, it is all about opportunities, and it is not easy to find them. We would all be extremely wealthy if we could do so. Let's go back to my Netscape story from Chapter 3. Imagine in the early days of the Internet around 1994, when I came upon the Mosaic browser and Netscape at this Bellcore meeting. I was working for Stentor, which was the consortium of Canadian telephone companies. I remember specifically Nick Ciancio at Pacific Bell bringing this opportunity to our attention. He said it would revolutionize the Internet by providing a user-friendly interface. It generated a lot of excitement at the meeting, and we all took the opportunity back to our home companies for consideration. As mentioned previously, not only did others not see the potential, but it was viewed more as a minor threat to our long distance business that could potentially displace some international toll traffic. Even though we were responsible for new business opportunities, it was difficult to make the case for why we should invest, especially with this mind-set and our entrenched long distance and data divisions.

This opportunity was shipped off to another group and eventually became the foundation of the Canadian Internet service provider Sympatico. Of course, Nick was right. It did revolutionize the Internet, and hindsight is 20/20. Yet, one can only imagine where the telephone companies would be today if they could have seen that the Internet was much more than displacing high-priced international long distance traffic. Recognizing opportunities is difficult, but articulating them in a way for others to see them is even more of a challenge.

In case you are wondering since it was such a long time ago . . . the word 'Internet' did exist in the early 90s. In fact, according to Wikipedia, the first use of the word internet was in a scientific paper in 1974 as an adjective and, in 1982, it became the noun it is today. Once again, another word, like innovation, that goes back in time and was used in a different context, as early as 1883! Interesting piece of trivia, now back to opportunity recognition.

Learning how to recognize opportunities requires building up skills to gather and scout for ideas that can then be shaped into attractive opportunities. People who are good at this we call *opportunity recognizers* or *innovation catalysts*, as we saw in the case of Dylan and Nick, or even me. They typically demonstrate a high level of technical sophistication to understand the potential of the technology, with a worldly market savvy to connect the dots with market needs. These people are often the mavericks in your company. You know who they are. Are you one of them? We push up against the status quo and are motivated to make a difference and stretch the company in new areas. We also know each other and play critical roles in conducting an informal sanity check of an opportunity's potential, within our well-connected internal and external networks.

Once opportunities have been uncovered, an initial evaluation should take place involving team members with senior management credibility, innovation project experience, deep technical expertise, business development experience, and, perhaps, even specialized expertise from outside the company. The initial decision criteria and assumptions should focus on:

- How the technology will unfold.
- How the markets will develop.
- How the company will respond.

It is important to be clear on the assumptions you are making, given the uncertainty of these early opportunities. Often, these assumptions are misinterpreted as facts, only to surface at the most inopportune time in the innovation life cycle to seriously undermine the potential of the business opportunities. This happened to us at Nortel with our NetActive venture. The team came from the residential broadband area and we believed that residential broadband deployment was imminent. Of course, it is standard today, but it was clearly an assumption that we accepted as a fact in the late 1990s. I will elaborate upon this story in Chapter 10.

Remember the ABCs: Admit what you don't know. Assumptions count on this mind-set. The outcome of this evaluation process is to decide what to do next. Should we invest in this opportunity to move forward to Incubation and learn more from the market? Does it require additional Discovery work or scoping before this decision can be made? Should we look for revenue streams via licensing, especially for Discoveries that do not fit with our strategy? Or should we simply not pursue it at this time and put it on the shelf or back burner, knowing that there might be a better time or alignment of ideas in the months or years to come. See Figure 6.1 for a summary of decision criteria and decision options.

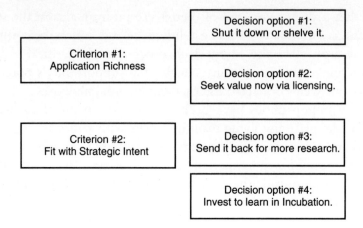

FIGURE 6.1   Discovery Criteria and Decision Options
Source: RPI Phase I Research

This last point about timing is best illustrated by another story. How many times have you seen seemingly unrelated ideas come together to form a compelling business opportunity? I have seen it happen over and over again. This is why we put certain ideas and opportunities on the shelf, not in the delete file. One of our greatest contributions to a Nortel business division in the late 1990s was a bridging or gateway solution to enable the emerging Internet protocol (IP) network and the public switched telephone network (PSTN) to communicate, as illustrated in Figure 6.2. This business opportunity came to Dylan by combining a fourth idea he was screening with three others he had already screened and rejected. He did not build out this business concept alone, but worked with the originators of the first three ideas and the fourth, who had become key players in the informal opportunity recognizer network. This would have been unlikely to happen without our ideas repository, the opportunity recognition skills we had developed, the richness of our internal networks, and Dylan's organizational memory. What is even more interesting is that discussions are taking place in 2013 to see if now is the time to retire the PSTN networks and transition to networks running IP only. Clearly, the PSTN to IP bridging or gateway concept provided value for a very long time.

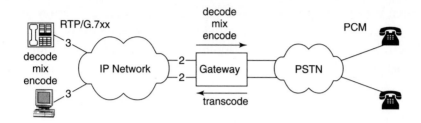

FIGURE 6.2 PSTN to IP Bridging Concept
Source: Canadian Department of Telecom

Application Generation and the Business Vision

We introduced Discovery as the place where we Plant a business vision of what *could be*, not what will be, since we do not know yet. So how do we get the game in play, when we most certainly do not have answers to standard product development questions? We do not even know what the product is yet!

This is where the business vision comes in since we are betting on future potential. How do we tell the story in a compelling way to at least have some room to play and experiment with business concept options? The answer is that we require a broad range of application areas to maximize our options since many of these applications will result in dead ends once we test them in the market. With an extensive list of application areas, we can then make an assumption, based on order of magnitude, not detailed market size calculations, that the market is big enough to warrant our attention. We also need to link the opportunity with the company's future ambitions or strategic intent, as Moen did such a superb job in defining. This way we can offer some level of confidence in the potential of the business opportunity, in the absence of a credible business case. It is worth emphasizing that as part of communicating the business vision, applications need to be articulated in terms of the end game of what value they could bring to the market, not necessarily what value would accrue to the company; often it is too early to know.

In generating applications, it requires divergent, not convergent, thinking to generate as many applications as possible. A repository of applications is required. Most often, it takes many application ideas to identify opportunities that could become Incubation projects. So how do companies uncover application ideas? The following are some of the techniques companies have used (and you can, too):

- Interview anyone you believe can be a source of applications ideas. This is how opportunity recognizers, such as Dylan, uncover and shape their opportunities through their specialized networks.

  - Interview the originator of the idea.
  - Interview others with deep technical or market expertise in the same area of science or business in industries other than the company's.
  - Interview others with deep expertise in adjacent areas of science or business involved in your company's industry and in other industries.
  - Interview lead users or early adopters of technology.

- Monitor what is going on in the thought leader networks and on the fringes where the disruptions occur. Our Nortel neural network venture, to detect fraud in telecommunications, originated from leading-edge research at a UK university.

  - Review governmental requests for proposals or competitions.
  - Investigate programs taking place in research institutes and universities.
  - Read widely: technology, innovation, business, science, and other publications. Innovation happens at the intersection points.

- Attend professional conferences focused on emerging trends to inspire you. I attended a smart card conference in the early 1980s to develop our Calling Card strategy, long before the commercial application of smart cards.
- Work with companies able to match your Discovery quests with the outside community of experts. Westinghouse and other companies are doing this to tap into the Small Business Innovation Research (SBIR) companies through the Innovation Development Institute.

For the early evaluation of applications that you generate and positioning of your business vision, there are two major criteria to help you consider the overall business potential:

1. *Application richness or robustness.*[5] Is there enough richness to enable a variety of applications and promote an options mentality?

   - Are there many product or process opportunities? Are there whole families of products?
   - Will exploration of the application connect the company to new partners? New market domains?
   - Are there several differences that the application market values, not just one?

2. *Strategic fit.* Does it fit with the company's strategic intent—its ambition of where it wants to be five to 10 years from now?

   - Could we deliver upon our strategic intent through the pursuit of this business opportunity?

Discovery provides the foundation and Plants the initial business vision of what could be, which is likely to shift over time based on what you learn (see Figure 6.3). This business vision is important to provide you with the credibility and strong footing from which to Pivot in Incubation. Four key insights to carry forward with you from Discovery to Incubation are:

1. For *idea generation*, ideas come from many places. The frequency of "aha's" or the lightbulb going off is very low. This is the reason for the emphasis on perspiration versus inspiration based simply on hard work.
2. *Opportunity recognition* is about connecting technical ideas with business possibilities.

   - Skills are required to combine, elaborate, and develop ideas into opportunities.
   - The most important critical success factor is the ability to tap into informal internal and external networks.

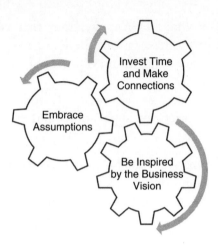

FIGURE 6.3   Discovery Insights for Plant

3. In *initial evaluation*, making explicit assumptions regarding technology, markets, and company strategy is the only way to move forward.
4. The *business vision* gets the game in play by communicating in a compelling way that there is a richness of applications, that the market is big enough and growing enough to warrant further experimentation, and that there is the promise of furthering a company's strategic ambitions.

THE DISCOVERY TOOLKIT IN BRIEF

With these Discovery principles and insights in mind, the Discovery Toolkit has been developed to help you transform your ideas into opportunities and learn how to make the case for why more investment is required in Incubation to test business concepts in the market. We want to avoid analysis paralysis in Discovery. The fact is that there will be more questions than answers. Therefore, we need to get the questions right. The answers come by engaging in market experiments during Incubation and doing this as early as possible. This is the only way to uncover the true potential (or lack thereof) of higher-uncertainty innovation opportunities.

Standard Tools

The Discovery Toolkit is available on our website at www.innovation 2pivot.com. We hope you take the time to experiment with these tools and maybe even make some progress in turning your idea into an opportunity. The following tools make up the Discovery Toolkit, and each is described in the following subsections:

- Idea Uncertainty Assessment Tool.
- Genesis Pad Opportunity Description.
- Opportunity Screening Criteria.
- Opportunity Potential Questions.
- Uncertainty Identification Checklist for Discovery.
- Opportunity Stakeholder Positioning Steps.
- Plant or Discovery Value Pitch.

Idea Uncertainty Assessment Tool

Are you unsure how to determine the level of uncertainty you face with your idea? The Idea Uncertainty Assessment Tool in Table 6.2 has been developed to help you decide. If you are facing medium and high levels of uncertainty, then the D-I-A approach is the right one for your idea and you will benefit by using the Discovery Toolkit. If you are facing low uncertainty, then you are likely dealing with only an incremental improvement, which should be sent to your product development process for consideration. It should also be a lot easier for you to position the value of your idea, since you know a lot more. If you do happen to be struggling with this positioning or with making your case, the Discovery Toolkit might still be able to help. We have been told throughout the years that the principles guiding these tools also help in the incremental innovation space. While this was not our intent, try it on and see if it works for you.

Genesis Pad Opportunity Description

Are you having trouble translating your idea in to an opportunity? The Genesis Pad Opportunity is a tool that enables you to take your raw idea and translate it into a potential opportunity hypothesis. The structure of the Genesis Pad, and the information requested,

TABLE 6.2 Idea Uncertainty Assessment Tool

	Uncertainty Level		
	High	Medium	Low
Technical Considerations			
Technology Feasibility or Business Model Viability	Unknown	Feasible and/or Viable	Product Defined
Intellectual Property (IP)	Unknown	Known and Not Filed	Known and Filed
Market Considerations			
Market Type	New Market	Market Unfamiliar to Company	Existing Market
Market Landscape	Unknown	Market Entry Options Known	Market Entry Option Selected
Resource Considerations			
Funding Source	Unknown	Known, Partially Available	Available through Funding Process
People and Competence Fit	Unknown or No/Low Fit	Some Internal Fit, External Partnerships Likely Required	Good Resource Fit
Organization Considerations			
Strategic Fit	Unknown	Beyond Current Strategy	Current Strategy
Commercialization Timeline (Industry Specific)	Long-Term	Medium-Term	Near-Term

Note: Uncertainty at shaded level for ≥ six items is an incremental innovation project.
Source: rInnovation Group—inspired by work with Westinghouse

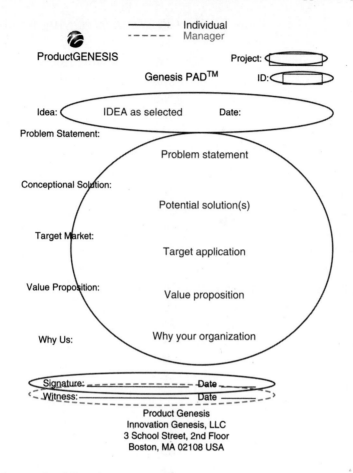

FIGURE 6.4 Genesis Pad Opportunity
Source: Product Genesis LLC.

guides you on how to flesh out your idea in sufficient detail to describe it as an opportunity, without a lot of time and effort on your part!

Questions to help you get there, as covered in Figure 6.4, include:

- *Problem statement.* What is the problem that needs to be solved?
- *Conceptual solution.* What are some possible solutions to the problem (or at least solution directions)?

- *Target market.* Who gets the value from solving this problem—who cares about it?
- *Value proposition.* What is the value of solving this problem?
- *Why us.* Why is this our problem to solve? Why is this our opportunity rather than someone else's?

Opportunity Screening Criteria

Are you wondering how to conduct an initial screening of your idea to compare its potential as an opportunity with your other ideas or those of colleagues? The Opportunity Screening Criteria are used to quickly evaluate the relative merits of multiple potential opportunities. This tool uses high-level criteria that are relatively easy to apply as a frame of reference without extensive time and effort. The Opportunity Screening Criteria in Table 6.3 include indicators of a given opportunity's potential from a market perspective; its fit with the company's technology, resource, and organization capabilities; and its alignment with the strategic or innovation intent.

TABLE 6.3   Opportunity Screening Criteria

Criteria	+1	0	−1
Market Magnitude Indicators	Large	Moderate	Small
Market Health	Growing	Flat	Declining
Market Value Proposition Indicators	Many	Some	None
Problem Definition	Good	Moderate	Limited
Conceptual Solutions	Some	Few	None
Company Value Proposition Indicators	Many	Some	None
Technical Capabilities Fit	Core/Adjacent	Stretch	None
Market Capabilities Fit	Core/Adjacent	Stretch	None
Organizational Capabilities Fit	Core/Adjacent	Stretch	None
Resource Capabilities Fit	Core/Adjacent	Stretch	None
Convergent Trends and Drivers	Multiple	2	1 or none
Countertrends and Drivers	1 or none	2	Multiple
Intellectual Property (IP) Activity	Some	None	Intense
Strategic Intent Fit	On Target	Stretch	None
TOTAL SCORE			

Source: Product Genesis LLC

To score your opportunity, treat all criteria equally. We are not trying to build a computational model! Remember we are in the world of uncertainty and just want to get a sense of whether there is any potential. Score each criterion as either +1, 0, or −1, and then sum up all your scores, adding or subtracting as you go. If you score above +5, then your opportunity has potential, so keep working through the tools. You might also want to include a hard disqualifier for certain criteria, where you must score +1. If you don't score +1, then you set this particular idea or opportunity aside. Grundfos did this to ensure that an opportunity contributed to its innovation intent pillars of Concern, Care, and Create. A positive score was required on at least two of these three pillars to qualify as part of its organizational commitment to sustainability.

Opportunity Potential Questions

Are you having trouble making your case and being heard in a culture that focuses on the short term? The Opportunity Potential Questions in Figure 6.5 are designed to help you think about what you can reasonably address during Discovery based on the uncertainty you face. From our research, getting from idea to business opportunity is the first discontinuity to be overcome to achieve commercial success. You will need to make a number of assumptions to move forward. This will help you to present your opportunity in a compelling way so you can at least make the case for why your opportunity is worthy of consideration based on its richness of applications, a big enough market, and a clear business vision.

I want to mention this vision thing. With hundreds of coaching sessions to reinforce this message, most people struggle with defining a business vision. What we do now is discuss what is possible and what is more likely to occur in the shorter term. We then develop a road map of strategic options, which become more uncertain over time. It is difficult to step out of your comfort zone and challenge the status quo. We are uncomfortable describing any business opportunity without the facts. However, as explained in the story of Dylan and Frank, this is the world of possibilities. We have to paint the picture of what could be based on assumptions, not facts. Do not be afraid to admit what you don't know (remember the ABCs) and step out!

Uncertainty areas	Yes	No	Maybe	Why
Technical considerations				
1. Is there the potential for significant improvements and/or cost reductions in what already exists or the creation of something new to the world or markets?				
2. Do you have confidence that technical challenges can be overcome and a learning prototype can be developed?				
Market considerations				
1. Can you identify a number of application possibilities?				
2. Can you provide a clear value proposition for the market?				
3. Do you have a sense of the market potential?				
Resource considerations				
1. Do you have the competencies internally to pursue this opportunity?				
2. Do you see the need for strategic partnerships?				
3. Is there a place to go in your company to make the case for funding?				
Organization considerations				
1. Does your opportunity fit with your company's strategic intent?				
2. Can you provide the rationale for why it makes sense for your company to pursue this new opportunity?				

FIGURE 6.5 Opportunity Potential Questions

Source: rInnovation Group

Uncertainty Identification Checklist for Discovery

Are you having trouble identifying your uncertainties or even knowing how to think about them, especially in the resource and organization areas? The Uncertainty Identification Checklist for Discovery in Tables 6.4 and 6.5 is a complement to the Opportunity Potential Questions to help you think through technical, market, resource, and organization uncertainties. It has been developed based on the experiences of many projects and has two parts. It identifies areas for you to consider and setbacks or potential showstoppers that could get in the way of your success.

Opportunity Stakeholder Positioning Steps

Are you unsure how to position your opportunity to get your stakeholders on board? The Opportunity Stakeholder Positioning Steps in Table 6.6 help you with this positioning. It is your homework to clarify the messages in your value pitch that your stakeholders need to hear. They all have different motivations and expectations, so you need to understand this to put together an effective value pitch, as described in the next subsection.

Plant or Discovery Value Pitch

Are you struggling with your value proposition and how to deliver it in a compelling way so it can be heard? The Plant or Discovery Value Pitch (or "reason to believe," as some companies use in their strategic intent development) is a powerful communication tool and becomes your value proposition intricately linked with your business vision. The goal is to attract interest in further discussions, not provide a detailed explanation of the opportunity's merits. All team members and key stakeholders should be able to deliver an effective value pitch, which evolves and becomes more effective through iterative learning. You should be able to develop an effective value pitch early in the life of your opportunity, even if it is based only on assumptions. If you cannot, you should ask yourself why. Is there an underlying problem with finding the potential value drivers? Or do you perhaps lack the skills to put it together and deliver it effectively?

Our Plant or Discovery Value Pitch guidelines have been adapted from the startup world for the corporate audience. The objective is to

TABLE 6.4 Discovery Uncertainty Identification Checklist—Areas to Consider

Categories	Technical Uncertainty	Market Uncertainty	Resource Uncertainty	Organization Uncertainty
Uncertainty Focus	Understanding technology drivers, value, and economic feasibility	Learning about market drivers, value creation, and business viability	Accessing money, people, and organizational competencies	Gaining and maintaining organizational legitimacy
Discovery Areas to Consider	• Completeness and Correctness of Underlying Scientific Knowledge • Articulation of New Benefits That Are Enabled • Potential Cost Saving Advantages	• Clarity of Value Proposition • Size of Business Potential • Potential for Multiple Market Applications	• Availability of Internal and External Funding • Requirements for Money, Team, and Partnerships • Business Concept Lead Choice	• Strategic Context for Innovation • Commitment of Senior Management

Source: rInnovation Group

TABLE 6.5 Discovery Uncertainty Identification Checklist—Setbacks or Potential Showstoppers

Categories	Technical Uncertainty	Market Uncertainty	Resource Uncertainty	Organization Uncertainty
Uncertainty Focus	Understanding technology drivers, value, and economic feasibility	Learning about market drivers, value creation, and business viability	Accessing money, people, and organizational competencies	Gaining and maintaining organizational legitimacy
Discovery Setbacks or Showstoppers **Technical = Specific to Discovery** **Market = Too Early To Know** **Resource and Organization = Any Stage**	• Technology or Business Model Proof of Concept Setback		• Major Funding Loss Due to Reversal of Overall Corporate Performance • Team Limitations • Inability to Attract Required Talent • Lack of Partnership Strategy • Failure of Alliance Deal or Technical Partner • Undefined Partnership Exit Conditions	• Loss of Champion • Change in Senior Management and/or Strategic Imperatives • Change in Senior Champion or Sponsor • Transfer of Responsibilities at Transition from Business Concept to Project • Lack of Strategic Communications • Inappropriate Portfolio and Project Level Metrics • Insufficient Runway to Demonstrate Business Results

Source: rInnovation Group

TABLE 6.6   Opportunity Stakeholder Positioning Steps

Strategic Communication Steps	Positioning Questions
Objectives	What is required to build organizational alignment and manage stakeholder expectations for your opportunity?
Organizational Value	What is the perceived and actual value of your opportunity?
Stakeholder Identification	Who needs to be influenced and why? Senior leadership and peers. Supporters and resisters.
Stakeholder Motivations and Expectations	What is important for your stakeholders to get their support?
Compelling Messages	What are the most important messages to effectively influence your stakeholders?
Communication Options	How do you best reach your stakeholders? Face-to-face, social media, other.
Positioning Plan	What will you do, by when, and how?

Source: rInnovation Group

address organization and resource uncertainties up front by addressing strategic and organizational alignment issues early. It is amazing how effective it can be when done well, and yet many people struggle with its purpose. Many great ideas go nowhere because the idea originator lacks the skills to make the pitch. Of course, not everyone will be prepared to invest the time to learn this skill. However, if you believe in the potential of your business opportunity, then you should invest that time. If you want to get important stakeholders on board to build organizational support, then you need clear messages. This tool helps you to get there.

It is based on the principle that if one runs into an important stakeholder in a hallway, cafeteria line, airport, or elsewhere (even the elevator, although less likely in Denmark since there are few tall buildings, as I joke with my colleagues there!), you have the amount of time during a brief encounter to convince this person that a meeting would be worth his or her time.

It is now time to build upon the work you have done to translate your idea into an opportunity through Genesis Pad Opportunity, evaluate the potential of your opportunity based on the Opportunity Screening Criteria and Potential Questions, and identify

---

Who: Identify Targeted Stakeholder.

What and Why: Primary Messages (The "Wow" Factor)

1. Describe opportunity (brief description of what it is, not how it works).
2. Identify why it is important (strategic rationale/strategic intent, solve a market problem, etc.).
3. Define benefits such as order-of-magnitude performance improvements (factor—2 times, 5 times; etc....), cost savings (range in percentage terms) and/or new-to-the-world performance features (why never been done before).
4. List application possibilities across the most promising markets.
5. State order-of-magnitude market size and/or revenue potential.

FIGURE 6.6   Value Pitch Checklist for Plant
Source: rInnovation Group

your messages in the Opportunity Stakeholder Positioning Steps to develop your value pitch. Refer to Figure 6.6 to help craft your value pitch and the following tips for its delivery:

- Delivery time should be one minute or less, yet there will often be only 30 seconds before the listener tunes out.
- The pitch needs to start with a point that will attract that person's attention. Therefore, value pitches need to be tailored to the expectations of the listener. This is done through homework by understanding the potential audience, practicing the pitch, and being able to adapt accordingly when encountering a key stakeholder in an impromptu situation.
- It requires developing three main messages that would appeal to a broad interest base. The three most commonly used are linking your opportunity with the company's strategic drivers, describing the opportunity's market attractiveness, and making assumptions about its potential economic value. You should be able to start with any one of these messages and loop back to the other two, depending on the person or group being addressed. This is what we call the media technique, which is what we learn when we answer questions in a potentially intimidating inter- view situation. One wrong answer could make the company's shares topple!

- The value pitch addresses, as you move through Discovery and Incubation, the following critical questions:[6]

  - What is the market problem that you are looking to solve?
  - What would be the economic value of solving that problem?
  - Who has the problem?
  - Do they have money, and how much would they be willing to pay (Note: Most often, this can only be addressed in Incubation)?

Advanced Tools

We have also designed more advanced tools for the innovation professional, such as the Innovation Ambitions Spider Chart, the Opportunity Scan with Market, Technology, and Intellectual Property Dimensions; the Opportunity Recognition Tool, Opportunity Discovery, the Discovery Questions, the Discovery to Incubation Transition List, and the Business Concept Template. Once you have mastered our standard tools, then you can move to these more advanced tools, available on our website.

Innovation Ambitions Spider Chart: This tool helps you and your organization define the playing field or landscape that you want to explore for new opportunities. The Innovation Ambitions Spider Chart is composed of Opportunity Dimensions (axes) and Opportunity Characteristics (tick marks on the axes). Opportunity Dimensions describe the major attributes of potential opportunities, from a market, technical resource, and organization standpoint. Opportunity Characteristics describe specific capabilities that are needed in each dimension. Capabilities are plotted along each dimension axis, starting at the center with capabilities that are core to your organization today, and moving outward into stretch capabilities and then opportunistic capabilities. The outer bounds of the core and stretch regions are outlined on the chart. Opportunities that use only core capabilities are the easiest to execute on (and may belong in the core business). Opportunities that require some stretch capabilities are the likely target for Discovery activities. Opportunities that require capabilities outside the stretch zone should be approached very cautiously.

These are often so foreign to the company that they cannot be evaluated for practical purposes.

Opportunity Scan with Market, Technology, and Intellectual Property dimensions: This set of tools allows for the structured identification of potential opportunities, and provides a framework for conducting these high-uncertainty investigations. These investigations start with defining the playing field or landscape based on a delineation of organizational capabilities, visualized in a spider chart. This is followed by a structured research mining approach to learn how to extract future-oriented information based on meaningful trends and drivers that could create potential opportunities. Convergence screening is then conducted to identify convergent trends with strong potential, divergent trends with weak potential, and fractal trends with unknown potential due to very high uncertainty (this might require use of a scenario-based analysis rather than direct trend and driver analysis).

Opportunity hypotheses are developed from logical combinations of problems to be solved, potential solution approaches, target markets or applications, and market and organizational value propositions that are indicated based on the convergence of trends and drivers. Additional validation research is conducted to fill in gaps in the available information to complete the Opportunity Selection Criteria evaluation. More in-depth opportunity screening is then undertaken to score opportunities based on the Opportunity Screening Criteria in Table 6.3 to decide on which opportunities show the most promise.

Opportunity Recognition Tool: This tool builds upon the Opportunity Potential Questions. It is focused on a more detailed consideration of project initiation requirements. The intent is to stimulate and sustain the flow of ideas generated by internal and external scouting activities into the project initiation pipeline. It lists by order of importance the issues to be considered across technical, market, and strategic areas to make a compelling case for further investment. It is designed to help technical, marketing, and innovation resources work together to make a strong case for pursuing this opportunity.

Opportunity Discovery: This set of tools is designed for both individuals and teams to perform structured exploration of the voice of the market. The approach begins with a carefully crafted research strategy, designed to facilitate the translation of opportunities into market needs, potential solutions, and business concepts. The research strategy is driven by sequential passes of in-market in-depth interviews. The research starts with thought leaders and industry experts to gain an understanding of high-level value drivers in the market, trends creating new needs, and general operating characteristics of the market. From there the research spirals into lead users and lead stakeholders, individuals who represent the extreme-need case within the potential opportunity, and informs the researcher about the strength and depth of the market value drivers, potential early adopter segments, and market entry points. The final spiral of research includes core users and stakeholders, those who may have some needs today but who are much less motivated to action. This research layer helps identify the potential market timing and the total solution requirements for broad adoption within the market.

Discovery Questions: These more in-depth questions help you work more systematically across technical, market, resource, and organization considerations. They are designed to ensure that the right questions are asked during Discovery, with the objective of reducing these four uncertainties to prepare an opportunity for Incubation.

Discovery to Incubation Transition List: This list ensures that all the appropriate Discovery issues have been considered to increase the chances for a successful transition from Discovery to Incubation. It will help with completing the Business Concept Template and building confidence in the business vision, feasibility of the opportunity, and the organizational alignment process.

Business Concept Template: A more formalized Business Concept Template facilitates the decision-making process when faced with high levels of uncertainty. Companies often attempt to design these processes to remove the risk from the equation. This alone will curtail the flow of opportunities and impede the progress of innovation. We promote the principle that uncertainties must be clear up front to reduce them, since the risks are not even identified yet. The Business Concept Template is developed from Discovery learning to provide the rationale for moving an opportunity from Discovery to Incubation.

Words of Caution

The purpose of the tools is to enable your learning. If they are used as a means to control opportunities, innovation will be stifled and application of these learning aids will be perceived as simply another bureaucratic process. You must be mindful of the careful balance between people and process. This is why we focus on the D-I-A mind-set versus process and try to stay away from too much reference to process. Market exploration and experimentation by their very nature require that variation be maximized to gain an understanding of the landscape.

Learning is not a sequential experience, nor is it ad hoc. Rather, it requires situational learning where flexibility, fluidity, and improvisation are the name of the game. These tools and methodologies are to be utilized to enable the process of recording what needs to be or has been learned, identifying where to focus next, and determining how much to invest in terms of money, people, and partnerships. Keep these words of caution in mind as you use the tools throughout the D-I-A model. I have been known to go into coaching situations and reset teams since the process was getting ahead of learning objectives—it's not a good idea to put the cart before the horse!

PLANT YOUR VALUE PITCH: MAKING THE TRANSITION TO INCUBATION WITH YOUR OPPORTUNITY CONCEPT

Now it is time to put together your organizational story for why your opportunity has potential and is ready for Incubation. This is your opportunity concept, developed from the elements that make up your value pitch as follows:

- *Concise market value proposition.*[7] This is a statement of what your opportunity could do for or to the market, *not* necessarily for or to the company at this point, since it is often too early to know.

- *Potential lost value.* This is a clear statement of what *ignoring* the opportunity could do for or to the company. Often, the consequences of not pursuing an opportunity are more easily understood than its potential.
- *Compelling business vision.* Your opportunity is big enough to warrant attention. Some companies even ask, "Is it 'millionable' or 'billionable'?"—interesting terms. It could possibly become a new business opportunity or technology platform for your company. Do not be afraid to step out. Remember, if it is only an incremental improvement, then you should proceed to your product development process. We are in the game of uncertainty reduction first, then managing the risks of product development.
- *Market size, growth rate, and application richness.* You will most certainly need to make assumptions about market size and growth rate, yet you will also need to look beyond them for a thorough listing of potential applications to ensure robustness of the opportunity. Higher uncertainty leads to higher failure rate. We need to know if there are a number of options to draw from.
- *Identification of critical uncertainties.* Be clear on your most pressing challenges and potential showstoppers, along with your level of confidence they can be overcome, where low confidence is less than 50 percent, medium is 50 to 75 percent, and high is greater than 75 percent. We want these uncertainties identified up front so we can address them in Incubation.

Are you *now* ready to Plant your value pitch and move to Incubation?

I hope you are now starting to get a feel for what Discovery is and what it is not. The goal is to help you avoid the ominous valley of death between conceiving of an idea and seeing it realized commercially. Discovery is the first part of your innovation journey to create a common language for and understanding of the innovation life cycle. As we have seen, Discovery can start with any insight, whether it is of a technical nature from scientific work or other. This insight alone is insufficient for you to be heard, and this is where opportunity recognition skills and value articulation come in to help you attract organizational attention. The Discovery Toolkit helps guide you through the uncertainties others have faced in crossing this valley.

In addition to all the principles we have already covered in Discovery, there are two of these principles that you need to bring with you to Incubation—the D-I-A learning mind-set and a razor focus on "learning per dollars spent" (spend the least to learn the most).

Think of "learning per dollars spent" as your Incubation mantra. The phrase came from the vice president of strategy at Air Products, but Dorte Bang Knudsen at Grundfos was the first to call it a mantra. It is now time to move on to Incubation (Pivot). This mantra will become much clearer in Chapters 9 and 10. I am confident you have made a compelling case for transitioning to Incubation, and we are now ready for this next step! Are you?

First, let's see what Remy has to say about opportunity and the entrepreneur in the following chapter and what Gina and Lois have to say about our perspectives on the pursuit of opportunities in Chapter 8.

NOTES

1. Material from this chapter is drawn from Rensselaer Polytechnic Institute (RPI) Phase I and II research; Richard Leifer, Christopher M. McDermott, Gina Colarelli O'Connor, Lois S. Peters, Mark Rice, and Robert W. Veryzer, *Radical Innovation: How Mature Companies Can Outsmart Upstarts* (Boston: Harvard Business School Press, 2000); and teaching, training, and coaching experiences.

2. Gina C. O'Connor, Richard Leifer, Albert S. Paulson, and Lois S. Peters, *Grabbing Lightning: Building a Capability for Breakthrough Innovation* (San Francisco: Jossey-Bass, 2008), chap. 3.

3. Procter & Gamble website.

4. Mark Rice, Donna Kelley, Lois Peters, and Gina Colarelli O'Connor, "Radical Innovation: Triggering Initiation of Opportunity Recognition and Evaluation," *R&D Management* 31, no. 4 (2001); and Gina Colarelli O'Connor and Mark P. Rice, "Opportunity Recognition and Breakthrough Innovation in Large Established Firms," *California Management Review* 43, no. 2 (2001): 95–116.

5. Gina Colarelli O'Connor and Mark P. Rice, "New Market Creation for Breakthrough Innovations: Enabling and Constraining Mechanisms," *Journal of Product Innovation Management (JPIM)* 30, no. 2 (2013): 209–227.

6. Adapted from "Every Entrepreneur a Salesperson," MIT Entrepreneurship Development Program (EDP) 2003, Ken Morse, senior lecturer and managing director, MIT Entrepreneurship Center.

7. Gina Colarelli O'Connor, "Market Learning and Radical Innovation," *JPIM* 15 (1998): 151–166.

CHAPTER 7

OPPORTUNITY AND THE ENTREPRENEUR

In Chapter 6, Joanne discussed opportunity recognition in the context of corporate entrepreneurship. In this chapter, I discuss opportunity recognition in the context of entrepreneurship and will refer back to some of the content in Chapter 6.

One of the more elusive aspects of entrepreneurship is opportunity recognition, the process by which an opportunity is identified. In Chapter 6, we stated that ideas are only the beginning of the journey; I couldn't agree more. When I write about opportunities, I am not referring to ideas. I get approached with new ideas every day that never amount to an opportunity. I could get all philosophical on you and delve into the historical meanings of an idea from Plato to Hume, but I prefer to take a more direct approach and state that an idea is a concept or thought that comes to an individual mind. Ideas are easier to come by than opportunities. You get them as you ride the subway, walk through an airport, take care of your kids, and just live your life. Ideas are not opportunities; instead they serve as the building blocks for opportunities. In Chapter 6, we defined an opportunity as a match between a need in the marketplace (hidden or explicit) and a product or service offering that fills that need. I like to think that an opportunity transforms an idea to the point where it has the promise or potential to be converted into an innovative market offering.

OPPORTUNITY RECOGNITION

Last year, two students, Jake and Kyle, approached me about an idea for a web platform that allows users to buy tickets on behalf of their friends and then get reimbursed by those same friends. The problem that Jake and Kyle were attempting to solve was the age-old problem of collecting money from family and friends after you laid out the money for some event like concert tickets or a ski trip. At this stage the students had an idea, not an opportunity. Up to this point, they had gone through only the first three steps of the opportunity recognition process. As you can see in Figure 7.1, the first three steps are Background, Solution, and Idea. The background is the organic step that every entrepreneur takes. It includes the entrepreneur's knowledge and experience. The next step is where the entrepreneur sees a problem and unconsciously seeks a solution. Maybe it's a mom who can't stand the car seat for her child because it clamps down on her hands. In the back of the mom's mind, she begins to seek a solution to this problem. At some point, the mom comes up with a solution, and we have the next step, a eureka moment: an idea. This is a moment we have all experienced in our lives. That's the step Jake and Kyle were at when they entered my office. Jake and Kyle had yet to do any work to evaluate the idea—a key component of the opportunity recognition process.[1]

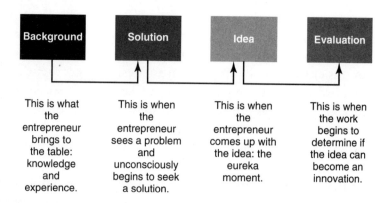

FIGURE 7.1   Opportunity Recognition

As we can see from Jake and Kyle's story, the idea is only the start of the opportunity recognition process. After my meeting with Jake and Kyle, they began to go through the evaluation step. It is during this step that the rubber meets the road. It is the point where the entrepreneur has to be brutally honest about the idea. During this step, ideas may be tested with feasibility analysis, market analysis, financial review, and feedback. Also, entrepreneurs may make use of concrete experience, observation, and imagination to gain meaning. I followed Jake and Kyle on their entrepreneurial journey and saw how they began to mull things over after our first meeting, which was followed by market and feasibility activities. For example, the students began to search the web for other competing services and to get feedback from their friends and professors. Kyle and Jake also entered business plan competitions and startup events, and—wouldn't you know it?—the idea began to evolve. I will come back to Jake and Kyle later in the book.

There is a concept known as "knowledge asymmetries" in the area of opportunity recognition that provides us with an understanding of why one entrepreneur may see an opportunity, while another does not. The idea dates back to opportunity recognition studies performed in the 1980s. In these studies, researchers were attempting to find out the main reason entrepreneurs recognized opportunities. Was it serendipity? After all, when asked, many entrepreneurs would cite serendipity as the main reason. However, the research turned up a different reason. It turned out that even though founders of startups cited serendipity as the main reason for recognizing opportunities, the true factor was work experience. Follow-up studies pointed to experience in general as an important factor in recognizing opportunities.[2] You may be thinking, "They needed a study to tell them that?" Remember this was the 1980s and entrepreneurship was an unknown field at the time. What these studies pointed out was that each person has a unique experience that allows him or her to see a unique opportunity. This is known as knowledge asymmetry, which essentially means that every entrepreneur has a unique stock of knowledge that leads one entrepreneur to see an opportunity while another does not. In other words, our mothers were right in stating, "You are special and unique."

TECHNOLOGY TO MARKET OPPORTUNITY

The opportunity recognition process we discussed to this point assumes an organic approach to recognizing an opportunity. In other words, it is about the natural process that takes place when an entrepreneur comes upon an idea. In contrast, there are times when an entrepreneur is asked to determine the best opportunity for a technology. In this section I present a framework for identifying the best opportunity for a technology.

One common misconception among would-be entrepreneurs is thinking that a technology in and of itself is an opportunity. This often occurs with a startup that is focused on commercializing a university's technology. However, a technology is not a solution that customers will buy. It may serve as the basis for a solution, but it is rarely if ever a solution in and of itself. Think about it. When was the last time you bought a technology? Did you buy the iPhone because it was a technology or did you fall in love with the apps, music, and phone features? Customers do not buy technologies—they buy solutions. A technology can serve as the basis for an idea. The iPhone has numerous embedded technologies, including material and software technologies. However, customers do not buy technologies; they buy what the technologies can do for them. A technology is often too raw for the end user and needs to be first transformed into an opportunity and then next into a solution. Let me clarify. When I was the CEO of a software firm, we had two computer scientists who came up with some very smart algorithms. In their raw state, these algorithms were nothing more than technologies. When I attempted to license these technologies to medical imaging firms, I quickly found out that they had no interest in the technologies. What they wanted was a piece of bulletproof software based on those technologies that was customized to their applications. They wanted a solution that could be easily plugged into their systems.

Now that you know that a technology is not an opportunity or a solution, you may be wondering what it is. The word *technology* has long been over-used to describe anything that is new. How often do we hear a CNN report on a new iPhone technology that does this or that? But are these really new technologies or innovations? According to the National Institutes of Health's website, "[t]echnology is a body of knowledge used to create tools, develop skills, and extract or collect materials. It is also the application of science (the combination of the scientific method and material) to meet an objective or solve a problem." This is a very broad definition that may not be useful to most entrepreneurs. I find it more useful to describe technologies in terms of their characteristics. One of the key technology characteristics is not being ready for the market, while being applicable to many different markets. For example, a new material made up of nano–springs with a unique property of glowing in the dark might be used in the fashion industry as a sneaker material, the bicycle industry as a coating, or any number of other industries that find this unique property compelling. For each of these market opportunities, the technology would have to be worked on before it became a product or solution.

So, what can you do to determine a technology's market viability? Over the years, I have developed a methodology that helps me do this. I have converted the methodology into a tool named Technology to Market Assessment Tool (TMAT). Figure 7.2 gives a high–level overview of TMAT. The figure depicts different inputs to TMAT. Along the top of the figure, we start with a portfolio of technologies, the kind you might see at a university or research center. From there, you select a single technology that will be assessed. Along the bottom of the figure, you have the different market opportunities that exist for this technology. To the right of the market opportunities, you have the key success factors (KSFs or customer needs) for each market opportunity. Once the KSFs have been identified, you map the KSFs to the resources and capabilities (R&Cs) of the startup team. This is an important step, as every startup team has different R&Cs and is in a different position to bring a product to market. With the mapped R&Cs in hand, you perform a competitive analysis of the proposed market opportunity against other products in the market. After all markets have been analyzed, you put the results together in a Market Assessment Summary. The purpose of this explanation is not to give you an in–depth review of the tool; instead my hope is to give you a high–level review of what it takes to do a proper assessment. It is very

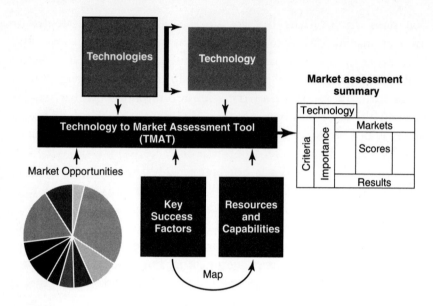

FIGURE 7.2 Technology to Market Assessment Tool

hard work that cannot be done overnight. It requires an in-depth understanding of each market opportunity, competitive landscape, and the R&Cs of the startup team.

THE CHALLENGE FOR UNIVERSITIES TO COMMERCIALIZE TECHNOLOGIES

In addition to educating students, many universities are in the business of developing technologies. The U.S. government funds a significant portion of the research and development of technologies. The ownership and management of a university's technology intellectual property rights have become a critical responsibility for all research universities. This was not always the case. It was only after the passing of the Bayh–Dole Act in 1980 that universities have had the option to retain title to technologies developed under federally funded research programs. To manage these new rights, universities around the country have created departments to control the process of transferring these technology rights from the university to the market. The goal of these technology transfer offices is to transfer technologies from the university to firms by licensing the technology rights to the firms. The rights licensed are generally patent rights with the university receiving a royalty in return. This requires the ability to manage these rights, as well as to market and ultimately to license these rights. To help transfer these technologies to the market, some universities encourage university startups that will commercialize these technologies. The professor or researcher who is developing the technology often launches a university startup. However, there are often times where a venture capitalist will license the technology and create a startup around the technology. There may also be times when the researchers will go out and find an experienced entrepreneur to launch the startup on their behalf. In one of my most recent startups, I was hired by the university's researcher to launch the startup based on a technology developed by the researcher at the university. The researcher remained with the university, working with the startup during breaks in the school year.

As was discussed in the previous section, regardless of where the technology originates from, the first big task in assessing a technology is determining the different market opportunities for the technology. This is an incredibly challenging task for an experienced professional, let alone a first-time entrepreneur. Universities are challenged with this task. All technology transfer officers attempt to determine the market viability of a technology that is being handled by their office. If one considers that a single technology transfer officer may handle upwards of 200 cases at one time, then it is clear that it would be impossible for a technology transfer office to determine the best market opportunities for every technology. Instead, a good office will have programs in place to assist entrepreneurs with assessing the markets. For example, a university can launch an entrepreneurship center to help students and faculty launch startups, or they can sponsor events to bring technologists and businesses together.

The Big XYZ

So I have an idea—now what? That's one of the first questions I get asked by aspiring entrepreneurs. As we discussed previously, an idea is not an opportunity. Also, there are times when an entrepreneur organically comes up with an idea and other times when a university, research center, or R&D department needs to find the best opportunity for a technology. One of the first steps in fleshing out an idea is to come up with a summary of the startup's concept. Guy Kawasaki, a well-known entrepreneur and founder of Garage Technology Ventures, often speaks about coming up with a mantra for a startup. According to Kawasaki, the number of words for the mantra should be few and get to the heart of the startup. Guy is not alone in believing in a short and powerful phrase to describe a startup. Most books on entrepreneurship will refer to this short phrase as an excellent way to quickly communicate the essence of your startup. I don't disagree with this advice. However, I disagree with the advice that this is something that a startup can do on day one. It can take a very long time before a startup is clear on what its mantra should be. As we have discussed in this book, a startup is surrounded by a high level of uncertainty. Stating that you know what your mantra is when you don't even know your market is only going to lead to greater confusion. Instead, I propose that at this stage of development the startup should focus on coming up with a very practical and useful statement of what it thinks it will be offering the marketplace. I call this statement the Big XYZ.

I have listened to thousands of startup ideas over the years. Over that time I have noticed a pattern used by people presenting their ideas. It generally goes something like "If we develop/create/build X, customers will Y at a rate of Z." I have labeled this concept summary pattern as the Big XYZ. The elements of the Big XYZ are given in Table 7.1. For example, let's revisit the story of the two student entrepreneurs I introduced earlier in this chapter, Jake and Kyle. Jake and Kyle had an idea for a group payment platform that would allow users to shell out money and get reimbursed for a group event like a ski trip. The Big XYZ for this startup could have been: "If we develop an online group payment service, group

TABLE 7.1 Big XYZ Elements

Big XYZ statement: If we develop/create/build X, customers will Y at a rate of Z.
X: This is the product or service that is going to be created.
Customers: This will be a specific market segment that the X will be marketed to.
Y: This is what you want potential customers to do to obtain X.
Z: This is the market adoption/traction over a specified time.

organizers, ages 18 to 29, will sign up and pay a transaction fee at a rate of 100 signups and 20 transactions per day over the first six months." In this example, X = an online group payment service; customers = group organizers, ages 18 to 29; Y = sign up and pay a transaction fee; and Z = 100 signups and 20 transactions per day over the first six months. It's amazing how many startups are unable to state their concept in terms of the Big XYZ. It generally points to a lack of understanding on what the startup is looking to accomplish. By describing your startup in these terms at the very start, it becomes a very useful way to communicate what you intend on creating, who you intend to market to, what you want from customers, and how quickly you plan to grow.

THE VALUE PROPOSITION

What about some of the other concept summary terms you may have encountered like *positioning statement* or *value proposition*? How do these terms relate to the concept summary?

Let's start with the term *value proposition*. If you have ever attempted to launch a startup, then someone most likely asked you, "What is your value proposition?" I have always wondered if the people asking the question know what a value proposition is. According to the *McKinsey Quarterly* article entitled "Delivering Value to Customers,"[3] two McKinsey staffers, Michael J. Lanning and Edward G. Michaels, originally coined the term *value proposition* in the late 1980s. At the time, I was working at General Motors. I remember that the big movement afoot in the late 1980s was a way to align all the processes within a firm to deliver exactly what the customer wanted or needed. GM, like so many other American firms at the time, had lost sight of the customer and was losing market share to firms like Toyota, which seemingly had an insight into the customer's needs and wants. A tool known as Total Quality Management (TQM) appeared during this time. TQM was used by companies to help them build quality into all of their operations. Another tool at the time was Quality Function Deployment (QFD), which was also used to build quality into an organization. The effort needed for a corporation to undertake the implementation of either tool was enormous. These tools required mapping each and every customer need or benefit, for every product line, back through the organization. I was part of the GM team that helped developed some of these tools.

While I was working on quality tools at GM, McKinsey was working on some tools of its own centered around building value into the organization. Note that the words *value* and *quality* were essentially being used in the same way then. The process of building value was known as the value proposition process (VPP). The goal was to make sure that every employee of the organization fully understood how he or she was going to deliver value to the customer. Lanning and Michaels defined value as the difference between the price a customer was willing to pay for a benefit and the price the customer actually paid. For example, if you were willing to pay $5 for the taste of a Starbucks coffee but paid only $3, then you would net $2 in value. Other experts define value as the total benefit you received from buying the cup of coffee.

I believe that TQM, QFD, and VPP are related, and the term *quality* in TQM and QFD serve the same purpose as *value* in VPP. Fast-forward 25 years, and it seems that every venture capitalist and angel wants to know the value proposition for a startup. To determine this you need to know exactly what your product is going to be, who your customers are going to be, and what the most important benefits are. This is something that a startup is often unclear about during the Discovery phase, and it is only during the Incubation phase that the startup can begin to clearly define it. This is why I prefer the Big XYZ at this stage of a startup's development. I want to compare this with the use of the term *value proposition* in

Chapter 6. Its use has evolved to focus more on stakeholders and what could be rather than on the customer, which works well in a corporate setting.

THE POSITIONING STATEMENT

As an entrepreneur, you might also encounter the term positioning statement. According to *Positioning: The Battle for Your Mind*, a classic book on positioning statements, Jack Trout and Al Ries wrote that "positioning is not what you do to a product. Positioning is what you do to the mind of the prospect."[4] The positioning statement is a marketing tool to help the startup focus on how to best position the startup relative to both the competition and the market. Geoffrey Moore in his book *Crossing the Chasm* put forth the following framework for developing a positioning statement:[5]

For	[target end user]
Who wants/needs	[compelling reason to buy]
The	[product name] is a [product category]
That provides	[key benefit]
Unlike	[main competitor]
The	[product name] [key differentiation]

Here is a fictitious positioning statement for a mobile app:

For on-the-go professionals who need up-to-the-minute stock tips, the StockTipper is a mobile app that provides stock tips from billionaires like Warren Buffett; unlike StockTips, the StockTipper brings you tips from successful billionaires.

This type of exercise is valuable and important, but probably not in the same way most experts suggest. Instead of the positioning statement serving to position the startup in the marketplace, I suggest that the positioning statement be used as an input to the Pivot activities we will be reviewing later in this book. It is a good exercise to determine some of the most important assumptions that are driving the startup. The preceding positioning statement is filled with assumptions—from whether on-the-go professionals really want tips from billionaires to whether the startup can get the billionaires to give tips.

NOTES

1. G. T. Lumpkin, Gerald E. Hills, and Rodney C. Shrader, "Opportunity Recognition," in *Entrepreneurship: The Way Ahead*, ed. Harold P. Welsch (New York: Routledge, 2003).
2. Andrew Corbett, "Experiential Learning within the Process of Opportunity Identification and Exploitation," *Entrepreneurship Theory and Practice*, 2005.
3. Harvey Golub, Jane Henry, John L. Forbes, Nitin T. Mehta, Michael J. Lanning, Edward G. Michaels, and Kenichi Ohmae, "Delivering Value to Customers," *McKinsey Quarterly*, June 2000.
4. Jack Trout and Al Ries, *Positioning: The Battle for Your Mind* (New York: McGraw-Hill, 1981).
5. Geoffrey A. Moore, *Crossing the Chasm* (New York: HarperCollins, 1991).

CHAPTER 8

ENTREPRENEUR AND CORPORATE ENTREPRENEUR PERSPECTIVES: PURSUIT OF OPPORTUNITIES

We (Gina and Lois) are back to offer our commentary on the Plant or Discovery Chapters 6 and 7. As part of building on the Plant, Pivot, and Propel concepts, it was clear in reading these chapters that the term *plant* means to plant a seed that could grow, not plant your feet on the ground and don't move. This chapter covers the perspectives of the entrepreneur and the corporate entrepreneur in how they transform ideas into opportunities and position to attract interest in those opportunities.

GETTING FROM IDEA TO OPPORTUNITY

What comes through very clearly is that an idea is not an opportunity. Opportunities require recognition of a match between a need and a potential technology or solution. They also require development and elaboration of how this may flesh out. In other words, they take work. They are not "aha" moments.

Who are opportunity recognizers? Lately there's talk about T-shaped people. These are people who know a little about a lot of things (broad) and a lot about at least one thing (deep). Remy talked in Chapter 7 about how opportunity recognizers have experience in a domain and across domains. They develop their T-shape that way.

Who are opportunity elaborators? Joanne's story in Chapter 6 about Dylan and Frank highlights the required characteristics for elaborating opportunities. Dylan thought about possibilities. Imagination and curiosity and openness and lateral thinking are some of the skills and characteristics we see in people who elaborate opportunities. They may not even recognize the opportunity in the first place, but once it's uttered in even the most innocuous way, these people can run with them.

Who are opportunity evaluators? There's Frank, the opportunity evaluator. Some venture capitalists (VCs) think like Frank, and some don't. When you have uncertainty, how does one adequately evaluate an opportunity? We have found that good investors and good corporate sponsors evaluate opportunities not on the basis of probabilities, as Frank did based on his risk reduction and financial return mind-set. Rather, they consider the robustness of the opportunity. They recognize that Pivots will likely occur, and ask, "If this direction won't work, are there enough others such that we're likely to find gold there somewhere?" Richness of the application possibilities is what drives opportunity evaluation in the world of uncertainty, rather than net present value (NPV) calculations. And that's true for both environments: startup and corporate. Of course, this is easier said than done. We've heard from many venture teams in both contexts that finding the right investor or sponsor who can evaluate an opportunity in this manner is a rare thing indeed. That's why we offer the tools: to help develop opportunity recognizers in this counterintuitive manner.

The opportunity elaboration process is turbocharged when there is continuity of people doing it. For example, Remy's claim that an opportunity recognizer has experience can be interpreted to mean that that person can connect an idea he or she encountered last month with one he or she sees now and another heard from a friend. This is the same person picking up and connecting disparate pieces of information.

On the corporate side, we don't have to rely on the same single person. Some of the companies we've studied put opportunity-screening panels together and try to keep the same people on the panel over time. That small team reviews ideas and can begin to detect patterns in ideas over time, or can connect one idea today with one that came through last month, much like we rely on one person in the startup world to do. Here, organizations have an advantage over the entrepreneur. But the entrepreneur's VC team is a different matter. They operate much like the opportunity-screening team would in a company. The primary difference is that the VCs cannot force two independent startups to join forces if they see a symbiotic relationship between those opportunities. But a company can. The other difference is that VCs do not always see opportunities as early as the corporate opportunity-screening team might.

In Chapter 7, we talked about how knowledge asymmetries can impact an entrepreneur's ability to recognize an opportunity. Many would-be entrepreneurs are scared to discuss their ideas openly and prefer to work in what they call "stealth" mode. This mode requires utmost secrecy and minimal interaction with the market. One can easily see the problems of operating in such a mode, as the aspiring entrepreneur runs the risk of launching a product or service that nobody wants. The studies discussed in Chapter 7 should put most would-be entrepreneurs at ease, because even though an idea can be shared with others, the outcome of going through an innovation process cannot. Also, the fear of stealing an idea cannot outweigh the benefits from testing an opportunity in the marketplace.

ATTRACTING ATTENTION

Finally, once an entrepreneur can get past the fear of an opportunity being stolen and the corporate entrepreneur looks for potential synergies, there's the issue of attracting attention. Both Joanne and Remy address this issue because startups and internal venture teams have to articulate a compelling story about this new breakthrough possibility, and sell investors or company leadership on the promise of the business. In this situation, startups may have the upper hand. They can articulate a dream and, as long as they have some beginning results to demonstrate or some market interest, they have a solid foundation. The world is their oyster, their marketplace. If they have a big enough market potential, investors are interested. Investors then look to the entrepreneur's ability to manage the startup and build upon this market interest with the right team, in the right environment, and with the right advisers.

Not so in the corporate world. You have to show that you fit the strategic intent of the company or you have to work behind the scenes to mold that intent in a way that fits your vision or opportunity. And that's only in the case where companies actually think about or work on developing a strategic intent—indeed, very rare in our experience. They have to provide a rationale for why the company should invest in this opportunity, and the criteria are not just about market potential but about strategic fit, robustness of the opportunity, and resource fit.

We learn that companies are more likely to respond to perceived threats, such as "If we don't do this, then our competitors will eat our lunch" than opportunities such as "If we invest now we can lead this technology market domain as it emerges." But even then, you don't want to be the person who is perceived as crying wolf all the time. And if you couch your vision only as a threat, people will get tired of listening. There is a delicate balance in how to articulate opportunities that are not right up the company's alley today but are huge veins to mine for the future. This is particularly true when the vein for the future will cannibalize today's business, as noted in the story about Nortel and the Internet, or Kodak and the digital camera that Joanne mentioned. But one way to do it is to talk about possibilities, and multiples of them. It is also about understanding your stakeholders and how to position opportunities in a way that they can see the potential.

In contrast, Remy talks about the importance of the Big XYZ in Chapter 7, which boils down to a very clear set of expectations about what the venture will deliver to the market and what the market should then return to the venture in terms of revenues, adoption, and growth. That helps the team clarify the opportunity and drives some of the ambiguity out of the picture. The positioning statement helps articulate how this opportunity differs from competitive offerings. Both tools force an entrepreneur to get very specific about one single possibility, rather than sell the robustness of the opportunity at a higher level of abstraction. And we think that's why Remy along with Eric Reis, author of *The Lean Startup*,[1] and others are so focused on the importance of pivoting. There's more commitment to a direction in the opportunity articulation stage in the startup world than is necessary in the corporate world. And that's driven by the need in the startup world to satisfy investors, who, sadly, can't seem to live with the ambiguity that early stage companies in actuality face. The strategic intent of most investors is not about market domain leadership; it's about making money. So, the tools for describing and developing an opportunity are a little different. Hmmm . . . maybe we need to develop tools to help investors in the startup community evaluate early stage opportunities drawing upon insights from the corporate world!

NOTE

1. Eric Reis, *The Lean Startup* (New York: Crown, 2011).

PART THREE

PIVOT = INCUBATION—THE MISSING LINK

CHAPTER 9

———

INCUBATION—
DISCIPLINE TOGETHER
WITH CHAOS[1]

Do you have time for a few more stories about the corporate entrepreneur before jumping into the Incubation principles? In my days as a corporate entrepreneur, I learned only too well that this world of uncertainty requires thick skin. After my experiences at Nortel, I wrote an article remarking that there is a unique passion and commitment (along with an element of masochism) required to ride the wave of chaos, change, and uncertainty. Change is not easy. Getting someone to believe in the potential of your opportunity is the easy part, or at least it was for our Nortel team.

It is also the view of Alan Schrob, who was director of new business development at NOVA Chemicals, when we worked together. As he described, "Incubation for us was the most critical phase. The learning we did during Discovery was incredibly important in terms of understanding the opportunity, but Incubation is when the risk profile changes dramatically, investments begin, agreements are constructed, and prototypes are tested in the marketplace."

While we did not call it Incubation in our early Nortel days, this is what we were aiming for. It is where the rubber hits the road, and a long and winding road (borrowed with appreciation from the Beatles) at that, due to all the uncertainty we have to deal with. It is the time when patience wears thin because people are looking for more immediate results.

This goes back to all those resource and organization uncertainties that we were not good at describing back then . . . if I had only known then what I know now. I wanted to get these points raised now, as we step into Incubation. This chapter and the next provide insights and tools for living with this inevitable chaos.

I have asked Alan and other colleagues to share their Incubation insights and stories to make this as real for you as possible. I selected three companies committed to getting Incubation right that I know well—NOVA Chemicals, Moen, and Grundfos. Let's start with Grundfos, one of the world's leading pump manufacturers. Some of you will be "out there," as Lars Spicker Olesen, chief incubation officer at Grundfos, will explain next, and some of you will not. We call it the missing link in companies for a reason. There are still too few who do it well, and this becomes a large contributor to the high failure rate in product development. How many meetings have you been in where you speak of learning loops and uncertainty reduction? Incubation is about getting out in the market to learn. It requires the ability to learn quickly, redirect, and improvise. It is about reducing uncertainties early to increase the success rate of product development.

Lars shares three of his many Incubation experiences to best illustrate these points.

> *Engage the experts—thinking behind a desk has a limit.* In one of our projects, we were targeting an application relevant for dairy farming. To assist in getting to the very first technical solution, we contacted a consultant. He brought with him a colleague who had established an entire business around the exact same concept (based on another technology, though), and from her we learned all about market drivers and barriers, technical benchmarks, relevant progressive first customer partners, and how to tackle legislation for our new approach. Needless to say, luck also came into play, but it is difficult to get lucky if you do not play or, in other words, are not out there.
>
> *Decide—often.* I made a motto after having run several projects of a highly uncertain nature. One should not underestimate the effect of

actually doing something, instead of just talking about it. Sometimes (quite often in these projects, actually), we simply cannot think it up. But by trying just something, we get a little bit wiser and understand more about what it is we don't understand. Short learning loops and building on learning are the easiest things to say, and the hardest things to actually do. So decide also about things that are not nice, like closing a project; but still, decide. The Learning Plan (described later in the chapter) has been a great tool for helping us to do this.

Go with the flow of learning. To keep an open mind and keeping options for a business in play is difficult, once one gets the first few successes. When something is not working, it is easy to try something else. When something is working, it is hard to not hammer only on that thing and perhaps not see the full potential. In developing a concept that had interfaces toward two existing systems, owned by different entities, we learned that our exact same technical solution could be used in another application, where marketwise we only had to convince one entity. And yet, we still went after our first, more complex market positioning concept because we were already on this path with a functional, technical prototype. I am still not sure whether that was the right idea.

Lars must be wondering if this could lead to yet another failed product development or, at the very least, an opportunity that is incrementalized in terms of its overall business potential, because the opportunity to revisit the scope and redirect to, perhaps, a better learning application area has not been fully considered.

Let's see how these experiences carry over to the Incubation principles.

INCUBATION PRINCIPLES[2]

While Discovery is about the conceptualization of business opportunities, Incubation is a competency based on experimentation to uncover latent or hidden needs and next generation concepts. This requires the ability to experiment with multiple technology and business concepts or models *simultaneously*. The objective is to arrive at a demonstrated model of a new business opportunity and bring game-changing value to the market and, consequently, to the company. Integrating the technology and market learning together differentiates this approach from the serial product development process, where, most often, the product is developed and then brought to the market.

There is an acceptance of failure as integral to the learning process—failure by design, as it is often called. Despite these failures, we expect experiments to continue. Incubation reinforces the need for the creation and pursuit of options, with movement in multiple directions simultaneously. There is a focus on learning and redirecting. Critical to this is enriching and extending internal and external networks. This is required to enlarge the scope of the company's knowledge base and commercial opportunity space. This must be done in the market to really be "out there," as described by Lars.

In Incubation, many application possibilities are tested, yet few enter Acceleration. Incubation requires working through tests in parallel through iterative learning, not the serial product development or phase gate approach many companies have in place today. The Incubation competency encompasses strategic coaching, opportunity and relationship brokering, portfolio thinning and enriching, and nurturing skills.

Coaching is required to help people make strategic linkages and to understand the uncertainty-reduction process and how to deal with an ambiguous environment. Brokering provides connections to sources of knowledge, resources, and politically important players to build project support and to access the right internal and external networks. Thinning and enriching of the portfolio are undertaken frequently, due to the high churn rates associated with iterative or spiral learning. Options are tested, then redirected or eliminated, as this learning occurs. This is difficult to manage, because the need for failure is not well accepted. We see evidence for this by the corporate pressure for high success rates. There is also a tendency toward incrementalization by force-fitting a concept to what is known, to lower the risk and, therefore, the potential for failure. When faced with all this uncertainty, teams need to be nurtured through compassionate leadership and by establishing the line of sight, with the company vision to provide a sense of direction and a reason to believe.

Let's revisit a few stories to illustrate these points, starting with coaching based on Alan's experiences. "We leveraged coaching sessions with project teams to work through uncertainties and ensure the correct learning took place. These sessions allowed the project teams to step back from the detail and project activities to review their progress in uncovering uncertainty, in the technology and the proposed market, as well as resource and organizational uncertainty. We designed these sessions to not be critical but more to allow the teams to think more strategically about the opportunities they were working on."

And how do companies deal with failure and tap into expertise?

Steve Pierson, chief business innovator at Grundfos, shares this story with us.

Learning loops were invaluable for reducing uncertainty in an efficient manner. Learning loops can yield success, failure, and learning.
The first learning loop for one of our projects was a complete
failure, but we didn't want to admit it. We should have made the
call to kill the project as soon as the project began to show it
would not be a good learning platform, but this would have created
embarrassment and an admission that we didn't take into account
the unknowns in our planning. While we did identify them, we
dismissed them and went on with business as usual. As our experience grew in the use of the D-I-A approach, we actually focused on
addressing these unknowns and embraced failure as much as success,
because we viewed it as learning.

From our failures, we decided to experiment in our second learning
loop and use an external partner who specialized in building controls in the wastewater and water treatment industry. This partner
built what we needed in a fraction of the time and cost that it
took us in our first learning loop, and it performed as specified.
By sensoring the system to measure key performance indicators
we determined that the project was a complete success and saved
between 30 and 40 percent in energy costs for the commercial
building owner. Furthermore, we had an unintended consequence
of our experimentation and found a faulty component with one heat
pump, which would not have been discovered without sensoring
the energy usage of each heat pump. Now the facilities manager calls

me to ask how his system is performing. He has put trust in me that I have his back and will let him know if any issues arise. We have also found an internal ambassador who values what we do.

Hmmm . . . Have we also uncovered another opportunity, a service business model for monitoring system health?

The story Lars told us also reinforces that you cannot always think it up; you need to be "out there" experimenting. There could even be unexpected positive outcomes. In Incubation, we also legitimize failure as a source of learning and that success can be just as much about uncovering what will not work as what will.

Incubation Objectives

Based on the principles, let's spend a little more time on the "learning per dollars spent" mantra. Remember Dorte Bang Knudsen calling it a mantra in Chapter 6. This really sets the stage for our Incubation objectives. Business concept or project costs should increase through the early, middle, and late stages of Incubation commensurate with learning. This is an excellent test of whether we are truly focused on reducing uncertainties. The focus is to maximize learning and minimize spending, and to test a number of market-entry options to arrive at a market-entry strategy. As uncertainties decrease, we can then feel more comfortable spending more, because we know more. This mantra is also tied to how we manage the number of learning loops and the length of each one, which we cover in the next section. I simply know by the budget assumptions if someone has a D-I-A or product development mind-set, and in coaching sessions I have forced teams to reevaluate what they really need to spend to learn! Developing a learning prototype requires significantly less investment than building a product prototype for development. When we get to Soren Bro's story in the next section about the German research institute, which mind-set do you think it had?

One time, I almost jumped out of my chair when one young, recently hired entrepreneur, lacking corporate experience, recommended building 10 prototypes in early Incubation at over $100,000 each. In the software world, it is easier to test many options since the costs are lower, yet even these tests need to be carefully managed. If too many variables are being tested simultaneously, then how do we really know what the tests are telling us?

With this philosophy of maximizing learning and minimizing spending, we aim for the Incubation objectives to be about uncovering and nurturing a portfolio of opportunities (or options) of a highly uncertain outcome yet with immense possibility for the market and the company. With the higher failure rate, we need more options to test, yet we have to be creative in the ways we do it, to keep the costs down. This portfolio or options approach also provides the foundation for the development of a serial corporate entrepreneur. When one fails, it is time to move to the next opportunity, building on the skills already developed and leveraging networks to bring in the new expertise required. Since we are still facing too much uncertainty, we also want to develop *proposals* (not plans) for new business areas based on the outcomes of experiments in the market, with the technology, production processes, value chain, and potential customers. We seek to clarify new strategic growth opportunities for the company and to gain clarity of the value proposition for the market, as well as for other stakeholders. We also look to establish market or customer pull to measure market interest, validated through early trial revenue with customer partners or cost-sharing arrangements with development partners. If others are willing to invest early, this helps to build the case for why we should.

Incubation Activities and Processes

In terms of Incubation activities, our goal is to experiment on many dimensions, including market, technology, and strategic impact. We begin by investigating promising Discovery opportunities where technical feasibility is proven, or we have confidence that it can be, and applications seem robust. Often, the market needs to be educated about the technology or business model. How the technology or business model evolves comes from what is learned in the market. We are looking to interact with the market through application trials in two or three domains to test our options. We work with partners and potential customers to test whether the perceived value founded on assumptions aligns with the team's expectations through the probe and learn approach, which will be described in Chapter 10.

Additional activities include stimulating new market creation and value chain development via partners. This is required because it takes time and money to create a new market, so it is better to share the risks. It is important to emphasize that as business concepts and formulations continue to evolve during Incubation, iterative technical development is required based on what is learned in the market. Remember Lars wondering whether they should have gone after a potentially easier learning application or stayed the course as they did. We do not lock in technical specifications until the end of Incubation. Throughout Incubation, we focus on developing learning simulations or prototypes to test concepts, not develop products.

In mid to late Incubation, once uncertainties have been significantly reduced, we can then conduct credible business case analyses based on the outcomes of market and technical experimentation, with the objective of clarifying the economics of the potential business model. There could also be some initial yet very small revenue generated through trials, along with more substantial partner investment. It is time to establish revenue targets and start the calculations for how this business opportunity could be profitable. While strategic fit and market interest remain the main discussion points, it is now time to start focusing on more traditional financial measures.

Before that, we focus on keeping the game in play by clearly outlining what this opportunity *could* be. This is why the business vision, as described in Chapter 6, is so critical. By design, higher-uncertainty investments are more strategic. We need to tell a compelling story of what is possible until we have sufficient learning to convert assumptions into knowledge. Finally, as the last of our Incubation activities, we must not lose sight of our near-term and longer-term options in terms of applications, markets, and products to deliver upon our business vision.

As you might expect, the processes to support these activities are nontraditional. They have little resemblance to phase gate processes and involve:

- Learning Plans, which are described in the next section.
- Early market participation with lead users, partners, and innovative customers.

- Market probes that become market launches by creating a potential path to market, and where the company can begin to commercialize early market opportunities. Market probes help to:

  - Identify potential new applications to enhance the business vision.
  - Build internal credibility due to external interest.
  - Learn about cost structures and partnership options.

- Creating a pipeline of opportunities, accepting that failure is part of the design. When one shuts down, there is a better or more promising one to work on. This pipeline helps:

  - Provide psychological safety to teams working on projects that are not working out—serial corporate entrepreneurs mentioned earlier.
  - Make stop or put on shelf decisions much easier and more efficient since there is more to draw upon. The decision to stop a project should come from the project leader and team since they are in the best position to know.

Let's be clear. Shutting down projects is not easy. The corporate culture is to keep projects alive, even if they have to go underground. I have seen millions of dollars or euros wasted on development projects that seem to have a life of their own. My observation is that once a project is being managed through the product development process, there is incredible pressure to pass each gate and a reticence to ask the difficult questions. Again, it's this fear of failure thing.

Companies also set inappropriate metrics for measuring success. Soren Bro, an Incubation manager at Grundfos, shares the story of his project shutdown experience.

My boss asked me to participate in a meeting with a prominent German research institute. The project was about developing our own microwave UV system together with this institute—a high-uncertainty project on all four MOTR (market, organization, technical, and resource) levels. I was asked to challenge the process with my D-I-A mind-set, and I had a lot of critical questions! A few months after the first meeting, I was put in the project management role. The project was facing fundamental technical uncertainties at that point, and essential benchmarks had not been done.

The institute suggested addressing the performance uncertainty by designing and building a $200,000 test rig and doing the benchmark in the lab. The D-I-A mind-set and tools pushed us to look for an alternative way to test the assumption about whether we would be able to compete with existing players. We knew we did not need to spend $200,000 to figure this out, especially since we were early on in the project. We found an expert in Russia who knew the fundamental limits of the core technology we were utilizing, and in a single phone call and a little e-mailing, this person provided us with the evidence to make the decision to close the project. A great and very fast learning, for little cost!

In the middle of the project, Grundfos introduced personal incentives for all its employees. My personal incentive was decided by my boss and sounded like this: "Finish the scheduled test rig according to time plan." When the time came to discuss if I had fulfilled this target incentive, I was first told, "You did not make the test rig, which means no incentives." Of course, I argued that I had actually saved Grundfos a lot of time and money by making the decision to close the project. After further discussion, my boss corrected the result to "full incentives."

This story I use now to exemplify what the mind-set can do for our organization and that traditional metrics are not suited for this uncertain world of business. The closedown of this project led to investigation into other UV opportunities and finally our Enaqua competency-based acquisition.

So shutdown was not easy for Soren, yet it did lead to an important strategic investment. Fortunately, with his powers of persuasion, which I have seen in our coaching sessions, he did get the incentives he deserved. More often than not, however, this is not the case. This is either because people are not quite so skilled in making their case or because companies simply refuse to accept that traditional metrics are inappropriate when dealing with high-uncertainty projects.

Therefore, the objectives for moving from *Incubation* to *Acceleration* are to:

- Ensure that the "learning per dollars spent" mantra has been successful in reducing uncertainty.
- Validate market interest through partner investment, emergence of new applications, invited lectures, press inquiries, technical leadership, and so forth.
- Establish revenue targets and secure early revenue, if possible.
- Provide market evidence that the business opportunity can be profitable.
- Find and develop people with the competencies for growing these business opportunities.
- Revisit strategic fit.

See Table 9.1 for the Incubation Focus Areas from Table 3.3, Innovation Business Opportunity Evolution, in Chapter 3.

TABLE 9.1   Incubation Focus Areas

Pivot	*Incubation* Experimentation Output = Concept Proposal
Technical Uncertainty	
Understanding technology drivers, value, and economic feasibility	Technology Prototypes, Simulation, IP Strategy and Plan Execution, Product or Solution Specifications
Market Uncertainty	
Learning about market drivers, value creation, and business viability	Early Adopter Experience, Market Learning, Business Model and Market Entry Strategy
Resource Uncertainty	
Accessing money, people, and capabilities internally and externally	Innovation Talent and Partnership Development
Organization Uncertainty	
Gaining and maintaining organizational legitimacy	Structure and Process to Support D-I-A Mindset and Effectively Transition Concepts or Projects

Source: rInnovation Group

INCUBATION AND LIVING WITH CHAOS:
THE LEARNING PLAN[3]

As covered in the previous section, Incubation is about maintaining alignment with and influencing the strategic intent via the business vision. It also requires ensuring that the right type and level of resource commitment is in place and that the pacing of projects is driven by learning and redirection. Projects should be assessed based on Incubation (not traditional) evaluation criteria and metrics. Internal and external networks are essential to access new sources of knowledge and capabilities, and we cannot lose sight of the importance of uncertainty reduction in market and technical areas as well as resource and organization ones. This is certainly a tall order. How do we manage all of this chaos and uncertainty? This is where the Learning Plan comes in.

First you must accept the premise that chaos exists and we can bring some order or discipline to it. At a presentation I made in London many years ago, I had a discussion about the difference between *complicated* and *complex*. I was basically told that we were making innovation complicated, whereas it was not complex. This conversation has stayed with me throughout the years. In the dictionary, the two words are considered synonyms, yet I think of them slightly differently. I agree we do make things complicated. On the other hand, complexity just is. I have tested this over the years. What we are dealing with is definitely complex, when considering four dimensions of uncertainty, having more questions than answers, shifting capacities for innovation, and so forth.

The Learning Plan methodology provides a disciplined approach for managing this very chaotic world by acknowledging its complexity and seeking a way to make it as simple as possible. This methodology is specifically designed for the Incubation environment. We are experimenting with options to uncover the best path for market entry. This is unlike the commercialization focus of product development, which is specific to a target market. This testing of options runs counter to most corporate cultures, yet is essential prior to making the large investments required to commercialize a business opportunity. This is likely why we see such high failure rates in product development and mostly incremental innovation investments.

Short, Quick, Inexpensive Learning Loops

Let's get back to Louise Quigley, director of strategic innovation, and Mike Pickett, vice president of global strategic development, at Moen, from Chapter 3. Louise, Mike, and I spoke of their experiences with the D-I-A systematic approach to learning. Mike has seen a big difference in learning speed.

> There is a perception that Learning Plans are slow, but in my experience they can be incredibly fast. In the early stages of development, Learning Plan methodologies can improve the speed of execution by a factor of 10 over typical Stage-Gate processes. The Learning Plans keeps us focused on what we need to know next. We can systematically and iteratively test and reshape our market hypotheses until we arrive at the right solution. In my 25 years of product development experience, this is the most effective tool I have found for working on highly uncertain innovative projects.

Moen has also added an interesting twist to keep up its speed of learning. Louise facilitates regular Learning Plan sessions and explains:

> In our Learning Plan sessions, we start with an initial plan and focus on what is most critical to learn next. We go out, conduct learning loop exercises against critical unknowns, review the outcomes, and use the learnings to adjust our hypotheses. Then we go through the process again. You could say we have big learning loops when there is a significant change and small learning outcome loops when there is not. This iterative approach enables us to learn quickly and helps us arrive at the most compelling innovation opportunities.

We are finding that companies are adapting the Learning Plan methodology for their unique circumstances, while respecting the principles of the methodology. With Moen's consumer product focus, it makes sense to consider which steps are essential to maintaining and accelerating learning speed in a fast-paced market. This might be about regularly reviewing learning outcomes but not designing a new Learning Plan until there is a change in course brought on by learning. However, before deciding which approach might work for you, I would highly recommend you first read what the methodology is all about and consider the benefits of training and coaching addressed in Chapter 10. Moen has been on this journey for some time and has been through a number of these sessions to get to where it is today.

The Learning Plan Methodology

The Learning Plan in Figure 9.1 has been designed as the project management mechanism for higher-uncertainty innovation projects. The objectives are to help with the articulation of project value, serve as a communication vehicle, establish a common language for innovation, and make the learning process more efficient by having a record of the past and a clearly defined path forward. The Learning Plan is to be used for learning at the project level. It is a tool to work through uncertainties. The Incubation Uncertainty Identification Checklist in Table 9.2 is a complement to the Learning

	T	M	R	O
Learning Approach				
Known				
Unknown				
Assumptions				
Assumption testing (learning per dollar spent and unit of time invested)				
Tasks and timetable				
Objectives/evaluative criteria for the test				
Learning Outcomes				
Assumptions converted into knowledge				
Impact across TMRO				
Impact on overall concept/project progress and risks				
Influence on next steps				

FIGURE 9.1   Learning Plan Design Template
Source: RPI Phase I Research

TABLE 9.2 Incubation Uncertainty Identification Checklist—Areas to Consider

Categories	Technical Uncertainty	Market Uncertainty	Resource Uncertainty	Organization Uncertainty
Uncertainty Focus	Understanding technology drivers, value, and economic feasibility	Learning about market drivers, value creation, and business viability	Accessing money, people, and organizational competencies	Gaining and maintaining organizational legitimacy
Incubation Areas to Consider	• Approaches to Solving Identified Technical Problems • Manufacturing and Software Development Requirements	• Initial Market Entry Application and Follow-on Applications • Initial Customer Partners • Other Required Value Chain Agents • Existence of Other Technical/Potential Competitive Solutions • Business Model Appropriateness	• Team Competencies Aligned with Business Concept Requirements • Talent Attraction and Development • Competency Acquisition In-House or External Partnerships • Partnership Identification, Formation, and Management	• Nature of Innovation Guidance Process • Relationships with Internal Stakeholders • Potential Organizational Resistors • Influence with Corporate Strategy/Management • Expectations of Senior Management and Transitioning Units • Organizational Design

Source: rInnovation Group

145

Plan to help teams think through technical, market, resource, and organization uncertainties. It was developed based on the experiences of many projects and serves to identify areas to consider and setbacks or potential showstoppers.

The Learning Plan is designed in two parts. The first is the learning approach, and the second is the learning outcomes. The learning loop is the combination of these two parts. The design also ensures that one considers all four uncertainties—technical, market, resource, and organization. Uncertainties will be further elaborated upon in the next section.

In the *learning approach*, we focus on identifying what we know, what we do not know, and our assumptions. We confirm what we know by asking if we have evidence to support it. If we do not have this evidence, we are likely making an assumption, which becomes an unknown. Based on what we do not know and our assumptions, we then decide what is most critical to address next. We convert our assumptions into hypotheses to provide insights into what tests might be conducted. The nature of these tests can also help define what is most critical. We confirm what is most critical by asking ourselves whether, if we do not address it, it will it get in the way of learning progress and success or have the potential to become a showstopper. We also factor in the amount of learning that can come from these tests and the time needed to get that information.

These become our tests. We set them up based on "learning per dollars spent"—how can we learn the most and spend the least? The goal is the most quality learning for the least amount of time. We also define the tasks and timetable. The timetable is defined by what we need to learn, not a calendar event. How long will it take us to learn this? Therefore, learning tests can take one week or a number of months. Some showstopper tests do take time, or you might have a number of yellow or red flags but no obvious showstoppers in the beginning. This gets back to the focus on what is most critical for us to learn next. We need to develop objectives and evaluative criteria for these tests so we know how to evaluate the learning outcomes to determine if we have been successful.

In the *learning outcomes* part, we evaluate assumptions that have been converted to knowledge and review their impact across the four categories of uncertainty. We also evaluate the outcomes of our tests to see how they are different from what we expected. Learning in one area will have an impact on another, due to their interdependencies. We also need to step back and look at what this learning is telling us about overall project progress and risks. This is where we ask ourselves if we should stay the course or redirect, which will then have an influence on next steps (or even stop the project). These next steps then become the starting point for the next learning loop. With this approach, project reviews are driven more by learning loop completion than by calendar events, as mentioned previously.

This methodology was designed with the steps of a scientific research method in mind: Loop 1—Assumptions or background, hypotheses, data gathering, analysis, results, and their impact on future hypotheses to be tested in Learning Loop 2; Loop 2—Assumptions or background, hypotheses, data gathering, analysis, results, and their impact on future hypotheses to be tested in Learning Loop 3; and so forth. The basis is that we are systematically testing cause and effect around not only technical considerations, but also market, resource, and organization ones, which means we are testing perceptions to see if they have any basis in fact.

Let's get back to another insight, courtesy of Jesper Ravn Lorenzen, Incubation manager at Grundfos, which confirms this.

> Many people consider innovation and NBC (new business creation) as quite fluffy, "the fluffy front end." My reflection is that the D-I-A mind-set and methodology are actually a replication of the scientific method, albeit on another abstraction level.
>
> 1. We define hypotheses or assumptions.
> 2. We set up experiments to test those assumptions.
> 3. We describe what we expect to learn.
> 4. We carry out the experiments.
> 5. We reflect on what we learned from each experiment and how it was different from what was expected, and then, based on what was learned, stay the course or redirect and restart the learning loop cycle.
>
> I acknowledge that NBC requires special professional and personal traits to handle the uncertainty, but my observation of what makes

me an efficient and competent innovation manager is actually something else. I am not very creative in a conventional way; I neither draw nor play an instrument, but I am good at creative problem solving to develop and set up cheaper, quicker experiments than most others can. And this gives me an edge when reducing project uncertainties.

So it seems the Learning Plan is proving to be an effective tool to bring a disciplined approach to uncertainty reduction and make the innovation world a little less chaotic place.

Dimensions of Uncertainty

With all this discussion about uncertainty—even starting in Chapter 2 I said innovation is *all* about uncertainty—perhaps we should spend a little more time on this topic. I have already introduced the four categories of uncertainty—technical, market, resource, and organization—and we know, through the RPI research and our innumerable experiences with companies, that these resource and organization uncertainties are highly problematic. There are two other dimensions of uncertainty that we also need to address: latency, or what is hidden, and criticality.

Once again, for the categories of uncertainty, the technical component is about understanding technology drivers, value, and economic feasibility. The market component covers learning about market drivers, value creation, and business viability. The resource component covers accessing money, people, and organizational capabilities (internal and external). The organization component is about gaining and maintaining organizational legitimacy.

While we have spoken about the importance of identifying potential showstoppers and introduced the Incubation Uncertainty Identification Checklist to help with this, we have not covered how to surface them. This is where the second and third dimensions of uncertainty, latency, and criticality come in.[4] This is going to get somewhat technical, and many people still struggle with making these distinctions. See Figure 9.2 for a visual representation of this.

		Criticality	Criticality
		Low	High
Latency	High	Cell 2: Unanticipated but Routine	Cell 4: Unanticipated Show Stopper
Latency	Low	Cell 1: Anticipated and Routine	Cell 3: Anticipated Show Stopper

FIGURE 9.2 Latency and Criticality Dimensions of Uncertainty
Source: RPI Phase I Research

Latency is about uncertainties we can anticipate and those we cannot. Common latent assumptions are: "Our sales force can sell this" (despite this being a solution versus component sale) or "We can find the engineering resources for our project" (despite a limited number of people and skills in the resource pool). Criticality is about understanding what is routine and what are showstoppers. What is routine, whether it be anticipated or unanticipated, will not get in the way of success, but the showstoppers will. A common criticality assumption is: "This fits with our strategy." This is despite there being no clearly defined strategic intent, and we know lack of fit is definitely a potential showstopper. Therefore, converting the unanticipated showstoppers to ones that can be anticipated and addressing all anticipated showstoppers during a learning loop are priorities. Surfacing the unanticipated showstoppers is facilitated by the Incubation Uncertainty Identification Checklist in Table 9.3, which is a collection of showstoppers captured from the experiences of actual projects. While certainly far from comprehensive, it helps direct your thinking in what could get in the way of your success. Based on experiences over the past 10 years and a company's need to prioritize and focus, there will typically be no more than two to four potential showstoppers or most critical issues to address per learning loop.

TABLE 9.3 Incubation Uncertainty Identification Checklist—Setbacks or Potential Showstoppers

Categories	Technical Uncertainty	Market Uncertainty	Resource Uncertainty	Organization Uncertainty
Uncertainty Focus	Understanding technology drivers, value, and economic feasibility	Learning about market drivers, value creation, and business viability	Accessing money, people, and organizational competencies	Gaining and maintaining organizational legitimacy
Incubation **Setbacks or Showstoppers** **Technical and Market = Specific to Incubation** **Resource and Organization = Any Stage**	• Prototype Limitations • Cost Disadvantages • Technology and/or Application Development Issues	• Market Attractiveness Turns Out to be False • Market Test of Prototype Fails or Disappointing • Inability to Secure Appropriate Customer Partner • Lack of Robustness, Depth, Scope, and/or Number of New Capabilities Offered Resulting in Limited or Constrained Market Applications	• Major Funding Loss due to Reversal of Overall Corporate Performance • Team Limitations • Inability to Attract Required Talent • Lack of Partnership Strategy • Failure of Alliance Deal or Technical Partner • Undefined Partnership Exit Conditions	• Loss of Champion • Change in Senior Management and/or Strategic Imperatives • Change in Senior Champion or Sponsor • Transfer of Responsibilities at Transition from Business Concept to Project • Lack of Strategic Communications • Inappropriate Portfolio and Project Level Metrics • Insufficient Runway to Demonstrate Business Results

Source: rInnovation Group

Before moving on to the next section, where we look at the learning loop development process, Arun Ramasamy, chief innovator at Grundfos, shares his story of the value of focusing on critical uncertainties.

When I took over the responsibility of incubating our water heater opportunity, as is to be expected, uncertainty was fairly high in all four categories—technical, market, resource, and organization. Despite having an engineering background, I had never built or designed a heat pump, let alone led a very capable multidisciplinary team to build a radically innovative heat recovery system. The task was complex in every imaginable respect. The "simple" task of figuring out where one should start in the project would have been overwhelming but for the thinking behind the Learning Plan, a favorite part of the entire D-I-A framework. One of the key insights I drew from this experience was that being focused on critical uncertainties actually led to more clarity on the project. Let me illustrate this with an example.

We were preparing to design and build our prototype system when my boss and I had a difference of opinion. He felt that my claim of designing and building the prototype in 30 days was simply not possible. It should be noted that I'm a product of the software industry and a complete outsider when it comes to heat pumps. Perhaps I was being naive in my estimates. "Arun, you'd need at least four to six weeks to pull together the engineering drawings alone." To his credit, he let me proceed anyway with my "uninformed approach." After all, this was supposed to be the first learning loop of the Incubation phase.

What gave me confidence was that similar systems had been built by others and that the objective was to prove that the technology would work, not design a manufacturing-ready system. The engineering drawings, in my mind, were not relevant until much later in the Incubation phase. The prescription to focus on critical uncertainties provided additional impetus to move forward. To make a long story short, we ended up building our prototype in 30 days—and, yes, without one engineering drawing. By focusing on the critical uncertainty of developing a learning prototype to make it real and to demonstrate feasibility, this led us to more clarity than an engineering drawing would have provided.

Now let me jump in here and make a very important point. This discussion happens all the time, especially when people come from product development and operational backgrounds. Coming up with the engineering drawings would have been appropriate for the product development process. How would we get quality products out the door otherwise? Yet, that was not Arun's objective in the early days of Incubation. He was merely taking the next step beyond the proof of concept, knowing there were similar systems out in the market and focusing on what was most critical to learn next.

So everyone has been speaking about these wonderful learning loops. Let's get to it.

Learning Loop Development Process

There are three steps involved in the learning loop development process, and they can seem academic. I encourage you to experiment with this process. Practice makes perfect, and it takes time to perfect the process. It is intuitive for some and not for others. We are going to cover the basics. What is most important to focus on is being systematic. In preparation for a learning loop initiation session, the starting point is your opportunity concept or Plant Value Pitch from Chapter 6.

The first step is to initiate your learning loop.[5] The second step is to evaluate your learning outcomes. The third step is to understand the general guidelines to gauge the effectiveness of your learning loop development.

Initiating a Learning Loop

Let's start with your opportunity concept. For each of the four uncertainties, create a page (or use a flip chart) and divide the page into knowns on the top and unknowns at midpage. If you want to get creative, you might want to color code the uncertainties. I like to use black for technical, green for market, and bold colors such as purple and red for resource and organization so they stand out. We cannot forget that they are the ones that get in the way of success.

For each of these four categories of uncertainties, list each of your knowns and provide the source for this evidence of fact to ensure it is not an assumption. Now list your unknowns and your assumptions. Remember to work on what is not immediately obvious or latent using the Incubation Uncertainty Identification Checklist. You will need to go back and forth across the technical, market, resource, and organization areas since one thought will trigger a dependency with another.

Once you feel you have a good sense of what you know and don't know, then identify what is most critical to address next. Remember the test is: Will this get in the way of my success? Set up your tests for these most critical areas across the four categories with objectives and evaluative criteria for the tests. Then develop a plan for what resources are required, how much it will cost, and how long is required to learn what you need to know.

From this exercise, the objective is to identify your critical uncertainties and assumptions and the required tests for addressing them, including what it will take. Remember to use the Learning Plan Design template in Figure 9.1 as a guide. It might also be a good approach for recording your learning.

Evaluating Learning Outcomes

Once you have completed your tests, it is time to update your learning. As part of this, you want to look for any insights on the need to redirect or stay the course. You also want to see if any new uncertainties have emerged, as they invariably do. Remember to look across all the categories of uncertainties for the interdependencies. Now you are ready to complete your learning loop and set up the next one based on what are your next most critical uncertainties, associated tests, and resource requirements (people and money). The cardinal rule is that this process is learning dependent, not calendar dependent. You drive the direction of your learning. There are no predetermined gates. Set your time line always with this in mind. Your goal is not to go through set gates but rather to begin to determine what they might look like.

General Guidelines

Finally, let's consider a few guidelines to help you gauge the progress you are making. It typically takes two to three learning loops to see evidence of gaining traction or market interest and decide whether to continue with a project or application area. If you have multiple applications to test, you need to conduct a learning loop for each application that appears interesting. Combining two or more applications becomes difficult to manage since often different tests are required. Applications can still be tested in parallel, but I recommend you record them separately on the Learning Plan Design template should you choose to use this format. I say "should you choose" because you might even come up with a template of your own. We have experimented over the years on how best to record this learning. It is a very dynamic process that is difficult to capture in a static tool. We have developed Excel spreadsheets and Word documents. Grundfos is using a mind-mapping tool. We are now taking the next leap to an online tool that you will be able to play around with in its standard form or even choose to upgrade to its more advanced version. I will expand upon the Incubation Toolkit in Chapter 10. In the meantime, feel free to experiment!

The final guideline is that your project requires multiple learning loops to be ready for Acceleration. In our experience, there are no fewer than three and no more than seven. These are averages only. The number of loops required will vary by your industry, where software will require fewer loops than renewable energy, for example. It will also depend on your level of project uncertainty. Breakthrough opportunities will require more loops than evolutionary ones. Consider this a rule of thumb only. The final outcome of the learning loop process is the preparation of your concept proposal to move to Acceleration.

As you can see, Incubation is much more involved than Discovery. Let's move on to Chapter 10 so we can elaborate on the road map for getting to your concept proposal. As we tackle the management challenges of how to engage in market learning and think about business models, let's keep in mind this mantra of "learning per dollars spent."

NOTES

1. Material for this chapter is drawn from Rensselaer Polytechnic Institute (RPI) Phase I and II research; Richard Leifer, Christopher M. McDermott, Gina Colarelli O'Connor, Lois S. Peters, Mark Rice, and Robert W. Veryzer, *Radical Innovation: How Mature Companies Can Outsmart Upstarts* (Boston: Harvard Business School Press, 2000); and teaching, training, and coaching experiences.

2. Gina C. O'Connor, Richard Leifer, Albert S. Paulson, and Lois S. Peters, *Grabbing Lightning: Building a Capability for Breakthrough Innovation* (San Franciso: Jossey-Bass, 2008), chap. 4.

3. Mark P. Rice, Gina Colarelli O'Connor, and Ronald Pierantozzi, "Implementing a Learning Plan to Counter Project Uncertainties," *Sloan Management Review* 49, no. 2 (Winter 2008): 54–62.

4. Hollister B. Sykes and David Dunham, "Critical Assumption Planning: A Practical Tool for Managing Business Development Risk," *Journal of Business Venturing* 10 (1995): 413–424.

5. The term *learning loop* comes from the Sykes and Dunham paper, as referenced in Chapter 4.

CHAPTER 10

EARLY MARKET ENGAGEMENT: BUSINESS CONCEPT OPTIONS[1]

In this chapter, we focus on how the Learning Plan is applied in practice. This is difficult to make real on paper because it comes down to situational learning. You need to do it to experience it. The next best alternative is to share the experiences of others. Of course, we continue to carry through our mantra of "learning per dollars spent," which I hope has been ingrained in you by now.

Steve Pierson adds one more mantra, "good enough," and other insights based on his experiences.

> *It is not about being perfect.* It is better for us to have a working prototype, which allows for early learning and experimentation, than to strive for perfection in the Incubation phase. We often used the mantra "It's good enough" when making decisions to move forward with our ideas, concepts, and prototypes.
>
> *Fail fast and fail often.* Admit failures and move on. Do not blame, but look for learning opportunities from these failures. Failing often and early will improve our chances of success in the long run. While we could have learned much more by running multiple concurrent projects, our platform was constrained by resources and funding.

We worked with the capacity we had and the mind-set of "good enough," and we accomplished a lot.

You can't manage what you don't measure. Partners are very important in accelerating our market learning and improving the "learning per dollar spent" metric. Partnerships are essential to fill our competency gaps, share the risks, and help to validate market interest. The name of the game is to reduce uncertainty quickly in a methodical manner based on the hypotheses we want to test in short, focused learning loops. With partners, we can learn more, faster, and at less cost. We can measure this.

Steve raises a number of important issues. Of course, the idea of measuring and managing innovation activities is much larger than partnering, yet using partners as one of the measures of success is a very important one for many companies. Louise Quigley also makes the point that "conventional new product development metrics don't adequately measure the outcomes of innovation efforts. It is important to give the organization the tools to evaluate learning per dollars invested and progress toward strategic goals, in addition to traditional measures like financial success." In our work with companies, we emphasize that a big part of success depends on creating your own metrics to manage expectations, or the wrong ones might be created for you.

Let me reinforce his new mantra of "good enough." This comes up often in coaching sessions. We are seeking to build prototypes and simulations of concepts to learn, not to develop products. Again, this is a very different mind-set. We have already touched upon this in the Incubation principles, but there is a new twist: one of capacity. There will never be enough money and, more importantly, skilled people to go around. The good news is that we do not need a lot of people working on early stage to midstage Incubation opportunities to learn. What we need are people with the right skills and mind-sets!

INCUBATION PROGRESSION: MARKET LEARNING AND BUSINESS MODEL

In early Incubation, we focus on framing our experiments based on our opportunity concept and the uncertainties we need to reduce.

We start to develop market prototypes, pick applications to test, engage early adopters, pursue our business model options with partners, discuss strategic alignment with senior management, and ensure we have the right project leader and team in place to carry all of this through. Just as much as experiments start small, so do teams, as with the startup world. Throughout Incubation, we work through iterative learning loops to reduce these uncertainties. In late Incubation, we prepare for the transition to Acceleration and conduct one final learning loop to develop a plan for addressing the remaining uncertainties.

As we work through Incubation, how we go about market learning as described by Steve and others, and how we think of business models, is all-consuming. We need the skills and mind-set to do this. If you do not have them, go find them. People and companies spend too much time wandering around because they do not know what to do, rather than finding someone who does. You would not ask me to build an energy smart grid, so why do we expect people to just figure out how to manage these higher-uncertainty innovation opportunities? Of course, with time and a lot of learning, people do get there; yet what about the time and, often, careers lost in the process? What we experienced at Nortel, and what remains a challenge today, is that the clock to demonstrate value starts from the beginning. There is limited patience for the learning cycle of innovation. Rather than trying to do it yourselves, leverage as many experts as you can to get it right, quickly. As Mike Pickett emphasized, "Organizations that choose to invest in innovation efforts expect to see a business impact over time. It is important that innovation teams stay focused on market outcomes, in addition to process. Ultimately, innovation teams will be measured based on business impact." What can you do to accelerate your understanding of the innovation process so you can focus on business impact?

In the market learning and business model sections, our goal is to help you at least understand why this is different from product development. This is critical for you to have the right business impact, at the right time. In product development, the markets are known, the product is defined, it has an organizational home, the technical hurdles are relatively low, and the strategic fit is clear.

We know this is not the case when faced with all this uncertainty. What should we do about it?

MARKET LEARNING[2]

There are two corporate models for market learning. The first is driven by the customer voice and is focused on today's business. The other is driven by the market, technology, new business model, or future voice and is focused on tomorrow's business opportunities.

Today's model is quite rightly about listening to the customer, addressing effectively and efficiently existing demand, and is characterized by lower market uncertainty. The result of this model is incremental new products and services to maintain the core business.

Tomorrow's model is about understanding market trends, visioning the market, and building and creating future demand, and is characterized by higher market uncertainty. The result of this model is major new products and businesses. These opportunities significantly grow and renew the company through initiatives that move the company beyond incremental innovation initiatives. They take the form of evolutionary and breakthrough innovation opportunities as described in Chapter 2.

In each of these worlds, different questions are asked and methods used to learn about markets.

For incremental innovation the questions are:

- How much market share can we capture?
- How fast will it grow?
- How can we segment the market?
- How should we position the product?

The methods for seeking these answers are through written surveys, product concept tests, focus groups, and secondary research. In this world, the products are real and customers can more easily assess their attractiveness.

For evolutionary and breakthrough innovation projects the questions are:

- What market applications will this enable?
- What is the potential impact of this technology or business model on the market?

- What hurdles must be overcome, and what uncertainties do we need to address?
- How can we demonstrate the concept via a simulation or learning prototype?
- What is the order-of-magnitude potential market size?

The methods for seeking these answers are through developing demonstrations and prototypes of the concept, attending forward-thinking industry conferences and trade shows, tapping into internal and external networks, observing and partnering with potential users, and the probe and learn process.

The insights we capture will also provide input to our strategic intent about visions of a future world and where the trends are driving us to envision new possibilities. They will not define this intent. It requires a much more involved (and necessary) process, as Grundfos, Moen, NOVA Chemicals, Novozymes, Westinghouse, and others have learned, to conceive of a strategy for the future.

Let's focus on one method that is very effective in finding answers: the probe and learn process. It is particularly attractive when working from an opportunity versus product concept, where market insights are based on trends and when targeted customers might not come from the existing customer base. The focus is on who could benefit the most from the application, not which market is the largest. We will spend more time on this later in the chapter, but often the best place to learn is in niche markets. We are also looking for where lead customers, partners, or even other stakeholders can be found who want to learn alongside your company. An early simulation or prototype is developed as a market learning tool rather than the final product, with the objective of obtaining the market's reaction based on a series of market experiments.

Before getting to Arun's story, I'd like to share a story of my own. Unfortunately, I have watched companies destroy innovation far too often. The most disappointing part is that, most often, it is out of ignorance, rather than a deliberate attempt to sabotage. It comes from using the wrong techniques to look for market validation.

We were working with a multinational imaging company in the early 2000s. Its research and development (R&D) team came up with a concept for sharing photos online. This was brought to its consumer business division for consideration. The division said it would use its standard product concept test to assess the likelihood of market acceptance. In order for this opportunity to be considered for the product development road map, it required a 25 percent favorable rating in the top box—definitely would buy. What do you think happened? Yes, it failed, but not because it was a bad concept. It failed because the wrong technique was used. It was far too early even to know what the product could be. So how can you even describe a *product* concept that the market could understand, let alone be willing to purchase? This was still in the early days of the Internet, so people could not even visualize what this could be. A demonstration was required to make it real by simulating an online community.

> *Products that fare badly in a market test can be canceled. In striking contrast, "probes" that fare badly, like the early GE CT scanners, serve as vehicles for generating information for subsequent iterations.*
> —Lynn, Morone, and Paulson, "Marketing and Discontinuous Innovation"[3]

Arun's experiences also help to reinforce these points.

We were at an important stage of incubating our SIGMA WATER-HEATER opportunity, when we decided to build a "field test" prototype. The primary purpose was to test the market viability of the articulated value proposition. The decision to build a prototype was based on the results of the preceding learning loop, which involved talking to qualified prospects in the Caribbean market.

These face-to-face discussions with key decision makers involved the use of an information brochure highlighting the features and benefits of our future product. While the brochure made the savings potential clear to the prospects, something else seemed to be missing. We learned that social proof (if others believe, then so should I) was a much more important factor in securing permission to field-test.

We resolved to build the prototype as a consequence and did so by focusing only on what we deemed were the critical uncertainties.

Reflecting the increased engineering complexity of the project, we began incorporating elements from our company's phase gate process whenever it made sense. This "haphazard" process perplexed colleagues closer to the company's core business who were more used to the rigor of the phase gate process than the flexible, iterative approach prescribed in D-I-A. However, every learning loop was producing meaningful results and aided us to move the opportunity ever closer to Acceleration. In less than a year, not only did we secure permission to field-test the prototype, but we also made our first sale.

This experience has convinced me that, for radical innovations, prototypes need to evolve with market feedback and phase gate type processes do not yield the required outcomes that we got from following the D-I-A framework.

And guess what—on April 18, 2013, and as I write this chapter, the SIGMA team at Grundfos found out it had won the 2012 International Design Award gold medal in the Sustainable Living/Environmental Preservation–Energy Conservation Equipment product design category. It engaged the design consultancy Dimensional Innovations to create the design in Figure 10.1.

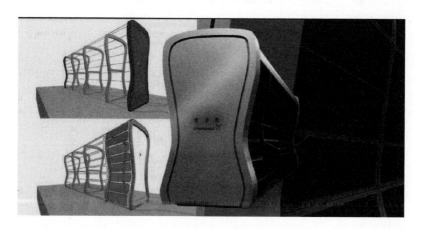

FIGURE 10.1   Grundfos SIGMA WATERHEATER
Source: Grundfos International Design Award submission

Business Model

Building a new business model in a company not only is a great management challenge but often threatens the status quo. This is often referred to as the tyranny or limitations of the current business model and, if not overcome, will lead to so-called incrementalization of business opportunities. In Incubation, we continue to test options, and arriving at a business model and market entry strategy is one of the most important outcomes to make the transition to Acceleration.

The four objectives of testing business model options are:

1. Finding the best path to market.
2. Deciding which parts of the value chain the company wants to retain versus outsource.
3. Determining how the company will form its value chain and value network (elaborated upon in Chapter 12).
4. Devising a plan for enticing value chain members to join.

In value chain development, examples of the questions we need to ask and answer are: Are we developing a product, service, or solution? Are we going to manufacture components or move up to systems? Do we need development or customer partners to build and test the prototypes, and, if so, who are they? How do we want to engage in marketing and sales—directly or via channel partners? How do we to want distribute the product, provide the service, or implement the solution? And so forth.

Again, as with market learning, different methods are required for discovering the appropriate business model. Business model design and development are highly experimental, requiring systems thinking, mechanisms for envisioning the entire value chain, and the logic of a puzzle to put the pieces together in different ways to create business model options.

Our experiences at Nortel were very much like this. In 1996, Jeff Dodge and John Andersen came to us with the concept of renting software over the Internet, which became our NetActive venture.[4] The initial vision was to deliver applications or portions of them over Nortel's residential broadband network, enabled by a unique

Internet authorization technology. At the time, the Internet and e-commerce were in their infancy. We actually had to create the back-office support to test the concept. We went from this vision to our first business model of providing the encoding capability between software publishers and e-commerce websites, which would then be the conduits to the customer. We didn't get much traction with the e-commerce providers at the time and uncovered bandwidth limitations in being able to deliver software. Our second business model was based on putting the encoding technology on CD-ROM, which then introduced CD-ROM manufacturers, a transaction website, and distribution requirements. Despite many experiments with the business model and significant investment, the business did not make it. Clearly, the concept was ahead of its time and we learned the hard way that it is not easy to experiment with business model options.

As we saw with Nortel, market learning will likely lead the company away from familiar business models. Value chain creation will stretch the company into new business areas that are not areas of natural strength. The business model will evolve as the company learns about the market and the market learns about the new technology and infrastructure requirements. The company may require a temporary infrastructure to educate partners and accelerate value chain development. We did this at Nortel, and Texas Instruments had to do this with its Digital Light Processing (DLP) component technology.

Developing business model options and testing them in the market requires training, coaching, and experience. Those who are good at testing various business models have done it before and have the benefit of bringing their experience to the unique situation. This reinforces the importance of situational learning. Knowing what I know now, I would have paid more attention to our critical uncertainties and looked for the showstoppers. In the end, looking back is far easier than being in the thick of it, so who knows whether we could have arrived at a different outcome back then.

It should be quite obvious by now that coming up with a business model is not easy, and finding the right one for your opportunity might not be a good match with what your company has in place today. Grundfos and other companies are using a tool called the

Business Model Canvas (found through search) to help work through their business model options. While it was not exactly designed with the world of higher uncertainty in mind, the principles are sound. As long as you remember that you are experimenting with options and will not be able to answer all the questions until later in Incubation, it is a good road map for helping you arrive at a business model and market entry or go-to-market strategy. Look it up to see if it can help you.

MARKET DEVELOPMENT CONSIDERATIONS

The challenges of finding effective ways to engage in market learning and conceive of new business models come down to understanding how markets develop. It is a given or certainty that you will have more questions than answers until you can find ways to reduce not only your market uncertainties but also your technical, resource, and organization ones. It is essential to embrace a new mind-set based on the "learning per dollars spent" and "good enough" mantras. I want to take this opportunity to recap a few important insights that come up all the time in our coaching sessions, before we move on to the Incubation Toolkit.

Learning versus Product Prototype

As mentioned in Chapter 3, Moen successfully introduced Motion-Sense in 2012. MotionSense is a hands-free digital faucet that started as part of the team's digital kitchen focus. The team followed the Incubation principles and enabling processes to bring this opportunity to market. Louise tells the story.

> We utilized "man behind the curtain" techniques to drive rapid prototyping and gain deep insights from consumers. [The phrase comes from the movie *The Wizard of Oz*, in which the Wizard portrays himself to Dorothy as having magical powers until the dog Toto exposes him as just a man controlling a computer and levers from behind a curtain.] We simulated the experience of a touch-free faucet by manipulating the controls from a remote

location. We could see what the user was doing and could adjust our settings based on the user's reactions. This allowed us to test multiple settings simultaneously and to observe consumers firsthand while they articulated what was important to them. Some of our original assumptions about the user experience were spot-on and others were wrong. "Man behind the curtain" allowed us to quickly react and extract these key areas of value to the consumer.

Our research into competitive offerings and the learning from using existing products in homes helped inform parameters for the simulated exercises. We developed an initial hypothesis of the consumer's specifications based on our early research and assumptions. The simulated experiment was done quickly and inexpensively through use of our *learning prototypes* versus product prototypes.

Mike went on to emphasize:

We use the market to inform our innovations. We let the users help shape the direction the product concepts take. We look for solutions that can activate consumers both rationally and emotionally. When we are successful doing this, we create true delight and passion with our users. This approach allows us to conduct short, inexpensive market tests before we start to develop the product.

The Moen team developed an inexpensive prototype based on product concepts. They did not lock in on a product specification and then develop the prototype for this. They were able to follow the mantra of "learning per dollars spent" by being clear on what they needed to learn and simulating the experiment with the "man behind the curtain."

Market Entry Approach

The idea of a killer application comes from the marketing world, where market knowledge is high (or at least it should be).

Forget about Finding the Killer Application

There is a niche entry strategy for entering new markets. The criteria for choice of the initial entry application for innovation projects are different. This runs counter to most product development organizations and operating units. The initial market entry strategy is likely to result in a smaller-than-expected niche opportunity where a so-called killer application is not pursued early on. Niche applications do lead to a killer business over time through the market learning and redirection that take place. Therefore, interim performance metrics linked to growth in market interest and attractive portfolio investments or activity, in terms of flow, pacing, and transitions, are critical to positioning organizational value.

There is a balance required between selecting an initial application as part of the market entry strategy and migrating to multiple applications. We do want to create a family of products or services over time to build out these new strategic areas. However, migrating to these other applications too early diffuses the focus of the project team. The team should enter the market with its first application and pursue follow-on applications over time once it has built a broader, more sustainable business base. There will be pressure to make big money and stretch resources across multiple market needs. This has to be avoided. Pick one application and stick with it until you have a solid foundation. Remember, more likely than not, it will not be a killer application, nor should it be. You are on the path to a killer business because you have many applications to draw upon.

Be Out There

The bottom line is that, in the world of innovation, a company's success depends on its ability to engage the market early.

Move from Office to Market

Business concepts need to get out of the labs or other sheltered environments to test market interest and build momentum. The objective is to create or visualize the experience. People do not know their needs if they do not know the possibilities. They require an experience to understand and see value. Remember the imaging company? Clearly, introducing imperfect products is countercultural.

Companies do not want to ruin their reputation for quality and do not want to give away their secrets. Yet this is the only way to interact with the market and learn. By carefully selecting market experimentation partners, we can manage expectations about what we are looking to *learn* from these market trials. In addition, the other concern about protecting intellectual property (IP) can also be managed, leveraged as a tangible asset, and even made better should valuable joint IP emerge.

Market Development = Market Learning

It is also *all* about "learning by doing," as I remember Hanne Arildsen always saying while working with Danfoss, a Danish-headquartered global producer of components and solutions for refrigeration, heating, and renewable energy.

Follow the Long and Winding Road

It is not about formal market launches. Rather, it is about "concept launches," "whispering in people's ears," and an "alpha, beta, ship" mind-set. The objective is to generate excitement about potential applications and uncover more beneficial applications. As Alan Schrob will point out later in this chapter, there is a tendency to move through Incubation too quickly or skip it entirely, as we see in most companies. Even when companies think they are incubating, they really are not, because they do not understand what it means to experiment. Success depends on resisting the urge to jump from discovery to execution or squeezing Incubation. Incubation is the missing link! It helps you have a robust business model and plan for growth. Are you up to the challenge of making the case in your company?

Innovation Roles

Who engages in "learning by doing," people, of course, so building the right team is pivotal to success.

Building the Team

Let's get back to our discussions at Moen. Another topic we covered was the importance of building the team and doing so not in the traditional manner, as Louise explains.

> Building the right team of strategic thinkers who understand the importance of a learning-based process and thrive in environments

with high levels of uncertainty is critical to sustainable success. Traditional product development manages risks, utilizing predictable, linear processes to take products to market. Typically, people coming from this space are uncomfortable with high levels of uncertainty. Their instinct is to manage risk and uncertainty out of projects. If people understand this dichotomy and are still excited to join the innovation team, they belong here. If they are uncomfortable with the unknown on a daily basis, it is not the place for them.

Transition (to Acceleration) teams are very important to our organizational alignment and to keeping projects on track toward commercialization. We need our business units to have ownership of incremental and category projects and we involve them during Incubation to do this. We view this as passing the project leadership baton through a transition phase, not a handoff or transfer point. Our transition outcomes have improved significantly. It is our collaborative approach that is making the difference.

An organizational challenge we face is maintaining a sustainable cadence of projects through our innovation pipeline, given the high levels of uncertainty associated with the projects we work on. That's why we take a portfolio approach rather than develop a product plan for strategic innovation. Not everything we work on in Discovery and Incubation will get transitioned to Acceleration. Consequently, we need to have more active projects in the pipeline than what are required to support the targeted cadence. We also need to take into account the unique skill sets required to do this. How do we build the organizational memory so that, as one of us moves on, the learning is preserved? We know our Learning Plans are an important part of this and we also need to be systematic in how we capture learning from one project to the next.

Mike has been very focused on another part of building the team, the importance of external networks.

Our success depends on our ability to develop rich external networks. Finding the right external partners is critical to our success. In our core business, we have the right internal resources to accomplish 95 percent or more of our key business unit objectives. For strategic innovation, we are working outside the core and we typically don't have the requisite skills and capabilities needed to successfully develop new areas. Partners bring skills and capabilities in the new areas that enable us to achieve our outcomes. We simply cannot afford the time and cost to develop them organically. Even if we could, there is a good chance that the next project would require a completely different set of skills and capabilities. This is the right model for innovation.

This is not the place to make a career; it is the place to be when you want to make an impact. Of course, people who assume these roles are in a much better position to move up in the core business because they have been exposed to the strategic direction of our business.

As someone committed to innovation as a sustainable capability in companies, I would like to see innovation become an attractive career path. Perhaps in some companies it will be more about having these roles acknowledged through senior management, and in others it will become a track alongside technical and business ones. This will likely be driven by company scale, scope, and culture. As mentioned, the innovation career path is integral to RPI's Phase III research,[5] and I am excited (and anxious) for the results. Regardless, it always comes down to people and what is the best model to support the corporate entrepreneur.

Success Depends on People

As much as we can offer a proven approach for uncertainty reduction and tools to help enable your learning, it all comes down to you and those around you. In our training sessions, we discuss the balance between people and process. Just like a venture capitalist would, we place a greater weight on the people. We have watched companies cycle through a number of people until they find the right fit. My colleagues at RPI are spending a lot of time researching this next key question about institutionalizing innovation through people. Let's hope this becomes the RPI team's third book!

In this book, I simply want to emphasize the *criticality* of people (yes, a potential showstopper) and the new roles required for market learning and market creation or development activities. For market learning, besides the traditional trend analysis groups, we need exploratory marketing groups that are different from more traditional marketing teams. Exploratory marketers combine observations and data that provide insight into the possibilities for market creation and evolutionary market options. There are also discovery scouts to make the connections with markets, partners, customers, universities, and other sources of knowledge not currently within the company's scope. They find new business opportunities and application areas for novel technologies and business models as well as breakthrough ideas. For market creation, opportunity brokers find takers for the opportunities outside the existing business areas or even external to the company if the mainstream business is hesitant. Innovation catalysts in the product lines can help accelerate the opportunity, even before Incubation is completed. They begin to build the internal business infrastructure; formulate the business model strategy; identify the resource strategy for partnering, funding, and filling competency gaps; and hire the right talent to accelerate the business.

We also see Incubation project managers, chief Incubation managers, innovation platform directors, and chief innovation officers. I am sure you are getting the picture. People are creating new roles and even inventing titles. Look at the number of Incubation titles Grundfos has for those who virtually do the same job. This importance of people is a central focus for me because it always takes us back to our resource and organization uncertainties.

Steve Pierson sees an effective innovation leader to be one who "has a great network, is an effective communicator, is a strategic thinker, and provides motivational leadership." As he so rightly points out, "A certain skill set is required to lead and motivate an innovation team." I trust you noted that Steve focuses on the softer skills required for effectiveness, not the tangible analytical ones such as technical design and financial modeling. In the end, for a leader, it is about listening, communication, and facilitating learning through experience and role modeling. Most importantly, it is about asking the right questions to guide teams in how to be creative in designing tests and executing their experiments.

The stepping-stones to change come in small increments. Each step you take makes a difference. You can learn to ask these questions and find the answers.

THE INCUBATION TOOLKIT IN BRIEF

With the Incubation principles and techniques for early market engagement in mind, the Incubation Toolkit has been developed to help you bring appropriate discipline to the chaos and propel your concept forward in Acceleration. By the end of Incubation, you should have more answers than questions based on what you have learned in the market and within your company.

Standard Tools

The Incubation Toolkit is also available on our website at www .innovation2pivot.com. I hope you find value with the Discovery and Incubation tools and will continue experimenting with these tools, designed for reducing your project uncertainties. The goal is to reduce your uncertainties enough to turn your business options into a clear market entry or go-to-market strategy. The following tools make up the Incubation Toolkit, and each is described in the following subsections:

- Learning Plan Design Template.
- Uncertainty Identification Checklist for Incubation.
- Technical and Market Concept Testing Approaches.
- Technical and Market Concept Testing Outcomes.
- Genesis Pad Solution Description.
- Transition Readiness Questions.
- Pivot or Incubation Value Pitch.

Learning Plan Design Template

Are you looking for a systematic way to identify and track uncertainties? As described in the Learning Plan Methodology section of Chapter 9, the Learning Plan is a project management tool for uncertainty reduction across the four categories of uncertainty as well as surfacing latency or hidden uncertainties and identifying dimensions of criticality. Traditional project management tools are not designed to address these types of uncertainty, which require a learning-based approach. Its purpose is to enable project teams to learn more about their projects and document project progress without having the answers typically required to complete a business plan. Ultimately, it guides the project team through the phases of project learning and maturation to reach the point where an opportunity proposal can be developed to present the project as an Acceleration candidate. See Figure 9.1 for the Learning Plan Design template.

Uncertainty Identification Checklist for Incubation

Are you able to sort through your uncertainties to identify what is most critical to address next? The Incubation Uncertainty Identification Checklist is a complement to the Learning Plan to help teams think through technical, market, resource, and organization uncertainties. It was developed based on the experiences of many projects and serves to identify areas to consider and potential showstoppers. The overriding objective is to use the checklist to help cover areas teams may not think of during Incubation and anticipate showstoppers, from which to develop action plans to reduce uncertainties before they become barriers to success. See Tables 9.2 and 9.3 for the Incubation Uncertainty Identification Checklist.

Technical and Market Concept Testing Approaches

Are you looking for approaches to test your technical and market concepts? In Tables 10.1 and 10.2, we provide a checklist for potential testing methods for both technical concept feasibility and market concept benefits. The key for both the tests is to realize that you have at least three audiences for each test—you have to be able to convince your target early adopters, your path-to-market partners, and your internal organization that both the technical and market concepts are valid. The key is to use the simplest concept testing approach that produces sufficient technical feasibility and market benefit learning. This is not the full-bore testing conducted before a new product development launch; this is a really bare-bones demonstration of feasibility at the lowest possible cost. And be particularly careful about the demonstration required by your internal organization, which should never require more technical feasibility or market benefit demonstration than the external market will! Use the "good enough" approach.

TABLE 10.1 Technical Concept Testing Approach

Target Audience	What is Required to Demonstrate Feasibility? (be very specific)	How do you Know this is Required? Use the simplest method that meets required demonstration!
Early Adopters	• Simulation results? • Lab breadboard test data? • Field prototype test data? • Multi-site test data? • Accelerated life testing? • Real life testing?	
Path to Market Partners	• As above	
Internal Organization	• As above	

Source: Product Genesis LLC

TABLE 10.2 Market Concept Testing Approach

Target Audience	What is Required to Demonstrate Benefits? (be very specific) • Who (gets the benefits)? • What (are the benefits)? • When (are the benefits delivered)? • Where (are the benefits delivered)? • How (are the benefits delivered)? • Why (is this a good value)?	How do you Know this is Required? Use the simplest method that meets required demonstration!
Early Adopters	• Sketches? • Story board? • Animation? • Simulation? • Looks-like model in use context? • Works-like model in use context? • Looks-like/works-like prototype?	
Path to Market Partners	• As above	
Internal Organization	• As above	

Source: Product Genesis LLC

Technical and Market Concept Testing Outcomes

Are you wondering what is required to validate the outcomes of your technical and market concepts tests? In Tables 10.3 and 10.4, we provide a checklist to get to "good enough" results from your technical feasibility and market benefit concept demonstration. As with the choice of testing approach, the required outcomes for demonstration of technical feasibility and of market benefit should match the high-uncertainty focus of Incubation. These are not final product launch certification tests; these are feasibility tests, designed to guide the evolution of the Incubation opportunity. And as with your choice of concept testing approach, the concept testing outcomes required by your internal organization should never be more stringent that those required by the marketplace.

Genesis Pad Solution Description

Are you wondering how to describe your solution concept once you move into the later stages of Incubation? In Figure 10.2, the Genesis Pad Solution provides a tool to create and document solutions concepts from individual or facilitated team ideation sessions. The tool keeps the concept development focused on solving a specific,

TABLE 10.3 Technical Concept Testing Outcomes

Target Audience	What has been <u>Tested</u> to Confirm Feasibility? (be very specific)	How do you Know Requirements were met? Provide evidence of assumptions converted into facts to support feasibility!
Early Adopters	• Simulation results? • Lab breadboard test data? • Field prototype test data? • Multi-site test data? • Accelerated life testing? • Real life testing?	
Path to Market Partners	• As above	
Internal Organization	• As above	

Source: Product Genesis LLC

TABLE 10.4 Market Concept Testing Outcomes

Target Audience	What has been Tested to Confirm Benefits? (be very specific)	How do you Know Requirements were met? Provide evidence of assumptions converted into facts to support benefits!
	• Who (gets the benefits)? • What (are the benefits)? • When (are the benefits delivered)? • Where (are the benefits delivered)? • How (are the benefits delivered)? • Why (is this a good value)?	
Early Adopters	• Sketches? • Story board? • Animation? • Simulation? • Looks–like model in use context? • Works–like model in use context? • Looks–like/works–like prototype?	
Path to Market Partners	• As above	
Internal Organization	• As above	

Source: Product Genesis LLC

articulated market problem, and encourages the individuals or teams to take more evolved concepts and flesh them out into effectively described (and diagrammed) solutions.

Transition Readiness Questions

Are you asking yourself what you need to know to transition to Acceleration? The transition readiness questions in Figure 10.3 help you to think through the final areas you need to address as you prepare your opportunity proposal to make the transition to Acceleration. The questions look across the organization, resource, market, and technical uncertainties to ensure you are ready. You will likely have a good sense of whether the product or solution concept is ready for further development. You might also have a

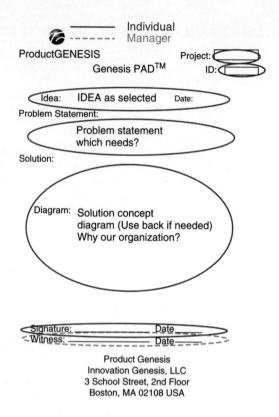

FIGURE 10.2   Genesis Pad Solution
Source: Product Genesis LLC

relatively good understanding of which application area to take to the market first.

On the other hand, you might be less aware of lingering organization and resource considerations. This is why they are at the top of the figure! I just had the discussion the other day about how a project transition was delayed because no one had budgeted for it. The same happened to us many years ago with a middleware software opportunity we sent to one of our divisions. In the end, the R&D budget had to pay for it because there was no other pot to draw from.

Organization: Business Vision and Innovation Maturity Level	Resource: Short Term Numbers Versus Investment Requirements
❏ What is the right home for the incubation concept or project, i.e., business unit (BU), strategic BU, or other? ❏ How does the project team address divisional or operational expectations?	❏ How does the concept or project team sustain funding during the transition? ❏ Who are the right people for the transition team to move to commercialization from experimentation?
Market: Niche Markets Build Killer Businesses	**Technical: Prototype versus Product/Solution Specification**
❏ Do expectations about market development match reality? ❏ How will applications and markets unfold? ❏ How does the concept or project team finalize the business model?	❏ Are the technical specifications set? ❏ How do manufacturing challenges impact market entry objectives?

FIGURE 10.3   Transition Readiness Questions
Source: rInnovation Group

Pivot or Incubation Value Pitch

Are you wondering what your value pitch should capture from your learning in Incubation? Your value pitch, or reason to believe, will have evolved by now, since you know more. This is covered in Figure 10.4. It is a powerful communication tool and becomes your value proposition. The principles covered in Discovery remain the same, yet the content of the value pitch will evolve significantly during Incubation, as more is learned about the market and the benefits of the technology, the business model, or both. We want to elaborate on your value pitch here more than in Discovery, to attract interest in further investment. Remember that you and other key stakeholders should be able to deliver the same value pitch. It is important to be singing from the same song sheet if you hope to build credibility and legitimize your opportunity. See Chapter 6 for the tips on how to do this well. This will become a key input to your opportunity proposal, covered later in this chapter.

Who: Identify Targeted Stakeholder.

What and Why: Primary Messages (The "Wow" Factor)

1. Describe concept or project (from the market's perspective, not in technology terms).
2. Identify why it is important (what is the market problem, where is your company's license to play, etc.).
3. Confirm business benefits based on feedback from market, partners, customers, or other.
4. Describe applications tested and business model options validated by market interest (partners, prototype feedback, etc.). Later stage—describe attractiveness of chosen market entry strategy.
5. State order-of-magnitude market size, revenue potential, NPV, and/or time to early revenue (too early still for profitability but need to have at least a sense that business can be profitable).

FIGURE 10.4   Value Pitch Checklist for Pivot
Source: rInnovation Group

Advanced Tools

As with Discovery, we have also designed more advanced tools for the innovation professional, such as the Learning Plan loops, Incubation Questions, Opportunity Experimentation, Partner Scan, Incubation to Acceleration Transition List, and Business Proposal Template. Once you have mastered our standard tools, then you can move to these more advanced tools available on our website.

Learning Plan loops: The Learning Plan Design template is a static tool. The Learning Plan loops are designed to take into account the dynamic nature of learning as you work through multiple loops and uncertainties.

Incubation Questions: These more in-depth questions help you work through your uncertainties more systematically. Once again, they are designed to ensure the right questions are being asked during Incubation, with the objectives of reducing your uncertainties to prepare a concept for Acceleration.

Opportunity Experimentation: This set of tools establishes an effective market and technical experimentation work flow for individuals or teams to follow. Research Strategy is used to establish the specific real-world learning required. Business Concept Breakdown identifies the technical and market uncertainties that need testing. Technical Concept Testing outlines the approaches and outcomes needed to demonstrate "good enough" technical feasibility (to early adopters, potential partners, and internal stakeholders). Market Concept Testing outlines the approaches and outcomes needed to demonstrate "good enough" market benefit to early adopters, potential partners, and internal stakeholders. Business Concept Refinement then helps teams internalize the outcomes from the concept testing and refine the business concept as needed. Business Proposal development then reflects that business concept refinement, as an opportunity is readied to leave Incubation and enter Acceleration.

Partner Scan: This set of tools helps teams identify where partnerships might be an effective means of filling capabilities gaps in the technology, market, and resource domains. Value chain analysis is used to identify likely opportunities for partnering. Then directed research efforts targeting specific partner characteristics uncover potential candidates to participate in the desired partnerships. The result is a well-structured partnership strategy for the Incubation efforts.

Incubation to Acceleration Transition List: This list ensures that all the appropriate Incubation issues have been considered to increase the chances for a successful transition from Incubation to Acceleration. It will help with completing the business proposal, reinforcing the business vision prospects for growth, building confidence in business viability, and navigating the organizational alignment process.

Business Proposal Template: A more formalized business proposal facilitates the decision-making process when the case needs to be made for more investment. This is a major transition point. Often, when companies see what it takes to commercialize these opportunities, they lack the courage or capacity to continue. In moving to Acceleration, we move from the world of uncertainty to risk, making it much more important to know clearly where we are heading. It also is the time to commit to more significant development costs, which we will address in Chapter 14. The business proposal is developed from Incubation learning to provide the rationale for moving an opportunity from Incubation to Acceleration.

As Alan at NOVA Chemicals explained,

> During incubation, we used processes to test various business models and better understand the potential value of the opportunities we were investigating. We also employed a number of Incubation tools, including the Transition Readiness Assessment Tool, to test our readiness to move from Incubation to Acceleration. Of course, we had expert project managers within our team trained on the Learning Plan process to ensure that project teams were working through uncertainty in a clear and objective way. It would have been very difficult to do this without an ability to follow the D-I-A approach and use the tools to bring the appropriate level of discipline to the chaos.

LEARNING APPROACH VALUE AND COACHING REQUIREMENTS

Let's go back to Alan's story about how important coaching was for the NOVA Chemicals team.

> Our inclination was to move more quickly through Incubation and into Acceleration, in some cases, before we were ready. Our Advisory Board, made up of senior leaders from within our company as well as independent advisers with either expertise in the areas we were investigating or experience in starting new businesses, provided us with a more strategic perspective. This allowed us to "see the forest through the trees" and to test our desire to move more quickly. Once we had built up a portfolio of opportunities, it also helped us in managing this portfolio.

Accelerated Learning to Achieve Faster Results

In the next insight, Steve Pierson describes his increasing understanding of the power of Incubation.

> Confidence comes from discipline to practice a process, just like attempting to perfect any activity.
> We were consumed with our individual platform responsibilities, which included identifying opportunities, developing business concepts, and field-testing these concepts to determine the feasibility

and stakeholder value for the potential target market segment. As a result of this intense focus and our novice status with the D-I-A process, we often strayed from our training and tools, which were intended to help improve the odds of success. Consequently, our team was not as productive as we could have been if we had taken a prescriptive approach to the methodology. This wandering took time and energy away from our mission of identifying, prioritizing, and creating new innovative business. It was very helpful to have Joanne lead regular coaching meetings to get us back on track and challenge our hypotheses. In retrospect, it would have been good to have had a strong internal project manager to ensure we were following the process as part of the deliverables schedule. We became more comfortable using the D-I-A tools as our team matured with our roles.

The moral of the story is that practice makes perfect, or at least improves with time. A coach needs to be around to guide the process, which Grundfos and others came to realize with time.

Over the years, we have tracked what people have to say about the value of D-I-A and the coaching experience. I am sharing these with you in the hope that the time you invest in learning this new practice or discipline is worth it. This disciplined approach enables the following to emerge with time:

- The D-I-A approach helps teams to develop a comprehensive view of project challenges and a more strategic perspective.
- A learning orientation is enabled and legitimized in the company. It also aids with prioritization and decision-making requirements.
- Project leaders and coaches develop new skills for managing innovation teams.
- Teams are encouraged to make connections to outside entities that can help them resolve uncertainties.
- Teams also learn how to clearly articulate what they know and do not know and come to realize that what people think they know is often based on assumptions.
- The process facilitates divergent and convergent thinking and expedites the decision-making process.

- It provides a path for guiding teams on the likely evolution of their project requirements.
- The more teams learn about all these uncertainties, the better prepared they are for the unexpected.
- The learning environment is clearly differentiated from the execution or product development phase, which reinforces the stages of learning and the purpose of Incubation.
- The process helps to identify the appropriate questions to ask and the tests to conduct to further learning, based on where teams are in the innovation life cycle of the project.

We have also seen how it has helped people work through resource and organization uncertainties. It aids with identifying when and how to move forward and enroll resources. People also learn how to address these uncertainties with senior management in less challenging ways, by asking for appropriate guidance. The value pitch thinking helps to communicate organizational value, link a project to the company's strategic intent, and manage organizational expectations. People also view the approach as relatively simple to use, and the principles, especially around these resource and organization uncertainties, could even work for lower-uncertainty innovation. Are you convinced?

Consistent and Timely Coaching Required

An outsider perspective is invaluable when critiquing opportunities and staying on course.

—Steve Pierson

Coaching is the glue that holds this approach together and makes it stick in your behaviors and company over time. You will need to decide if you would make a good coach—the one who asks the right questions, not the one with the answers. While this learning-based approach is intuitive for some, it is not for others. It is difficult to move from a mind-set based on what we know to what we need to learn, thereby admitting what we do not know. This is where the coach comes in. Learning how to coach people requires training and time to become adept in this new innovation practice.

We have designed the Learning Plan methodology for use in a higher-uncertainty innovation project setting. It is not appropriate for use until an opportunity has been scoped in Discovery and is ready for project initiation or testing of your opportunity concept in Incubation. It is typically overdesigned for incremental improvements, where there are many knowns. The exception to this could be in addressing resource and organization issues, as mentioned earlier, and which we will address in Chapter 14. For some, the template is too complex to follow when combined with four uncertainties and multiple steps in a learning loop. This is why coaching takes the experience to the next level when the dynamic nature of managing many uncertainties comes into play. Do we address them all simultaneously, one at a time, or in some combination? Each situation will be unique, yet there are patterns that become more obvious over time.

You have enough to get started for now without the benefit of coaching, but as you advance, you will likely have questions that are best addressed in a coaching environment. Remember the words of caution in the Discovery chapter, which also apply here—there is a delicate balance between people and process. Be careful not to put the process cart before the horse!

PIVOT TO YOUR EVOLVED VALUE PITCH: MAKING THE TRANSITION TO ACCELERATION WITH YOUR CONCEPT PROPOSAL

Now it is time to put together your organizational story for why your concept is worthy of more substantial investment and is ready for Acceleration. This is your concept proposal, developed from the elements that make up your value pitch and what you have learned during Incubation as follows:

- *Concise market value proposition.* Provide clear benefit statements of what this opportunity will do for the market, partner, and company based on what you have learned in the market.

- *Compelling business vision.* Reinforce through your market learning about how your concept could evolve into a business growth area with multiple generations of products, services, and/or solutions. Link this with your market and competitive landscape and your company's strategic intent.
- *Validation of the business case.* Select your market entry strategy based on the applications and business models you have tested. You now have enough information to provide a credible revenue forecast and identify a path to profitability. Of course, these numbers are based on assumptions. It would be a good idea to show mostly likely, conservative, and optimistic scenarios. You still have the risks associated with product development, so you want your stakeholders to think in ranges, rather than focus on a specific number.
- *Confidence in business viability.* Be confident in business commercial viability and that you can overcome the risks. Make the case for why your company can be a market leader.
- *Identification of assumptions and risks.* Be clear on your business risks and underlying assumptions. You might even have a few residual uncertainties to address, especially in resource and organization areas. We want these identified up front so we can address them in Acceleration.

Are you *now* ready to Pivot from your value pitch and Propel your concept into Acceleration?

We now move beyond our mantras of "learning per dollars spent" and "good enough" because we are done with experimenting. It is time for commercialization, and to do this well we need to bring in product development, lean thinking, and a quality focus. Since you have gotten most of your uncertainties out of the way, you stand a better chance than most of seeing your concept successfully commercialized.

First, let's see what Remy has to say about the entrepreneur in Chapters 11 and 12 and what Lois and Gina have to say about our perspectives on Incubation and hypothesis-driven learning in Chapter 13.

NOTES

1. Material for this chapter is drawn from Rensselaer Polytechnic Institute (RPI) Phase I and II research; Richard Leifer, Christopher M. McDermott, Gina Colarelli O'Connor, Lois S. Peters, Mark Rice, and Robert W. Veryzer, *Radical Innovation: How Mature Companies Can Outsmart Upstarts* (Boston: Harvard Business School Press, 2000); Gina C. O'Connor, Richard Leifer, Albert S. Paulson, and Lois S. Peters, *Grabbing Lightning: Building a Capability for Breakthrough Innovation* (San Francisco: Jossey-Bass, 2008); and teaching, training, and coaching experiences.
2. Gina Colarelli O'Connor, "Market Learning and Radical Innovation: A Cross Case Comparison of Eight Radical Innovation Projects," *Journal of Product Innovation Management (JPIM)* 15 (1998): 151–166.
3. Gary S. Lynn, Joseph G. Morone, and Albert S. Paulson, "Marketing and Discontinuous Innovation: The Probe and Learn Process," *California Management Review* 38, no. 3 (1996): 8–37.
4. Rensselaer Polytechnic Institute (RPI) 01-001, "The Path to a Spin-Off—Nortel Networks to NetActive, One Form of Corporate Entrepreneurship," November 2006.
5. Gina Colarelli O'Connor, Andrew Corbett, and Ron Pierantozzi, "Create Three Distinct Careers Paths for Innovators," *Harvard Business Review*, December 2009.

CHAPTER 11

BUSINESS EXPERIMENTS

The great philosopher Mike Tyson once stated, "Everyone has a plan, till they get punched in the mouth." Unfortunately, far too many entrepreneurs, including me, have gotten punched and knocked down. I learned the hard way that plans are valuable only if you recognize the fact that plans are snapshots in time as to what you intend to do in the future. Business plans are filled with assumptions, and it is your job as an entrepreneur to uncover assumptions and convert them into knowledge. Blindly executing on a business plan filled with assumptions may make you feel like you accomplished something, but truth be told, all you are likely to do is waste your time and your investors' money. Don't fall into the trap of executing your way to failure.

Converting assumptions into knowledge takes work. Maybe that's why so many entrepreneurs continue to go from idea to prototype to launch to failure. Many of these entrepreneurs are engineers and scientists, who follow the bad advice of friends and family and create products that the market shuns. I find that scientists and engineers are very comfortable in creating experiments to test their technical assumptions, but shy away from running business or market experiments. I am not suggesting that we should ignore running technical experiments; after all, technical is one of the uncertainty types. However, it is just as important to reduce market, organization, and resource uncertainty. The only way to convert market assumptions into knowledge is to define and execute business experiments that will either boost or deflate your confidence in the assumptions.

In Chapter 9, Joanne introduced the Learning Plan methodology—a disciplined approach for managing higher-uncertainty innovation projects. As discussed, the Learning Plan is a tool for corporate entrepreneurs to work through uncertainties. Likewise, in this chapter I will introduce a structured approach to working through the uncertainties in a startup, The Pivot Startup. The Learning Plan and The Pivot Startup are sibling methodologies. They share many common concepts, including technical, market, resource, and organization (TMRO) uncertainties; converting assumptions into knowledge; and validated learning. This chapter and the next were written to stand on their own. However, if you reread the previous chapters, you will find many common themes and gain deeper insights.

KNOWLEDGE CONSTRUCTION

Experts will tell you that market learning is a key startup activity. But what is market learning? To that end, what is learning or, more importantly, how do we learn? Whenever we learn something, we are actually constructing or building knowledge. For example, when you learned to drive, you built upon the knowledge you already had. In other words, the knowledge you had after you learned to drive is greater than the knowledge you had before you learned.

I met Jacob Brix, a doctoral student at the Danish Technological Institute and Aarhus University, while I was writing this book. He was a visiting scholar at Rensselaer Polytechnic Institute (RPI) with an office across from mine. Jacob is a tall, 6 feet 3 inches man with straight blond hair and a smile that melts away your defenses. He is an expert at learning and innovation and has worked as a consultant for a number of years with dozens of firms, large and small, on innovation. He came to innovation by first investigating learning, whereas I came to learning by first investigating innovation. One day when I stopped by his office for a chat, the conversation turned toward the book, and, by the time I was leaving his office, it became clear that his research and mine had many common threads. At the top was the conclusion we both came to independently that one cannot innovate without learning, or, as he puts it, without a capability to construct knowledge. "Learning is the process, while knowledge construction is the result," Jacob stated in my office later that same day. I couldn't agree more, which is why I refer to the learning loop as a knowledge construction loop (See Figure 11.1). After all, considering the fact that a startup knows very little at the start, the goal of any startup should be to construct knowledge.

According to Jacob, "knowledge is first constructed when it has been through an individual thought process of reflection where it is put into a context the individual learner can recognize and relate to."[1] In other words, information is not knowledge, and can become knowledge only if the individual or startup acts upon the information through analysis and reflection. For example, I can gather the information that $E = MC^2$, but that does not add to my knowledge. However, if I dig into this equation and begin to

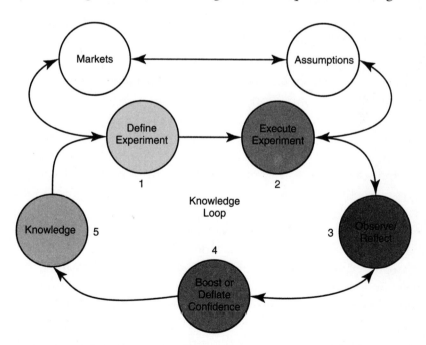

FIGURE 11.1 Knowledge Construction Loop

understand its underpinnings, and can relate this to the world I live in, then I will have added to my knowledge or, said differently, constructed knowledge.

Another insightful moment occurred in my discussions with Jacob when he used the word *illusion* in the context of our discussion on assumptions. Based on Jacob's work with dozens of firms and my work with startups, it became clear that startup firms and corporations often create a collective illusion when they base their actions on so many assumptions. It is a collective illusion shared among team members regarding technical, market, resource, and organization issues that leads to poor decision making and ultimate failure. One example of this was the startup I launched around 2002, IronSilk. The big assumptions we made were that:

- The online advertising revenue model would be similar to that of my previous startup.
- Revenue generated would be sufficient to split with our content partners.
- Content partner support would be minimal.

These assumptions had the startup team working under a collective illusion that the assumptions were facts. In retrospect, the decisions we made were poor and could have been improved if we had worked on constructing knowledge up front by testing the assumptions.

One concept that most learning experts agree on is that learning depends on feedback. For example, when I drive my car I keep my eyes on the lines and the center of my lane. If my car begins to move away from the center of my lane, my eyes catch this and feed it to my brain, and my brain makes the needed adjustments and sends a signal to my arms to correct. In order to learn from the market, the entrepreneur must get out of the office and into the market. This may sound like an obvious task, but most entrepreneurs are unwilling or unable to do this. Many find this type of activity intimidating, as it opens them up to rejection. Others find market learning activities to be daunting, too much for them to handle. Most are just unsure of what they need to do.

Unfortunately, those who do take the time to go out into the market usually squander the opportunity to learn; instead they end up chatting with potential customers and convincing themselves that customers are interested in their startup. They end up forming a collective illusion that gets shattered when they enter the market with their product or service. Some will waste time handing out surveys that ask potential customers hypothetical what-ifs. These potential customers try to be encouraging and to guess what answer the entrepreneur wants. In my experience, surveys about what a customer might want if a startup were to offer some product or service are not useful. You are asking too much of potential customers in the market to put themselves into some future situation in which they might buy some unknown product. Studies have shown that customers often do not know what they want, and the higher the uncertainty of the innovation opportunity, the more unreliable the answers.

Figure 11.2 depicts the learning process by which knowledge is constructed. It starts with defining assumptions and the markets that

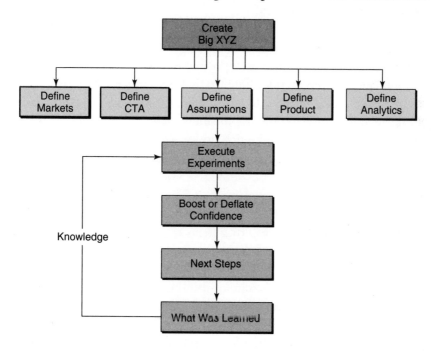

FIGURE 11.2   The Pivot Startup Flow

the startup is targeting. Next the startup will define and execute the experiments to validate the assumptions. The startup will then analyze the results (observe and reflect), which will lead to either boosting or deflating the confidence that the startup has for these assumptions. This leads to new knowledge, which can then be used to define and execute the next set of experiments. These steps are detailed in the following sections.

I will introduce The Pivot Startup methodology for entrepreneurs to follow. The Pivot Startup is a framework that entrepreneurs can use to reduce the uncertainty that surrounds their startups. It helps the entrepreneur define assumptions, markets, and experiments—and then execute the experiments in a validated knowledge loop (see Figure 11.1). The Pivot Startup helps entrepreneurs construct knowledge quicker and better, so that they are not guessing their way to a product launch.

DEFINE ASSUMPTIONS

Remember Kyle and Jake, the students who run a startup, Pay-WithMe, with the online group payment platform, PayWith.me? They recently came by my office to discuss several issues surrounding their startup. Like many other student startups, Kyle and Jake were thinking about entering several business plan competitions as part of their fund raising efforts. Jake was concerned about entering competitions. He felt that it might distract the team, which was made up of Jake, Kyle, and three other students. The concern was heightened by the recent launch of PayWith.me. The students were reviewing the web analytics of the online platform and were sifting through numerous features and marketing ideas to grow those metrics. I got a sense that they were somewhat confused, a bit apprehensive, and lost as to the next steps.

The PayWithMe team's state of mind is rather typical for a young Internet startup. A young startup will often focus on web metrics and ideas on how to improve those metrics. With nothing else to go by, a young startup begins the process of guessing features and markets. The startup team will enter prolonged discussions about which features to develop or what markets to enter next. These types of discussions always remind me of the time I was selling my home.

In 2001, my wife and I purchased a contemporary house in Sugarloaf, New York. Sugarloaf is a quaint village that has a great reputation for arts and crafts. The house we purchased sat at the top of a hill with floor-to-ceiling windows and 180-degree views of the village. It had been custom built by the previous owner. After we purchased the property, my wife and I gutted it and added several of our own custom features, including a stone fireplace, maple floors, tiled entry, and wooden doors. It turned into a spectacular house. Everything in it was custom and unique, and it reflected our tastes and personality. However, we put the house on the market when I decided to go back to school to get my MBA. We were soon inundated with advice on preparing the house for sale. Potential buyers would point out issues they wanted us to address. Real estate agents would give their opinions as to what needed to be done to sell the house. We would have these brainstorming sessions with agents, trying to come up with ideas to sell the house. These sessions did more to confuse us than anything else. Eventually, my wife and I realized that listening to everyone was a mistake, and we took over the marketing of the house. We needed to listen to only those buyers and agents who were serious about buying our unique house. We realized that buyers who loved traditional country homes were not the buyers to listen to. Their advice was useless and only served to confuse us.

The PayWithMe team was facing similar challenges. They were being inundated with advice on what to do next, which only served to confuse them. Furthermore, they had some disagreements about features and markets. The first thing I asked Jake and Kyle to do was to shift their focus from the web metrics to the assumptions that were driving the startup. As I explained to them, the focus of a startup has to be on the underlying assumptions that it is based on. As we previously discussed, a startup has four types of uncertainties that it needs to manage and reduce—technical, market, resource, and organization. These uncertainties are driven by the assumptions that a startup makes—the bigger the assumptions, the greater the uncertainty. It is up to the startup to reduce the uncertainties by going through a validated learning process that validates or invalidates the assumptions.

Here are two of the assumptions that they came up with:

1. College students are frustrated with group payment situations.
2. Fraternities and sororities are frustrated with group payment situations.

Both of these assumptions are market related, as they deal with potential PayWithMe customers. Next, I had them assign an importance to each assumption on a scale from 1 to 10, with 10 being critically important. If an assumption with an importance of 10 is unable to be validated, then the startup will be forced to Pivot. Figure 11.2 depicts an overview of The Pivot Startup's validated learning process. This is the process that I am mentoring Jake and Kyle on. As you can see from this figure, there are other steps that take place either with or after you define the assumptions—define markets, define product, define calls to action (CTAs), and define analytics. I review each in the following sections.

DEFINE MARKETS

A key step in launching a startup is assessing the marketplace (see sidebar, "What about Markets?"). Startups must ask important questions like:

- What market is being pursued?
- What are the size and the growth rate of the market?
- Which market segments will be targeted?

WHAT ABOUT MARKETS?

All books about startups and entrepreneurs cover the importance of markets. In fact, many books are dedicated to this subject matter. A quick Google search or Amazon book search will yield hundreds, if not thousands, of related resources, articles, and books on markets.

This section is not meant to be a substitute for an in-depth analysis of the market. Quite the opposite—I assume the entrepreneur will take the time to fully understand the market he or she will be selling in and the industry he or she will participate in. In my classes, I review three types of markets that an entrepreneur needs to fully understand: overall market, addressable market, and target market. In the case of Trade Shades, the overall market would be the sunglasses market worldwide. The addressable market would be the revenue generated by Trade Shades if everyone in the sunglasses market who could afford to buy Trade Shades did buy TradeShades. The target market would be the market that Trade Shades is targeting. You may have different definitions for these, but this is not important, as long as you do a thorough analysis before you begin defining market groups.

More importantly, a startup must get out of the office and into the marketplace to interact directly with the market. Although a search engine is an invaluable tool in gaining knowledge about a market, it is not a substitute for direct contact with the market. Over the years, I have become a bit of an expert when it comes to searching on sites like Google or Bing. My colleagues used to call me the Google ninja, for my ability to find out information about a market. This type of information is considered secondary research—information previously researched and made publicly available. In contrast, primary research is information that you gather directly. In general, secondary research leads to assumptions, while primary research leads to knowledge. There are of course situations in which secondary research can lead to insights and knowledge. For example, an assumption about competitors in the marketplace might be validated through secondary research.

A market group is a subset of a market segment. With The Pivot Startup's structured approach, the entrepreneur defines the market groups that he or she will experiment in within the Define Markets section. The market segments might have been highlighted during secondary research and the startup will then seek to find out information about these segments by experimenting in these market groups. Let me clarify by using another startup, Trade Shades, as an example. Two RPI students, Cory and Jonny, founded Trade Shades, which is focused on selling interchangeable and customizable sunglasses to young adults aged 15 to 29 through an online platform. The sunglasses frames are customized online by the user and manufactured by Trade Shades at their office using a 3-D printer. After the Big XYZ (covered in Chapter 7), the first step for Trade Shades was defining the assumptions and assigning an importance value to each assumption. The next steps were defining the markets and business experiments to validate these assumptions. Cory and Jonny wanted to run business experiments in two markets. One market group, labeled "free spirits," was defined as:

- 18- to 29-year-olds.
- Music lovers.
- Beachgoers.
- Attending a music festival in Miami.

The other market group, labeled "geek," was defined as:

- 18- to 24-year-olds.
- RPI students.
- Visitors to the student union.

DEFINE CTA AND ANALYTICS

To prepare for the business experiment, I asked Cory and Jonny to think about the call to action (CTA), which is an essential element of every business experiment. The CTA defines what you are asking of potential customers. CTAs can be intent to purchase forms, letters of intent, purchase agreements, arrangements to be beta testers, or financial transactions. A CTA serves as a substitute for the ultimate CTA—a request for money. It is important to remember that the goal of a business experiment is to give the entrepreneur an early indication of how the market will react when the startup is fully launched. In other words, will the market buy my product or service for a specific price at a specific rate over a specific time? The CTA is a critical piece of getting this answer. Without a call to action, the experiment turns into an affirmation of what the entrepreneur wants to hear, as opposed to an early indicator of what the market wants. One of the most common statements I hear from entrepreneurs is: "The market really wants my product or service." In turn I ask, "How do you know?" The response is generally something along the lines of "I met with a couple of potential customers and they said they were really interested." You can see where this is going. What does "really interested" mean? Are they willing to sign a letter of intent? Did they sign up to be beta testers? I find that people will often tell you what you want to hear. Entrepreneurs are optimistic by nature and will hear what supports their startup and ignore the rest. This combination leads to statements of certainty like "Customers can't wait until we launch." Really?

One of the CTAs that Cory and Jonny came up with was an intent to purchase (ITP) form on their website. With this CTA set up, Cory and Jonny then worked on the business experiment, which centered on the ITP form. The Trade Shades team came up with a number of business analytics that were tied to the CTA. One analytic was a question that was asked after the user filled out the ITP:

Which of the following most closely matches your interest?

a. That it is different.
b. That it is new.
c. That it is cool.
d. That it allows the changing of styles.

A positive result for this analytic is the answer "d."

Now you may be wondering how come it's okay to ask questions here but earlier I stated that surveys were useless at this stage. The reason is that here we are asking a question that is related to some call to action that a prospective customer completed. In other words, we are asking the customer questions related to why the customer performed some action. Surveys, on the other hand, tend to ask prospective customers questions about something they may or may not do about some product that may or may not be built. That is asking too much of the market and the results are unreliable.

There are many types of analytics that can be measured in a business experiment, including but not limited to web visitors, web conversions, positive language, and positive body language. A startup may end up with dozens of business analytics, which will be measured during the execution of experiments.

DEFINE PRODUCT

In his practice and research, Jacob has confirmed that regardless of the size of the organization it is important to test assumptions early on. He introduces the terms "preject" and "pretotype" to help the startup team manage innovation projects (see sidebar, "To Prototype or Not to Prototype?").

TO PROTOTYPE OR NOT TO PROTOTYPE?

Jacob's consulting firm refers to a "preject" phase that a new break-through innovation project goes through to test assumptions. In this phase, the team develops a "pretotype" that is far short of what a prototype would be. He described a meeting he was in where the team was struggling to convey an idea to the executive team using CAD drawings, so they decided to go with a part from a 3-D printer. The executive team quickly began to understand the value of the proposed breakthrough innovation project.

This "pretotype" reminds me of Eric Reis's minimum viable product (MVP) and is also similar to a learning prototype described in Chapters 9 and 10. In all cases, it is an early representation of the product or service that an entrepreneur presents to prospects and stakeholders. In order to run any business experiment, you must develop this type of early representation. The business experiment is intended to give the startup team a thorough understanding of how the market will react when they eventually launch their product or service. You don't do this through traditional market surveys and focus groups, which attempt to get answers to hypothetical questions about hypothetical products. You do this by simulating the value proposition through business experiments. We will discuss this further in the next chapter.

NOTE

1. Jacob Brix, "Improving Individual Knowledge Construction and Re-Construction in the Context of Radical Innovation" (unpublished working paper, 2013).

CHAPTER 12

VALIDATED LEARNING = KNOWLEDGE

As we discussed in the previous chapter, learning leads to knowledge. Ultimately, as entrepreneurs we want to launch a startup that will succeed. I was speaking with a former corporate vice president—a man with a considerable wealth of experience as a corporate executive and an angel investor. I will refer to him as Steve, as he is a very private person and I do not wish to impose on his privacy. Anyway, Steve and I were having a discussion on what startups should be focused on. In the past, I have heard Steve lecture on the importance of focus and execution, and while I always agreed with him on that, I disagreed with his take on what the focus should be on. Steve was always concerned with focusing on one market and looking at the bottom line. He tried to impose corporate management techniques on startups, which I believe led to many failures. Instead, as we have discussed throughout the book, the focus needs to be on building knowledge about customers, markets, team, capital, labor, and product. The approach should be centered on testing the validity of the most important assumptions.

The Pivot Startup approach discussed in Chapter 11 is a structured approach that an entrepreneur can use to construct knowledge. I am not proposing that this is the only approach, as I am always disappointed by books that tout their approach as the only viable option. Instead, I suggest that this structured approach has been vetted by over a decade's worth of effort in the real world and decades' worth of research in this area. The following sections outline how one goes about executing experiments to build knowledge.

BUSINESS MODEL

Before I get started outlining how to execute experiments, I want to emphasize that one key objective of the business experiment is to learn about the business model. You do this by essentially creating a market simulation that contains many of the key elements of a business model. Many of you have heard that term. If you are an entrepreneur who has dealt with venture capitalists (VC) or angels, then you have probably been asked about your business model. It's interesting to note that although a business model has been part of business from the very beginning, the term began to gain steam in the mid-1990s.[1] Since then, many experts have attempted to define a business model, which has led to so many definitions that most entrepreneurs are confused when asked, "What is your business model?" In the past, I have relied on the definition put forth by Henry Chesbrough and Richard Rosenbloom in their 2002 seminal paper on the subject titled "The Role of the Business Model in Capturing Value from Innovation: Evidence from Xerox Corporation's Technology Spin-Off Companies."[2] Richard Rosenbloom was a David Sarnoff Professor of Business Administration Emeritus at Harvard Business School (HBS) "whose teaching and pioneering research had a significant impact at HBS and beyond for more than five decades."[3] Henry Chesbrough is best known for his books on open innovation and is currently faculty director of the Garwood Center for Corporate Innovation at the Haas School of Business at the University of California, Berkeley. These two scholars identified the following six business model attributes:

1. Value proposition
2. Market segment
3. Value chain
4. Cost and profit

5. Value network
6. Competitive strategy

These attributes are straightforward, with the exception of value proposition, value chain, and value network. I covered value proposition in Chapter 7. I have often seen the terms *value chain* and *value network* used interchangeably, but they shouldn't be. Value chain refers to the internal structure of the startup required to deliver value to the customer. Value network, in contrast, refers to the industry and the startup's position in the industry that delivers value to the customer. The value network is often depicted as an ecosystem drawing with linkages between the players, and the relationships among all the players in the network are depicted through ellipses and arrows. See Figure 12.1 for a value network diagram of the pharmaceutical industry, which I created when I was doing an analysis of Big Pharma.

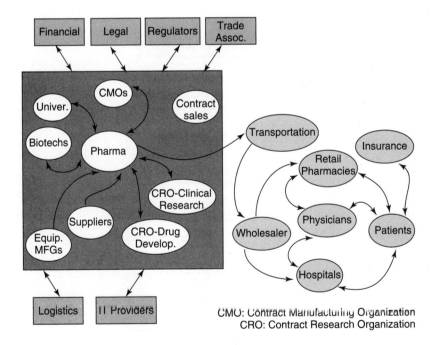

CMO: Contract Manufacturing Organization
CRO: Contract Research Organization

FIGURE 12.1 Value Network for Pharmaceutical Industry

When an entrepreneur first launches a startup, the startup is based more on business model assumptions than on knowledge. Many entrepreneurs are led astray to believe that all they need to do is fill in the blanks of some business model canvas and playbooks, and they are off to the races. In turn, entrepreneurs foolhardily fill in such playbooks with assumptions, which make them feel good but do nothing to improve their chances of avoiding the startup failure trap. A business model playbook, canvas, or table should be filled in with assumptions that over time are converted to knowledge. Put another way, these tools are holders of what you have learned, not an approach to constructing knowledge.

START EXECUTING EXPERIMENT

There are three pieces of information you need to start executing an experiment (see Figure 12.2). One is to determine which market

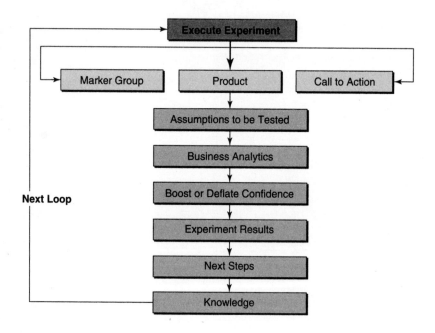

FIGURE 12.2 Execute Experiments Loop

group you will run your experiment on. The other is the product that you will show the market group. As discussed in the Chapter 11, a market group is a subset of a market segment. You should not attempt to test multiple groups under one experiment, as the results will be unreliable. For example, let's say that you develop a mobile app for orthopedic surgeons ages 28 to 40. A market group that you might run a test on is the orthopedic surgeons at a particular hospital in Manhattan, New York. Another market group might be orthopedic surgeons in a medical group located in Dallas, Texas. If you run one experiment and merge the results of the two groups together, you run the risk of failing to understand the differences between the needs of each group.

An example of a startup that is just beginning this process is Chase, an entrepreneur who is launching a startup named Green Energy Efficiency Solutions (GEES). Chase has developed a solar panel cleaning system that is waterless, inexpensive, and easy to install.[4] His Big XYZ (from Chapter 7) is:

> GEES will manufacture a solar panel cleaning system that contractors will buy for $800 and distributors will sell for $1,200 at a rate of 30 sales per month for the first year after launch.

There are three market segments that GEES is targeting:

1. Solar panel contractors (SPCs).
2. Solar panel distributors (SPDs).
3. Solar panel owners (SPOs).

EXECUTE: PRODUCT, MARKET GROUP, AND CALL TO ACTION (CTA)

Chase planned on creating what he called a "very rough prototype." As we discussed in the Chapter 11, this is an early representation of a product, which some experts call a minimum viable product (MVP) or a pretotype (or even learning prototype). In addition, he was going to run tests across all market groups at the same time and group the results. I suggested to Chase that he create a separate experiment for each market group, as combining results would skew or muddle the experiment. Chase felt that he could demo the pretotype directly to the SPC market group (contractors) and SPD market group (distributors). However, for the SPO market group (owners) he would create a video of the pretotype and display this video through his website to SPOs.

GEES had already defined the three market groups. The CTA is either a transaction or an early representation of a transaction. It gives the startup needed knowledge about the cost, profit, and value proposition. Chase came up with two CTAs, one for the SPC and SPD market segments and the other for the SPO market segment. For the SPCs and SPDs, Chase decided on having them sign an intent to purchase (ITP) agreement. For the SPOs, the CTA was to have them get their contractor to make the call to GEES. Here are the details of his first experiment:

- Market group: SPCs in the Albany, New York, area.
- Product: Live demo of a functioning prototype.
- CTA: Intent to purchase (ITP) agreement at a set price.

EXECUTE: ASSUMPTIONS AND ANALYTICS

In Figure 12.2 you can see that after you set the market group, product, and CTA, then you need to determine what assumption you are going to test. The assumption that was being tested was:

SPCs are willing to purchase a GEES system at a certain price to install on new solar panel installations.

There were also few business analytics to gather:

- The number of SPCs who viewed the demo.
- The percentage of SPCs who viewed the demo who signed the ITP.
- The level of positive language used during the demo.

For each analytic, GEES determined ahead of time what would constitute a validated result that would boost the startup's confidence about the assumption. The following was agreed upon:

- The number of SPCs who viewed the demo: 10 or greater would boost confidence.
- The percentage of SPCs who viewed the demo who signed the ITP: 50 percent or greater would boost confidence.
- The level of positive language used during the demo: Level 5 out of 10 or greater would boost confidence.

EXECUTE: CONFIDENCE, RESULTS, AND KNOWLEDGE LOOP

With the CTAs, product, market groups, assumptions, and analytics all set, GEES was ready to run the experiment through one loop. In Chapter 11, we discussed how knowledge is constructed through learning loops. Here Chase is ready to go through a loop. A loop is not one test on one assumption. It can be multiple tests on multiple assumptions, as with the learning loop process described in Chapter 9. In practice, I find loops to occur over time. By this I mean that a startup tends to wrap up a series of tests on several assumptions over a period of time. During this time the startup will learn a great deal about the customers, industry, competitors, prices, and markets by either boosting or deflating the confidence the startup has in the assumptions made. Some quantum physicists will tell you that we can never be truly 100 percent confident about an assumption. Instead, our confidence ranges between 0 and 100 percent without ever truly being 0 or 100 percent. Jacob, introduced in Chapter 11, is a bit of an expert on chaos theory, and he believes that startups are part of a chaotic system and that chaos theory applies. Regardless of whether you understand quantum physics or chaos theory, in my experience the idea that we are never truly 0 or 100 percent certainly rings true.

Figure 12.3 depicts how one can view a startup's confidence in its technical, market, resource, and organization (TMRO) assumptions. Even though we call these experiments business experiments, they

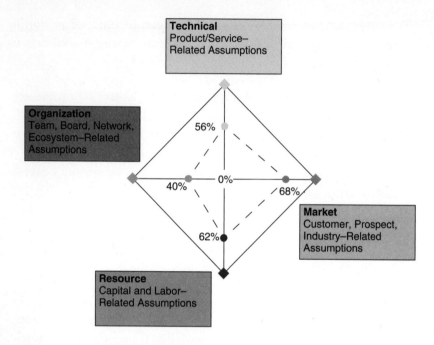

FIGURE 12.3 Diagram of Overall Confidence in Assumptions Across TMRO

can impact all of your TMRO assumptions. For example, during demos of your pretotype to potential customers, you may find that customers are drawn to certain features you assumed were not important, therefore impacting your confidence in technical assumptions. You may also discover that the capital needed to bring your product to market is higher than you assumed, therefore impacting your confidence in resource assumptions. How about organization assumptions? There was a time when I believed that the organization uncertainty that a corporate startup faced was much higher than what a regular startup faced. At the time, I focused my attention on organization issues that centered on the founding team, advisory board, board of directors, partners, and investors. I saw many startups fail because the founding team was at each other's throats a year into the startup's existence. Therefore, while I recognize that organization uncertainty was important, when compared to the issues a corporate startup faced, the complexity seemed to be lower. After years of mentoring startups, I no longer believe this to be true.

Instead, I believe that regular startups face high levels of organization uncertainty due to the interaction with the startup ecosystem in which the startup exists. I will go into the startup ecosystem at length in Chapter 15.

Now back to GEES's experiment. GEES ran the tests and ended up with the following:

- The number of SPCs who viewed the demo: 7.
- The percentage of SPCs who viewed the demo who signed the ITP: 57 percent.
- The level of positive language used during the demo: Level 6.

GEES wrote the following about the experiment results:

Our confidence in the assumption that "SPCs are willing to purchase a GEES system at a certain price to install on new solar panel installations" was boosted overall. We did have it somewhat deflated by our inability to get in front of more SPCs; however, we ended up with a higher percentage of ITPs and positive language than expected. Our next steps will be to run a similar experiment on SPCs in the Northeast and the Southwest.

After running several tests in the same loop, GEES wrote the following:

Our understanding of the needs of SPCs, SPDs, and SPOs in the Albany area is greatly enhanced. Our confidence was boosted with regard to our value proposition, market segment, value chain, value network, and competitive strategy. However, our confidence was deflated with regard to our cost and profit. Overall we gained a great deal of experience with prospects and the industry, and have a greater understanding of how we can deliver a product to the marketplace. However, there is a great deal more work to be done. We need to run several more loops to gain a greater understanding of the market segments across the country.

Over the years I have used Excel sheets to keep track of assumptions, experiments, tests, loops, and knowledge. It's doable but time-consuming and I find that information is lost. That's why we have developed The Pivot Startup cloud platform (www .ThePivotStartup.com). The software keeps track of all information, automatically calculates the confidence for each assumption, and generates an overall score for the startup. This overall score is an indicator of a startup's health. Startups that are working hard to construct knowledge and reduce assumptions obtain high scores.

BUSINESS PLAN

Creating a business plan and creating a startup are two very different things. A business plan is a snapshot in time that states where you are, how you got there, and where you are going. It is used to communicate the state of the startup to investors, board, and team. It is also used by many startups to participate in business plan competitions. A startup is not the business plan. A startup is an individual, or more likely a team of people, that is looking to commercialize a very novel invention or idea. A startup manages nonincremental innovation opportunities that are characterized by high degrees of uncertainty.

There was a time when a business plan was 20 to 30 pages long with an executive summary and appendixes. VC and angel investors used to ask for an executive summary, which was no more than two pages long. Times have changed, as most startups tend to favor more media-rich approaches to communicate the state of their startup. Many will create PowerPoint presentations, while others make use of platforms like Gust to communicate with investors (see sidebar, "Three Cool Startup Tools").

THREE COOL STARTUP TOOLS

Unlike the first time I launched a startup, today entrepreneurs have an amazing number of tools available to them. One of the best tools is Gust, an online platform where startups can create a startup profile, upload documents, and even create a video pitch. On its website (http://gust.com), Gust describes itself as "the global platform for the sourcing and management of early-stage investments." In a nutshell, Gust is an online service that connects startups with VCs and angels. Competing with Gust is AngelList, which can be found at https://angel.co. Both are essential for any startup. With this book, I developed an online platform (www.ThePivotStartup.com) that helps you manage The Pivot Startup process with your startup team, clients, board, or anyone else.

Many argue that a business plan is an essential part of launching a startup, yet many entrepreneurs never write one. Some studies have indicated that it can take as much as 200 hours to complete one business plan; my own experience with writing business plans supports this estimate. Why waste such valuable time on writing a plan for a startup that you know will change over time? Aren't entrepreneurs better served spending time speaking with customers and learning about the market? If business plans are a waste of time, then why do so many top universities, including Stanford University, supply business plan templates and business plan guides? An academic study at Babson College examined whether there was a link between the success of a startup and the writing of a business plan. The authors concluded that although they could not find a direct link, they were also unwilling to advise entrepreneurs not to write a business plan.[5] Another important study concluded "that business planning is a valuable activity, even in uncertain and ambiguous situations like firm formation." In fact, it went on to state, "Business planning may be a more effective tool during the start-up of a new business than during the maintenance of an established business."[6]

So, should you or shouldn't you write a business plan? I believe we are focusing on the wrong question. Whether you write a business plan is not as important to the success of your startup as the activities that take place prior to and during the writing of any plan. If you approach your startup with a structured approach like The Pivot

Startup, then whatever plan you end up writing will be based more on knowledge and less on assumptions. I was at a meeting where an entrepreneur was practicing his presentation for a local business plan competition. The entrepreneur is a research scientist at RPI who has come up with a novel material to help bone fractures heal more quickly. At the end of the presentation, he was getting feedback on his nonexistent financials. He said he felt uncomfortable putting in financials, as he would just be guessing. I explained that most of his business plan was based on assumptions in all areas, from technical to organization. I went on to say that it was okay, since most of the other entrepreneurs in the competition were in a similar situation. The fact is that when an entrepreneur first launches a startup, most things are unknown. If he or she creates a business plan upon launch, then guess what—most of the business plan will be based on assumptions. Over time, however, if the startup is properly managed, the assumptions will be reduced and all future business plans will reflect this knowledge. One of my colleagues commented that a good business plan should help the entrepreneur ask the right questions and lead the entrepreneur in the direction of compelling experiments. I agree with this if we interpret "in the direction of" to mean that the business plan can help the entrepreneur outline the assumptions in all of the key areas. In other words, the business plan does not drive the experiments; it only helps outline the assumptions that will in turn drive the experiments.

Are you curious as to what to include in a business plan? It depends on whom you are writing the business plan for. If it is for a VC, then go to the VC's website and see if it has a template or sample for you to download. You can also search for any blogs written by partners of the VC and see if any of them address business plans. The same advice holds true for angel networks. If the business plan is for a competition, then all competitions supply a template for you to follow. Make sure that you hit all the points in the template. I find that most judges at a competition tend to penalize an entrepreneur who gets too creative with his or her presentation. The judges don't mean to do it; it's just that they have a judging worksheet that is based on the template, and when you get too creative, they have a hard time scoring you.

A recent search for the exact phrase *business plan* came back with 27.5 million results. There are more resources and opinions on business plans than you can ever possibly go through. You can add the following suggested business plan presentation outline to the 27.5 million. Every startup is different and has different capabilities and resources; therefore, the business plan should reflect that. For example, if Bill Clinton is one of your startup's advisers, then it would make sense to put the team slide up front in the presentation. On the other hand, if your startup is bringing a very complex and novel technology-based product to market, then you might want to create a couple of slides for the solution to highlight the technology.

- *Cover slide.* Make sure not to waste this slide with just your startup name. Put your name, contact information, and a 10-word or less description of your startup.
- *Startup overview.* In this brief overview of your startup, you might include when the startup was founded, what funding stage you are at, how much money you have raised, and whatever else is important to your startup and your audience.
- *The problem.* The problem is not the same as the market. You might have a medical device that helps detect early onset of blindness. In this case, preventable blindness that goes untreated might be the problem.
- *How big is the problem?* Using the preceding example, the size of the problem would center on the number of preventable blindness cases and the cost to society.
- *The solution.* Here is where you describe how your product or service helps reduce the problem. You might also cover intellectual property issues here.
- *The market.* I often describe the market as a set of three concentric circles. The largest circle is the overall market, the next smaller circle is the addressable market, and the smallest circle is the target market.
- *Marketing strategy.* This section describes how you are going to make your market aware of your product and how you are going to sell this product. The 4Ps still provide a useful framework—product, place, price, promotion.

- *Business model.* We covered this subject earlier in this chapter.
- *Competitive analysis.* Don't write that you have no competitors. You always have competition, from either competing solutions or alternative solutions.
- *Milestones.* This slide shows what you have completed and what you intend to complete next.
- *Use of funds.* If you are asking for money, then put down how you intend to use the money.
- *Financial projections.* Generally these will be three- to five-year projections. What investors are looking for here is that you understand the assumptions that drive your financials.
- *Team.* Don't just put down names. Write down key information as to why they are the right people to bring this solution to market.

NOTES

1. Christoph Zott, Raphael Amit, and Lorenzo Massa, "The Business Model: Theoretical Roots, Recent Development, and Future Research," IESE Business School–University of Navarra, 2010.
2. Henry Chesbrough and Richard S. Rosenbloom, "The Role of the Business Model in Capturing Value from Innovation: Evidence from Xerox Corporation's Technology Spin-Off Companies," *Industrial and Corporate Change* 11, issue 3 (2002): 529–555.
3. www.alumni.hbs.edu/bulletin/2012/march/obituaries-0312.pdf.
4. GEES is a real startup that is deploying the methodology in the book. However, certain information has been changed to protect some sensitive data and for learning purposes.
5. Julian Lange, Aleksandar Mollov, Michael Pearlmutter, Sunil Singh, and William Bygrave, "Pre-Start-Up Formal Business Plans and Post-Start-Up Performance: A Study of 116 New Ventures," *Venture Capital* 9, no. 4 (October 2007): 237–256.
6. Frédéric Delmar and Scott Shane, "Does Business Planning Facilitate the Development of New Ventures?," *Strategic Management Journal* 24 (2003): 1165–1185.

CHAPTER 13

ENTREPRENEUR AND CORPORATE ENTREPRENEUR PERSPECTIVES: INCUBATION AND HYPOTHESIS-DRIVEN LEARNING

We (Lois and Gina) are back to offer our commentary on the Pivot or Incubation Chapters 9 through 12. In these chapters, it is clear that both corporate entrepreneurs (and teams) and the entrepreneur present proposals and plans that are laden with assumptions. While both types of entrepreneurs recognize the uncertainties of their situations, too often assumptions are ignored or not recognized and this leads to being "punched and knocked down," according to Remy, and, as Joanne states, requires the need "to ride the wave of chaos." Converting assumptions to knowledge about technical, market, resource, and organization uncertainties through experimentation is essential for both settings to avoid being ensnared in executing your way to failure. While the entrepreneur and the corporate entrepreneur have to face all four uncertainties, Remy highlights the importance of market uncertainty for the independent entrepreneur and Joanne reminds us that often it is the resource and organization uncertainties that come to haunt the corporate entrepreneur.

LEARNING IS THE ANTIDOTE TO UNCERTAINTIES

The basic point, though, is that learning is the antidote to the uncertainties. Learning is fundamental to innovation, and following a structured approach can help entrepreneurs avoid the traps of cognitive biases, overoptimism, and settling for the obvious, which often leads to weak businesses. Systematic approaches to learning and dealing with uncertainties are described for both the independent and the corporate entrepreneurship settings. The Pivot Startup methodology is proposed for the independent entrepreneur. The Learning Plan is recommended as the vehicle to address uncertainty challenges in the corporate situation. Both methodologies place importance on defining assumptions, executing experiments, and documenting what was learned. Iterative learning loops are also fundamental to each approach. Unbiased feedback is the holy grail.

Detailing what is really known and unknown to uncover assumptions that are sometimes overlooked and in other cases are latent or hidden because of our commonsense theories about the world is hard work. It requires a different sort of creativity than opportunity recognition. One needs to be on the lookout for the unanticipated "unknown unknowns" that are typically not thought about. Business experiments can help here. Yet, there is a reluctance to engage in them in both settings. The belief is that doing so takes too much time and money. But, as pointed out in previous chapters, this doesn't necessarily have to be the case.

LEARNING HOW TO LEARN

Being successful is about execution. But where does it make sense to put our full efforts in execution? To answer these questions, entrepreneurs and corporate entrepreneurs need to get out of the office and into the market or "out there," as Joanne and Remy have emphasized. They need to conduct experiments that systematically reduce uncertainties and address biases. According to Remy, most entrepreneurs are unwilling to proactively engage in experiments. Corporate entrepreneurs might be willing to conduct tests, yet they are predisposed to go to existing customers or those experts they know from mainstream corporate activity. When independent entrepreneurs do get out of the office, they are likely to end up chatting with customers. Both of these predispositions lead to doing biased experiments.

To move away from biased experiments, one needs to engage in action-oriented experimentation. This involves early representation of the product that allows the team to ascertain how a market will react to the product or service and the call to action, which embodies tests that highlight behaviors relevant to the entrepreneurial offering. In the corporate setting, the value of using coaches who continually challenge assumptions and help with designing experiments and the importance of exploratory marketing analysis are highlighted. Each of these roles can be deployed as an antidote to biases.

The nuanced differences between experimentation in the corporate setting and in the independent venture setting have to do in part with the differences in the fundamental drivers of engagement. While independent entrepreneurs are intent on building a business they don't have the time or luxury to focus on the organization, roles, and responsibilities per se. Their real driver is the initial product or service they need to get accepted in the market in order even to have the chance to build the business. In the corporate world, there are typically more options under consideration in terms of applications, so the early representation of a product is more in the form of a learning or concept prototype than a product prototype. Even startups are starting to reap the benefits of "pretotypes."

PIVOT STARTUP METHODOLOGY
AND LEARNING PLAN

The Pivot Startup methodology is centered on the assumptions that drive a startup. Its structured approach is aimed at helping entrepreneurs construct knowledge that helps them out of the mist of uncertainty about the startup. It leads to exploring the definition of markets based on the three types of markets the entrepreneur needs to fully understand—the overall market, the addressable market, and the target market. The methodology stresses the importance of experimentation to uncover how the market will react when the startup product or service is fully launched. Testing differences among market group behaviors will point the way about where to target. The call to action asks potential customers to do something or comment on something, which will indicate behavioral alignment with the product and show active interest in the product or service.

Emphasis is placed on getting entrepreneurs to go out into the world and begin understanding the ecosystem in which they may launch their startup. Although the experiments appear to be focused on evaluating the business model, they are much more. Unlike the corporate entrepreneurs, who may have a wealth of information about industries and markets at their fingertips, the entrepreneur generally does not. In Chapters 11 and 12, Remy proposed that an effective and structured way of gaining insight into the value networks and their place in the value chain is to create business experiments in these networks. This structured approach, therefore, does more than just give the entrepreneur insights about the market assumptions; it also helps validate technical, resource, and organization assumptions. How can the startup fit into its ecosystem?

The Learning Plan is specifically directed at higher-uncertainty projects, including evolutionary and breakthrough innovation ones, as Joanne continues to reinforce. The questions driving learning through experimentation are: How can this move us toward visions of a future world? How does this fit in with sociological and market trends? Incubation and the Learning Plan have different challenges than those of Incubation and The Pivot Startup. They operate at the program level, where an Incubation competence is focusing on a portfolio of projects going through Incubation and reducing uncertainties, and at the project level, where a particular opportunity is subjected to the Learning Plan. While detailing market complexities and market learning is important, experiments providing insight into adjacent markets and market creation are the challenge. How can the venture be leading-edge and deliver on a strategic intent?

In The Pivot Startup methodology, if an assumption with an importance of 10 is unable to be validated, then the startup needs to Pivot. However, there are additional considerations, including the strategy signed off on by the board of directors, board of advisers, angels, and/or venture capitalists. Furthermore, since startups are usually lean on resources, they need to consider whether they have the capabilities or resources to redirect. In the case of the corporate entrepreneur, projects can also change course. However, there is an additional complexity when there are several projects in Incubation; a critical assumption not being validated in one project can lead to the project being dropped and cause the Incubation portfolio to redirect its focus onto another project and another corporate entrepreneur. At the project level, if the feedback and reflection on learning do not suggest abandonment, then the team can proceed ahead and Pivot to Propel through Acceleration. On the other hand, the opportunity might not be ready yet, so the team Pivots by recasting or redirecting the project back to Discovery or through more Incubation learning loops first.

MAKING THE CASE FOR INVESTMENT

The goal of the Learning Plan is to find the right business model for the opportunity and also to provide an understanding of how it aligns or fits with the corporate context. Incubation helps you arrive at a business model and entry strategy. Late incubation prepares the opportunity for the transition to acceleration through conducting a final learning loop aimed at developing the concept proposal that can be used for gaining substantial investment for the future. Similarly, the goal of The Pivot Startup is finding the right business model for the opportunity and also to provide an understanding of how the startup aligns or fits in with the startup ecosystem and broader value network. At this stage some would say it's time to write a business plan. There is a debate, however, about how much effort should go into writing and executing the plan. After all, a plan can be the nemesis of fully achieving an entrepreneurial opportunity. While plans and also proposals are good for helping one to ask excellent next questions, they are just that: blueprints for the next stage of learning and reflection to validate knowledge that will be a sound basis for execution. Hmmm . . . will these uncertainties ever go away?

PART FOUR

PROPEL = ACCELERATION—THE BUSINESS RAMP-UP

PART FOUR

CHAPTER 14

ACCELERATION—
COURAGE TO INVEST[1]

You have made it to the other side of the "valley of death" and into a world that should be more familiar to you, product development. My goal was to get you to this point. Let's now focus on what you need to consider for making a smooth landing and ramping up your business.

Acceleration is all about propelling your concept forward, with sufficient momentum and investment to drive for success. Does your company have this courage to invest? I ask this because, when companies do spend the time experimenting and following the mantra of "learning per dollars spent," we often see that they lack the courage to make the more significant investments required in Acceleration. Or they starve these opportunities by providing only sufficient funds to keep them on life support. It is better to do nothing at all than to set these projects up for failure.

This chapter covers integration of the D-I-A approach with product development. It is not about the details of product development and phase gate processes since this information is readily available on the Internet. Our differentiation is about how to address higher-uncertainty innovation and make a smooth transition into the world of risk.

It is important that we complete the D-I-A framework with the Acceleration principles and tools. This will help you establish

225

a strong footing to propel your project in the right direction with the attention it deserves. Of course, I am making the assumption that you have secured the organizational support required to move forward. Even if not, this should be of value for the challenges you see in product development or to keep it on the back burner for your next opportunity—yes, as a serial corporate entrepreneur!

ACCELERATION PRINCIPLES[2]

In Acceleration, the objective is business growth. Whereas Discovery is about conceptualization of opportunities and Incubation is about experimentation to arrive at a development-ready concept proposal, Acceleration is about commercialization. Eventually, your project needs to grow to a point where it can stand on its own and compete for resources in an operational context. So how do we ramp up to a scale where this is possible? What does this look like for a corporate startup?

There are two key principles that are important to consider as you work though the stages of Acceleration. The first is that we are no longer looking to reduce uncertainties. That job is mostly done, and we now are embracing a new mind-set of risk. Of course, there is likely to still be a few residual uncertainties, especially in the organization and resource areas, but they are comparatively less than your experiences in Discovery and Incubation. The second is that we are also done with experimenting. It is time to set your technical and market specifications and start the development process. There will also be a few lingering uncertainties around scaling your product or solution to build the right foundation or growth platform for a family of products or even a new business area. In the end, we still need to be mindful that uncertainties do show up and then we need to determine how best to address them.

Moving from Uncertainty to Risk

As we learned in previous chapters, there is an important difference between uncertainty and risk. When we are dealing with uncertainty, the probable outcomes are not known and we use iterative learning to reduce uncertainties, one step or learning loop at a time. In Acceleration, we focus on risk because the probable outcomes are now known. I was in a coaching session in early 2013 and this exact topic came up. We were dealing with a project in product development. The project leader was calling the issues he was facing uncertainties, with his D-I-A mind-set. Yet he knew what the issues were. He could define the product and identify the probable outcomes. They were project risks. He also had uncertainties, but they were associated with the next generation of the technology and potentially new application areas. Once we sorted out the risks from the uncertainties, we were able to set the project on its right course. It is important to be clear on the definitions of uncertainty and risk to ensure we apply the best approach for addressing them. Thinking about uncertainty when it is risk creates the same project management challenges as focusing only on the risk and missing the uncertainties.

Moving from Experimentation to Development

Coming out of Incubation, you have developed your concept through your experimentation activities. The focus in Acceleration is turning this concept into a first product since it should be a road map for future market offerings. Remember all those applications still back in Incubation or Discovery. As you progress through Acceleration, you will work through iterations of your business plan from development to testing and validation to full production and market launch. Because you have reduced your uncertainties, you can now address the required criteria at each of the product development gates, described in the next section. These gates replace your learning loops and guide you in the evolution of your business plan and how to grow this into a business.

Therefore, the objectives for moving from Acceleration to operations are to:

- Ensure full integration with the product development process.
- Build a critical mass of sales support and establish the operational infrastructure for growth.

TABLE 14.1   Acceleration Focus Areas

Propel	*Acceleration* Commercialization Output = Business Plan
Technical Uncertainty Understanding technology drivers, value, and economic feasibility	Product Development Plan
Market Uncertainty Learning about market drivers, value creation, and business viability	Market Development and Sales Plan
Resource Uncertainty Accessing money, people, and capabilities internally and externally	Business Area Team Composition and Partnerships Aligned for Business Commercialization
Organization Uncertainty Gaining and maintaining organizational legitimacy	Organizational Commitment, Transition, and Final Home

Source: rInnovation Group

- Establish a market presence.
- Develop the management team.
- Work toward predictable sales forecasts, acceptable yields, and profitability goals.
- Mature the project to compete for resources and senior management attention on an equal footing.

See Table 14.1 for the Acceleration Focus Areas from Table 3.3, Innovation Business Opportunity Evolution, in Chapter 3.

ACCELERATION AND THE PHASE GATE PROCESS

In Acceleration, the project evolution continues across the technical and market dimensions and we keep a watchful eye on the resource and organization areas. On the technical level, we focus on the product or service development plan. We ask the question: "How will the enabling technology be converted into the right product based on what we learned from the market?" On the market level, we continue with the market development plan and integrate with it the sales plan. The question now is: "How will demand for this product or service be generated?" We also focus on product reliability and business scalability.

On the resource level, we focus on the team composition, ensuring that partnerships are aligned with our project's commercialization objectives and that we have sufficient funding to grow the business. On the organization level, our objectives are to ensure that the organizational commitment is in place, the transition issues have been addressed, and there is ownership of the project in a core business area (or support for a strategic business unit when moving into new business areas). The question here is: "What are the critical success factors for growth, and are they in place?"

Integrating with Product Development

As we make the transition from Incubation to Acceleration, we need to discuss where your concept fits in the product development process. We have seen the phase gate model implemented in different ways. The question of the fit between the D-I-A approach and phase gate models will vary based on implementation guidelines and strategic objectives.

The original phase gate model was Stage-Gate, introduced by Robert Cooper.[3] It has brought a necessary structure to the product development process that was missing in the late 1980s when I led a major service development project. What took us almost five years to implement could have been done in three to four years if we'd had this more structured process.

The objectives of the project were to implement a new database and signaling network to move from the analog to the digital world and thereby enhance our offerings for calling card and 800 services. Going back to uncertainty, we had low levels of market, resource, and organization uncertainty. It was a required enhancement for the market. We had a core team of 200 people and another 800 as part of our extended team, so there was no question about resources—people or financial. From an organization perspective, the strategic fit was clear. It was one of those must-do projects. While technical uncertainty was higher, we could have managed this with a more structured product or service development process. We did not need learning loops to test our market and other assumptions to evolve the technology.

There is a considerable amount of criticism about this phase gate structure being too rigorous. The effectiveness of its implementation is always in the details, yet the principles of stages and gates, as described in Figure 14.1, brought a much-needed disciplined approach to product and service development.

Debating the advantages and disadvantages of the phase gate process is beyond my objectives for this chapter. I do want to reinforce one very important point. Just as much as our D-I-A model is not appropriate for product development, the phase gate model should not be used for innovation opportunities facing higher levels of uncertainty. Through our stories in Chapters 9 and 10, you have read why different approaches are required, and I trust we have made the case for this. Thanks to this perspective, I was recently told, "It is great to meet someone who does not pray to Stage-Gate."

Of course, once the uncertainties are reduced, we do need to get a quality product or service out the door. We move from learning prototypes to product prototypes, from market probes to market launches, and so forth. After having followed the D-I-A model for innovation opportunity uncertainty reduction, companies drop into the product development process at Gate 1, 2, or 3 in the process flow. The point of entry depends on how they have implemented the product development process and on their level of maturity with the D-I-A model.

We universally agree that the Discovery and Incubation focus areas replace Stage 0, which has been introduced in recent years to

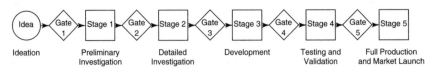

FIGURE 14.1 Stage-Gate Product Development Process

Source: Cooper (1993).[4] Stage-Gate® is a registered trademark of the Product Development Institute.

handle up-front ideation or early Discovery type work. Regardless of whether the entry point is Gate 1 or Gate 2, passing through Stage 1 of preliminary investigation and Stage 2 of detailed investigation should happen quickly and be more of a process check. Often, Gates 1 and 2 are combined as a quick sanity check. With Discovery and Incubation solidly in place, companies should be able to drop in at Gate 3, just prior to the start of development activities. Of course, with companies' aversion to risk, I suspect most will use Gate 2 or a "ready for Stage-Gate" session to ensure that all the development requirements are in place, before moving into Stage 3 of development. Regardless of how this is done, this review should be a process check, not a rethinking of what was done. With a collaboration model for transition and resisting the urge to adopt a "not invented here" (NIH) mind-set, this will position the project well for a successful development outcome.

Before leaving the product integration requirements, it is worth pointing out that we have changed the sequencing, or rather the philosophy behind market launch, with the D-I-A approach. We do pursue market launch activities in Incubation in the form of concept launches or other techniques, as described in Chapters 9 and 10. Our goal is to initiate the market development process early, especially for opportunities that require market creation work. This is unlike the product development process, where the product is developed and then moves to full production and market launch. In fact, in some phase gate processes, market testing is optional prior to market launch or the market information comes from product managers and developers. As such, the only testing is around technical validity, reliability, and scalability testing. Whether this is a good practice when dealing with incremental innovation concepts is one thing, but skipping market tests is the kiss of death for evolutionary and breakthrough innovation ones!

It is important to acknowledge that in Cooper's book *Winning at New Products*[5] there is market investigation in the early stages. However, based on our company experiences, the nature of market investigation comes more from the voice of the customer than from the voice of the market or the future. It comes down to validating (or not) what is already known, since the markets are clearer and the uncertainty is low.

I will leave you to consider how you have implemented your phase gate process and then decide where the D-I-A uncertainty reduction model fits. I also want to make one very important point. The overriding assumption is that you have reduced your uncertainty sufficiently to smoothly transition your concept to the product development process. However, for those concepts that do not fit with your business units, you will likely not be able to easily transition.

We are finding that, depending on your industry and what uncertainty means to you, integration comes in many forms. Some companies are able to use the D-I-A model to bring generational growth platform thinking to their phase gate processes. They do this by featuring the business vision prominently to always be considering the application migration path. This is more likely for concepts that are not too far removed from the core business. For others, where new business areas are emerging, they might need more of a business-building capability in Acceleration, rather than a product development process. You would benefit by reading Chapter 5 in the *Grabbing Lightning* book,[6] referenced earlier, for how to deal with opportunities that would typically be of a new business-building nature.

THE ACCELERATION TOOLKIT

With the Acceleration principles for business growth in mind, the Acceleration Toolkit has been developed to help you consider how to propel your concept forward in Acceleration and ensure it has a smooth landing in your product development process. The focus is on your first product, service, or solution, but we also want to keep in mind the applications back in Incubation or even Discovery. By the end of Acceleration, you will be at full production and market launch and considering what comes next.

Standard Tools

The Acceleration Toolkit is also available on our website at www .innovation2pivot.com. I hope you found value with the Discovery and Incubation tools and will continue using these tools for your next opportunities. The goal now is to ensure that your opportunity integrates well with the product development process. The following tools make up the Acceleration Toolkit, and descriptions follow:

- Resource and Organization Alignment Plan.
- Market and Technology Development Integration Plan.
- Propel or Acceleration Value Pitch.

Resource and Organization Alignment Plan

Are you wondering how to keep on top of your resource and organization issues? We know these carry through to Acceleration and are not well integrated with the product development process. The Resource and Organization Alignment Plan in Figure 14.2 provides you with a list of areas to consider for ensuring that resources and expectations are aligned with your project objectives.

Market and Technology Development Integration Plan

Are you wondering how to integrate the market and technical areas you covered in Incubation with product development requirements? This tool in Figure 14.3 will help you to be clear on what you have accomplished and how it fits. The "not invented here" (NIH) syndrome is alive and well in most companies. You do not want to have to repeat the tests you have already done!

Discussion points with stakeholders

- ❑ The potential of the opportunity for business growth
- ❑ Completeness of the marketing plan
- ❑ Expected pace of development of the market
- ❑ First application and application migration plan
- ❑ Level of demand/sales forecast for the first year and projected revenue
- ❑ Acceptability of the final business model and revenue sharing in the value chain
- ❑ Appropriate milestones and measures of success

FIGURE 14.2 Resource and Organization Alignment Plan
Source: rInnovation Group

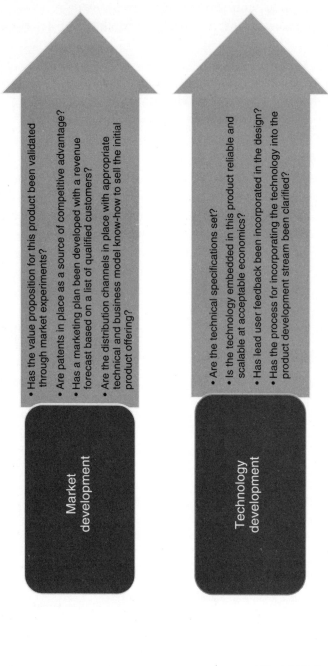

FIGURE 14.3 Market and Technology Development Integration Plan

Source: rInnovation Group

Market development
- Has the value proposition for this product been validated through market experiments?
- Are patents in place as a source of competitive advantage?
- Has a marketing plan been developed with a revenue forecast based on a list of qualified customers?
- Are the distribution channels in place with appropriate technical and business model know-how to sell the initial product offering?

Technology development
- Are the technical specifications set?
- Is the technology embedded in this product reliable and scalable at acceptable economics?
- Has lead user feedback been incorporated in the design?
- Has the process for incorporating the technology into the product development stream been clarified?

Propel or Acceleration Value Pitch

Are you wondering how to position your value pitch in Acceleration? The tips from Chapter 6 remain the same. We continue to change the content as we learn more about the product and market positioning, as described in Figure 14.4. Remember that you and other key stakeholders should be able to deliver the same value pitch. This is particularly important because you are now being integrated into the mainstream business. This pitch will become a key input to your business plan, covered later in this chapter.

Advanced Tools

As with Discovery and Incubation, we have also designed more advanced tools for the innovation professional, such as the Acceleration Phase Gates, Acceleration Questions, Acceleration to Operations Transition List, and Business Plan Template. Once you have mastered our standard tools, then you can move to these more advanced tools available on our website.

Acceleration Phase Gates: This tool covers the steps to be considered in the early, middle, and late stages of Acceleration. These stages are aligned with development, testing and validation, and full production and market launch.

Who: Identify Targeted Stakeholder.

What and Why: Primary Messages (The "Wow" Factor)

1. Describe product, service, or solution features and benefits (from the customer's perspective, not in technology terms).
2. Identify why it is important for the market and company (market positioning, competitive advantages, to deliver on business strategy, etc.).
3. Reinforce the product, service, or solution value proposition and business model (via feedback from market tests).
4. Describe how market demand will be generated and the critical success factors for market growth and legitimacy within company.
5. Provide your financial forecasts (revenues, sales, payback, margin, profit, etc.). Communicate the numbers that are important to build legitimacy in your company.

FIGURE 14.4 Value Pitch Checklist for Propel

Source: rInnovation Group

Acceleration Questions: These more in-depth questions help you to address your technical, market, resource, and organization risks. They are designed to ensure that your integration with the product development process goes well and your project has the right foundation for growth.

Acceleration to Operations Transition List: This list ensures that all the appropriate Acceleration issues have been considered to increase the chances for a successful transition from Acceleration to operations. It will help with completing your business plan and reinforcing your business strategy for growth, building confidence in the operations plan, and navigating the organizational alignment process.

Business Plan Template: A more formalized business plan is an important requirement to move through the product development process. It will go through multiple iterations through development to market launch. The business plan will provide the rationale for moving your project from Acceleration to operations.

PROPEL YOUR VALUE PITCH: MAKING THE TRANSITION TO OPERATIONS WITH YOUR BUSINESS PLAN

Now it is time to put together your organizational story for why your project is on a good trajectory for growth and is ready for operations. This is your business plan, developed from the elements that make up your value pitch and what you have developed during Acceleration, as follows:

- *Clear market value proposition*. Provide clear evidence for how your first product, service, or solution has been validated with customers, with any partners, and in your company based on your market launch.
- *Compelling business strategy*. Reinforce through your market development and launch activities how your initial market offering has positioned the company well for growth into multiple generations of products, services, and/or solutions. Link this with your market and competitive positioning and your company's strategic planning.

- *Strength of market and competitive positioning.* Describe how your product is positioned in terms of pricing model, sales support, distribution channels, and so forth, compared with your competition. Provide your sales forecast and time to breakeven point and profit, if these have not been reached yet. It is now time for profit and loss (P&L) management.
- *Confidence in the operations plan.* Be confident in your business strategy for growth and that your project is ready for operations. Make the case for why it is time for your product management people to take this over.
- *Identification of risks.* Be clear on any remaining business risks. There should not be many but there will likely be a few, especially around market positioning of follow-on application areas and staffing. We want these identified up front so we can manage them in operations.

Are you *now* ready to Propel your value pitch to operations based on your business plan for growth?

As corporate entrepreneurs, our journey is now complete. You have *planted* a business vision, *pivoted* to test your business concept options, and *propelled* your concept forward to achieve commercial success. I hope you also now have caught the bug to be a serial corporate entrepreneur. We need you to build innovation into a discipline that more companies will embrace. Our future depends on it.

In Chapter 15, Remy covers the entrepreneur's challenges in scaling a startup. In Chapter 16, Lois and Gina compare our independent entrepreneur and corporate entrepreneur perspectives on the challenges of growth.

NOTES

1. Material for this chapter is drawn from Rensselaer Polytechnic Institute (RPI) Phase I and II research; Richard Leifer, Christopher M. McDermott, Gina Colarelli O'Connor, Lois S. Peters, Mark Rice, and Robert W. Veryzer, *Radical Innovation: How Mature Companies Can Outsmart Upstarts* (Boston: Harvard Business School Press, 2000); and teaching, training, and coaching experiences.

2. Gina C. O'Connor, Richard Leifer, Albert S. Paulson, and Lois S. Peters, *Grabbing Lightning: Building a Capability for Breakthrough Innovation* (San Francisco: Jossey-Bass, 2008), chap. 5.

3. Robert Cooper, "Stage-Gate System: A New Tool for Managing Products," *Business Horizons* (May–June 1990): 44–54. The term *Stage-Gate* was first used by Cooper in the *Journal of Marketing*, spring 1988 issue.

4. Robert Cooper, *Winning at New Products: Accelerating the Process from Idea to Launch*, 2nd ed. (New York: Perseus/Basic Books, 1993). Note: The first edition in 1986 did not reference Stage-Gate.

5. Ibid.

6. O'Connor et al., *Grabbing Lightning*.

CHAPTER 15

PREPARING FOR GROWTH

In 1999, the dot-com bubble was filling up with one startup after the other. One of these startups, which I will refer to as ScaleNow.com, was experiencing tremendous growth. It was consistently ranked in the top 20 Internet sites for traffic. It was a content portal with die-hard members. The content was considered second to none in its niche and it had some seasoned publishing executives on board. It had begun acquiring companies left and right, and it was ruthless to the acquired executives. On the other hand, ScaleNow.com treated its own executives quite well. It bought its executives the most expensive chairs, threw them lavish parties, and even loaned them money to purchase real estate. It was scaling its operations on all levels and increasing the number of products it offered (scope). Within 12 months, however, it would be free-falling and selling off assets. Its executives managed to do well, but the rank and file had to scramble. It is a sad tale of mismanaged growth that I unfortunately had to see firsthand.

Assuming that the startup successfully executed the first two phases, Plant and Pivot, the next and equally demanding phase for the startup is Propel. Figure 15.1 depicts common startup growth curves. The dashed line is the classic hockey stick curve that every startup dreams of and every investor is skeptical of. It shows the startup losing money early on and then growing exponentially. The solid line

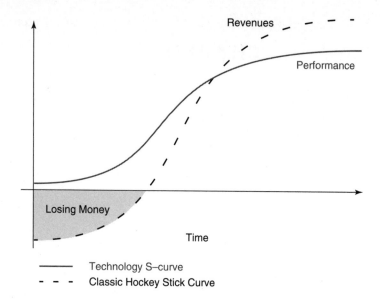

FIGURE 15.1   Classic Startup Growth Curves

is the technology S-curve, which shows the performance improving over time. These curves are useful for understanding what the startup is trying to achieve, but the reality is quite different. As the startup enters the Propel phase, it begins to scale its operations and increase the scope of its product lines. Issues associated with scale include, among other things, increasing the size of operations, employee base, manufacturing capacity, and server capacity. Issues associated with scope generally include increasing product line, marketing, and sales. The Propel phase is fraught with risk that can and usually does bring a startup to its knees. In the Plant and Pivot phases the entrepreneur is focused on reducing uncertainty across all dimensions—technical, market, resource, and organizational. The entrepreneur is attempting to find the best market fit for the startup's product. As the startup enters the late stages of the Pivot phase and enters the Propel phase, it is focused on finding the best scalable business model for the chosen application or market domain and then scaling into a large firm.

One of the reasons startups stall has to do with the environment in which the startup is launched, known as the startup ecosystem, which if unhealthy may stall a startup's progress. Another reason is premature scaling, where, like ScaleNow.com, the startup increases scale and scope before it is capable of managing growth and reaping the benefits.

THE STARTUP ECOSYSTEM

What is the first thing that comes to mind when you see the word *entrepreneurship*? I bet it is Silicon Valley. In my lifetime, entrepreneurship and Silicon Valley have been joined at the hip and for good reason. Silicon Valley has produced world-class startups like Google, Yahoo!, and Apple. Although we all know or should know that there are other startup ecosystems that produce world-class startups, we probably attribute more startups to Silicon Valley than we do to any other location in the world. But this is changing. According to the Startup Genome project report on startup ecosystems, the trend of startups emerging mainly from Silicon Valley has ended, and there has been "an explosion in the rise of new startup ecosystems around the world, and a new found [*sic*] maturity in others."[1] The report generates a ranking of the top 20 startup ecosystems based "more than 50,000 startups around the world."[2] Although there is no surprise at Silicon Valley ranking number one, there are many surprises in the top five, which include Tel Aviv, Los Angeles, Seattle, and New York City. Where is Boston or the Research Triangle? Times have definitely changed.

I love this report, because it challenges our thinking and assumptions while making us consider the factors that drive a healthy startup ecosystem. It is important for the entrepreneur to understand these factors as they affect the startup's organizational uncertainty. As we have previously discussed, when a startup brings a product to market, the startup is innovating. Investigating an ecosystem's startup capacity is closely tied to investigating the ecosystem's innovation capacity, which in turn is driven by the quality of the ecosystem's business environment. According to Michael Porter, an expert on the competitiveness of regions, there are four "structural and environmental conditions that contribute to the region's innovative capacity."[3] I find Porter's model[4] to be a great way to understand a region's competitiveness, and many of the elements are applicable to a startup ecosystem.

- *People, infrastructure, and capital.* The presence in the area of quality human capital, technologies, infrastructure, banks, angels, and venture capitalists.
- *Markets.* The presence of customers for startups to run business experiments on.
- *Competition.* The presence of other startups in a similar area leads to better products, investments, intellectual property (IP), and growth.
- *Suppliers.* The presence of suppliers to the startups in the region fosters improved understanding of the value chain and networks needed to compete.

In order for a startup ecosystem to grow, it needs to have quality people that it can form teams with; the infrastructure (information technology [IT], roads, airports, etc.) to facilitate startup activities; markets to sell to; and suppliers to work with. In addition, Porter points to governments, collaborative institutions, and attitudes[5] as having an impact. If you look to Silicon Valley, historically it has had:

- The support of the government with high levels of R&D funding.
- Formal and informal networks that universities and business leaders have developed and continue to support. Aspiring entrepreneurs can turn to these networks for mentoring, funds, and resources.
- Strong entrepreneurship attitudes in government, university, and business settings.[6]

Finally, Ravi G. Gupta, an expert at starting technology ventures, argues that there are eight organizational characteristics that need to be developed for an innovation ecosystem to thrive.[7] I have reduced these eight characteristics to six and applied them to the startup ecosystem as follows:

- *A unique strategy.* The startup ecosystem must offer something unique that draws startups to the region and keeps talent in the region.

- *Strong leadership.* University presidents, government officials, and business heads must demonstrate leadership to develop a region's startup ecosystem.
- *Long-term commitment.* Slogans need not apply. It is about committing resources and people to developing the startup ecosystem. Silicon Valley started its development in the 1950s and never looked back.
- *Benefits for the whole community.* It's not about creating a bunch of silos and wannabe heroes. It's about thinking about what is best for the community at large. Silicon Valley was able to accomplish this by leveraging Stanford University's resources to foster entrepreneurship, which helped keep talent in the region and improve Stanford's reputation.
- *Culture that supports the region's innovation strategy.* A Boston formal business culture would not do well in Silicon Valley and vice versa. The business culture needs to support the startup ecosystem's strategy to innovate.
- *Ongoing evaluation and adaptation.* Silicon Valley is aware of its standing in the world and is constantly trying to improve.

When I was launching my second startup back in 1995 and 1996, I got to see firsthand the positive effects of a robust startup ecosystem. As I wrote in Chapter 4, there was an area in Manhattan, New York, known as Silicon Alley where entrepreneurs gathered at cafés and offices. I would constantly hear entrepreneurs planning one dot-com idea after another in restaurants and stores. The net effect was an explosion of startups in Manhattan so big that the vacancy rate for office space at the time dropped to near-zero levels. The terms for office spaces were so bad that unless you were willing to sign a five- to 10-year lease, the real estate agents didn't even want to speak with you. An entrepreneur's best bet was to sublet space. In addition, there were clusters of startups that popped up in different areas. Along 20th Street right off of Fifth Avenue, digital imaging startups that could take your file and print it onto high-resolution paper or slides popped up everywhere. It was no wonder that these startups launched there, as the infrastructure for the broadband communications was in place, as well as a high-quality talent pool to work at these startups.

In addition, the suppliers for these businesses were located nearby. It's no surprise that the capital needed to launch and scale these businesses was located around the corner. The startup ecosystem in New York City was growing, but then came the dot-com crash and it all went away. Unlike Silicon Valley, which had been growing its ecosystem since the 1950s, Silicon Alley was only a few years old when the bubble burst. Therefore, it could not handle the crash. It would take another 10 years before New York City's startup ecosystem would rebound.

UNIVERSITY ECOSYSTEMS

As we can see from the preceding discussions, universities play a key role in a startup ecosystem. What about the universities' own startup ecosystem? How can a university play a productive role if it has a dysfunctional internal startup ecosystem? I believe that a university can't fully support a region's startup ecosystem unless it has a solid ecosystem. For example, when I joined Rensselaer Polytechnic Institute (RPI) as an entrepreneur in residence in 2011, I was struck at how the entrepreneurship ecosystem had changed in five years. When I was attending RPI, it was difficult for an entrepreneur at RPI to find other entrepreneurs there. I remember attempting to launch a startup and I felt that everywhere I turned, I was on my own. My professors were very supportive, but there was no one there to help mentor or work with my startup.

Partly as a result, the startup ecosystem in Albany, New York, was nonexistent at that time. There were a couple of VCs and a few experienced entrepreneurs, but there was no real ecosystem. I noticed a change in 2011. Dr. Gina O'Connor had become the director of the Entrepreneurship Center and her expertise with innovation gave her a unique insight into how to start elevating the startup ecosystem at RPI. Many of the elements that I mention earlier are also important in university startup ecosystems. What Gina provided was commitment and leadership. Her focus was on implementing programs that would improve the ecosystem throughout RPI. When I joined, I realized that in order to create a culture of entrepreneurship at RPI, we needed to implement programs that would give the students and faculty the capabilities and resources to launch startups. The culture at RPI could not be changed with some fancy slogans or incubator space; instead, culture would change only if people changed. People, in turn, were going to change only when they are given the capabilities and the resources to innovate. In addition, people change if they believe that their leaders are committed to the cause.

That's what I have been observing at RPI. As a professor, I have taught classes on startup management to give students the tools needed to launch and manage startups. As program director of the Entrepreneurship Center, I have developed startup workshops for students and faculty. I even created a "Teach the Teacher" course for training high school teachers to teach entrepreneurship. As I observe the ecosystem in the Albany, New York, area, I see hopeful signs that things might be moving in the right direction. The Albany Nanoscale College of Science and Engineering is actively encouraging and facilitating entrepreneurship.

In addition, RPI launched a peer-mentoring program for startup CEOs, which I managed this past semester. Not to be forgotten, the New York State government has put a lot of effort into stimulating entrepreneurship, including supporting economic development organizations. A little look back in history shows that in 1982 RPI provided the seed for entrepreneurial endeavors in the Albany area with the establishment of its incubator and the Rensselaer Technology Park. Since that time other institutions in the region have joined RPI in attempting to figure out ways to facilitate entrepreneurship. Fast-forward to today: RPI is engaging with the business community, and business leaders are stepping up to the plate to create incubators and lab space for startups. There is a long way still to go for Albany, New York, to challenge regions like Silicon Valley; however, it is hopeful to see so much effort from so many groups.

A TIME TO SCALE

One of my professors approached me when I was studying for my MBA with the question: "Remy, why do most startups stall at $5 million to $9 million?" It's a good question and one that may have some answers. Everett Rogers in his book *Diffusion of Innovations*[8] attempts to explain how the market adopts innovations. Rogers argues that the adoption of an innovation, like the iPhone, follows a bell curve model. Figure 15.2 depicts a generic bell curve with a time axis along the bottom. Rogers characterizes the customers in the market as innovators, early adopters, early majority, late majority, and laggards. Innovators are those who must have every new toy that enters the market. They are the ones who waited online when the first iPhone came to market. By contrast, laggards are the most skeptical type of customers. They don't want to take any risks, so they wait until everyone around them has the new product before they take the leap.

   To test this theory out with some popular startups, I used the Google Trends tool to find out the popularity of startups over time.

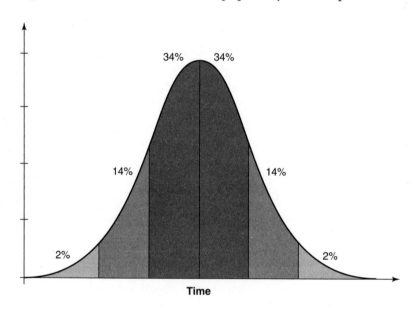

FIGURE 15.2   Generic Bell Curve

Google Trends is a tool that displays the popularity of a particular search term. I am using the popularity of a search term as a proxy for market adoption. I am comfortable with doing this, as marketing firms often use these types of searches to gauge the adoption of a particular product or service. The first search I performed was for MySpace. The result was a bell curve from 2005 to 2012, with a peak at July 2007. As most of you I am sure know, MySpace was the popular social network that preceded Facebook. I then typed in another Internet startup that soared in popularity and then came back down to earth—Friendster. Again we got another bell curve from 2005 to 2011, with a peak in November 2008. The idea that the product or technology adoption rate over time can be depicted as a bell curve is fairly well accepted in the entrepreneurship world.

Geoffrey Moore in his book *Crossing the Chasm* put a twist to Rogers's theory, noting that many startups stall when they get to the point in the curve that begins to quickly rise.[9] In other words, startups stall when they need to increase scale and scope rapidly. Moore argued that instead of the smooth curve, most startups experience a curve like Figure 15.3 and stall as if there is a chasm between those early

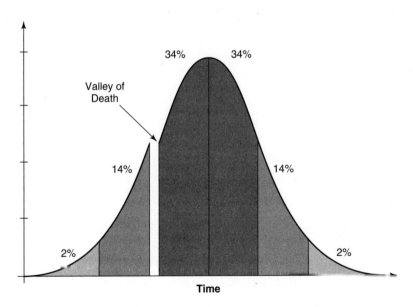

FIGURE 15.3   Valley of Death

adopters and the adopters who will help the startup rise up along the curve. Others call this hitting the growth wall or the valley of death (a slightly different twist from the corporate one of moving from research to the commercialization world, with Incubation as the missing link), where the startup is unable to increase both the size of the firm and the number of product offerings while simultaneously trying to control costs and improve quality. The stress that the startup team is under is so great that many startups are just unable to cope with the changes.

The Startup Genome project recently put out a report that attempts to answer the question of why startups succeed or fail. The report concluded, "More than 90% of startups fail, due primarily to self-destruction rather than competition. For the less than 10% of startups that do succeed, most encounter several near death experiences along the way. Simply put, we just are not very good at creating startups yet."[10] The reason I bring up this report is that it found that 70 percent of startups scale prematurely. It is one thing to have seen this happen in my career and to believe it to be true, but this report examined 3,200 startups and came up with the same conclusion.

An interesting point that the report made has to do with consistency of growth across all dimensions. The report concludes that startups that grow one dimension faster than the other dimensions tend to fail. The dimensions it references are different from the ones we use; however, I believe the concept still holds true. An example of premature scaling would be a startup that focused all of its attention on reducing the technical uncertainty, while not dealing with market, resource, and organization uncertainty. A symptom of this type of inconsistency might be a startup that is overspending on marketing to make up for the fact that it knows very little about the market.

As I read the Startup Genome report, I was impressed with how much the results support the concepts in this book. I put forth that if your knowledge across technical, market, resource, and organization dimensions is unbalanced, then that is essentially the point the report is making when it refers to inconsistency across dimensions. Throughout the book, I have discussed the importance of building knowledge across all dimensions. It is up to you, the entrepreneur, to make sure that you and your team become experts at bringing your product to market. To do this you need to identify the assumptions, test them, and build up the knowledge you will need to grow and scale. I realize that focusing on only one dimension may be easy, but it is also a surefire way to fail.

NOTES

1. Bjoern Lasse Herrmann, Max Marmer, Ertan Dogrultan, and Danny Holtschke, "Startup Ecosystem Report 2012," Telefónica Digital partnered with Startup Genome, 2012.
2. Ibid.
3. Remy Arteaga and Erica Coletti, "Entrepreneurial Growth: An Examination of the Entrepreneurial Growth Potential of Three of US's Top Entrepreneurial Hot Spots" (unpublished paper, 2006).
4. Michael Porter, "The Competitive Advantage of Nations," *Harvard Business Review*, March–April 1990.
5. Ibid.
6. Arteaga and Coletti, "Entrepreneurial Growth."
7. Ravi G. Gupta, "Eight Essentials for Success Lessons from Silicon Valley, Greater Boston, and Research Triangle," *Accelerating Innovation in Biotech, Life Sciences, and Hi-Tech*, May 10, 2003.
8. Everett Rogers, *Diffusion of Innovations* (New York: Free Press, 2003).
9. Geoffrey A. Moore, *Crossing the Chasm* (New York: HarperCollins, 1991).
10. Bjoern Lasse Herrmann, Max Marmer, Ertan Dogrultan, and Ron Berman, "Startup Genome Report: Premature Scaling v 1.2," *Startup Genome*, edited March 2012.

CHAPTER 16

ENTREPRENEUR AND CORPORATE ENTREPRENEUR: THE CHALLENGES OF GROWTH

We (Lois and Gina) are back to offer our final commentary on the Propel or Acceleration chapters, Chapters 14 and 15.

It is time to make an impact. You have vetted your business opportunity. Your technical, market, resource, and organization (TMRO) uncertainties have been explored, turned into learning, and provided validated knowledge about your opportunity. You are positioned to Propel. Reducing uncertainties ideally has resulted in confidence about pursuing a specific market or application space and business model. That business model has attracted initial customers—the innovators who, according to Remy (employing Rogers's view of diffusion), are those who must have every new toy. But that type of customer is not going to Propel you to grow. You need to attract a larger base of customers and build critical mass. Are the challenges of the goal of growth the same for both entrepreneurial and corporate startups? Well, yes and no.

THE ECOSYSTEM

On one level for both types of startups, successful growth is about aligning with the environment. But the environment is different for the two types. For many entrepreneurial startups, it is primarily the ecosystem in which they are embedded. The focus is often on leveraging that ecosystem to build a business. However, it could be the wrong environment—so then the issue is where to go. A university incubator or park or cosmopolitan area can be a nourishing environment for a new startup, but may not be the place to be when a large manufacturing facility is required. The point is that entrepreneurs should not assume that the best place to launch is where they live or go to school. Just like all other assumptions, where you launch should be tested prior to launching. In a new environment, there are new uncertainties.

For the corporate startup, it is also about aligning oneself with the environment. But this time the environment is the larger corporation. So how should you fit in? How will the processes that are appropriate for your business startup align with corporate standards and operating procedures that have led to corporate excellence? Does it make sense to create a new corporate division or business group, or is there an existing division or business unit that can take on the building of your new business, starting with your first product or service, and help it get to a critical mass? Each of these transitions will reveal new uncertainties. But can you really fit in with the company's strategic priorities? Maybe not. This will depend on your strategic intent and how far the company wants to stretch. If it is decided that your corporate startup is not strategically relevant, then you could consider a spin-out, which is aligned to a startup gravitating to a new community or ecosystem. You may have made these decisions in late Incubation or before the need to Propel. But often it is the very experience of growing the business that makes the appropriate landing zone apparent. For a corporate startup, a spin-out should be a secondary versus primary option, after serious consideration of how this business opportunity fits with the future direction of the company.

Entering into a different environment or ecosystem from where your business was born requires reevaluation and new activities that produce validated knowledge, essential for scaling the business in this new environment.

THE LAWS OF DIFFUSION AND RESISTANCE

According to Joanne, you have made it to the other side of the "valley of death" at the start of Propel and Acceleration. This valley is related to the ability to overcome the challenges of moving from a research to a commercialization world, with Incubation as the missing link. Remy, in turn, discusses "hitting the growth wall" or "crossing the chasm," where the chasm between early adopters and early majority is the challenge of Propel. It can also be another valley of death, yet different. The slight difference in orientation can be attributed to whether you are focused on a chasm caused by technology or market considerations or by resource and organization ones.

No matter the difference, in Propel there is likely to be a chasm brought about by some sort of customer resistance that must be overcome to grow big and make an impact. The early adopters are well-respected opinion leaders who find it easy to imagine, understand, and appreciate the benefits of the new product and business. These are the true believers who might have helped with sales or concept launches in Incubation or, at the very least, should be early targets as you begin to Propel. The larger target is pragmatists, those who deliberate before buying and must have real benefits demonstrated. They are important to entice because of their overlapping networks with other customer groups. Both the startup and the corporate entrepreneur must face the realities of new business and new product diffusion.

For the entrepreneurial startup, the resistance can come from the market or the startup's inability to scale. The corporate entrepreneur has to deal with two types of resistance: that of its organization and that of the market. Yes, each type of venture has some customers, but they probably have very different profiles, as indicated earlier, than those who will make the business grow. If you have a business that can demonstrate an order-of-magnitude improved solution compared to what is out on the market, with no increased price and no required change of behavior, you are lucky—resistance to adoption should not be a problem. But this situation is very rare. Most breakthrough, and even evolutionary, innovation opportunities will require people to give up their old ways and try something new. That is challenging. Old habits die hard, and people experience great discomfort in anticipation of change in status or recognition that their skills or capabilities are not up to date or are even becoming obsolete.

There is also the issue that your product or service may require replacement of legacy systems and new investment in infrastructure, making the initial cost of buying your product higher than antici-pated. Of course, your product or business is going to provide a great benefit, but often that benefit is delayed, compared with the initial cost. As Remy mentioned, instead of spending time on new product features and enhancing product scope, a mistake often made by the entrepreneurs he knows, it might behoove the startup to build a sales force or marketing organization that can address these issues and is suitable for the particular opportunity. For example, some high-tech products require a sales force that not only sells but also trains the buyer in the most effective way to use the product. Both types of startups face the challenge of managing the processes of adoption and diffusion of new products and businesses.

The corporate startup faces the previous problems but must also be concerned about how to integrate these new business opportuni-ties and align product specifications with the company's new product development processes. These processes have been honed over time for excellence and efficiency in the core business. For example, the mainstream business may require a product of 99.9 percent reliability and your new business will attract lots of customers even with 95 percent reliability. There are likely to be ongoing discussions of what is "good enough" (yes, this mantra could come back) for the first product to maintain the company's reputation in the marketplace, while at the same time supporting generational thinking. Future gen-erations will be focused on bringing costs down, adding new features, or even completely redesigning the product. There will be a clash with the company's pride of quality control. A compromise might be required to invest a little more in product development to meet the corporate requirement, as opposed to the market requirement that would have been the objective of the entrepreneurial startup.

Then also there will be the nonbelievers in the corporation—"This is not the kind of business we do"—or a mainstream existing business is growing and the prevailing view is that it is better to put the big bet and investment dollars in what is known and familiar. This harks back to the concept of innovation capacity and the priority placed on strategic intent. The corporate entrepreneur has to worry about not only the ecosystem capacity but also the innovation carrying capacity of the company at any point in time, which can change dramatically based on external and internal drivers.

SCALING

For the startup, scaling up to build a viable business is what Propel or growth is all about. For the corporate startup, as Joanne mentions, it may not be necessary to build a business per se. If the opportunity is not too removed from the core business, the challenge of growth and going from learning prototypes to product prototypes might be met by integrating the next phase of the opportunity development into the appropriate entry point of the company's phase gate or Stage-Gate process for product development. On the other hand, if the opportunity is really different from the company's core, then building a new business may be in order.

According to Remy, scaling is the phase where startups are usually brought to their knees. A business model might be good for innovators and early adopters but needs to be rethought for the larger customer base. Having given some thought previously into designing a business model that is scalable can go a long way. For example, choosing a labor-intense mode of product delivery might be okay for the first sales, but it is not likely to be effective for growth. Another issue of scaling is going for everything at once in a big way, as Remy describes was the case with ScaleNow.com. These issues will be similar for both types of startups when they need to build a business. Probably the temptation to scale too rapidly lies more in the entrepreneurial world than in the corporate one due to the pedal to the metal mentality that is still out there. In fact, we have seen the rate of scaling slowed down on the corporate side because of the organizational resistances described earlier.

BALANCING TMRO

In Chapter 15, Remy cites his own experiences and a report that found 70 percent of startups scale prematurely to reinforce the point that a balanced focus on TMRO is needed. Growing in one dimension has to be matched appropriately with the others. Scaling through enriching the scope of your product offerings has implications for resources and building the organization. However, Remy is not suggesting placing equal emphasis on each TMRO component all the time, as this would be inadvisable. TMRO has to be balanced in terms of the innovation capacity of the new business's environment and ecosystem. This often requires that both entrepreneurial and corporate startups focus on building critical mass in the Propel phase to address uncertainties related to the organization and resources. Yes, there are likely to be some technical issues—for example, how to best achieve production efficacy—but these are not likely to be the showstoppers that organization and resource constraints can bring about, as indicated by Remy and Joanne. What a shame if you have come this far and stall or fail because you do not scale at an appropriate pace or you mount an imbalanced approach to TMRO, given your operating context or ecosystem.

This completes the journey of the two entrepreneurial worlds and how they approach Plant, Pivot, and Propel. We hope you now have a good sense of how to Plant your business vision in Discovery, Pivot via your experiments in Incubation, and Propel to ramp up in Acceleration.

ABOUT THE AUTHORS

REMY ARTEAGA

Remy Arteaga is an entrepreneur with over 20 years' experience in commercializing technologies. Over this time he has spent most of his career on the early stage startup process, where he has founded and managed more than five startups.

As an entrepreneur, Remy raised millions of dollars in seed funding from angel investors, developed and negotiated investment agreements, built and managed startup teams, defined and negotiated licensing deals, and negotiated the multimillion-dollar acquisition deal of his second startup.

In his most recent experience, Remy helped launch a university-generated software technology startup, where he served as CEO for five years, before resigning to join Rensselaer Polytechnic Institute (RPI) as an adjunct professor, Program Director for the Severino Center for Technological Entrepreneurship, and Entrepreneur in Residence.

In his time at RPI, Remy has loved mentoring hundreds of students and aspiring entrepreneurs in The Pivot Startup methodology for managing startups. He finds inspiration in their pure enthusiasm and optimism.

Remy credits the experience early in his career at General Motors, where he helped create an internal new product development and innovation think tank, with giving him the tools to launch his first startup.

His most recent focus has been on the development and management of a startup management platform (www.ThePivotStartup.com) that will help those involved with launching and managing startups construct knowledge while reducing uncertainty. Remy specializes in working with startup firms that have the technical expertise to develop a great product but lack the experience to bring that product to market.

Remy received a bachelor of science degree in electrical engineering from the University of Rochester and an MBA from RPI.

JOANNE HYLAND

Joanne is the President of the rInnovation Group and former Vice President, New Venture Development, at Nortel Networks. As a founding partner in rInnovation, Joanne is working with major corporations to link innovation with strategy and to develop systems, leadership, and culture capabilities that drive growth and corporate renewal. The rInnovation Group works across diverse industries from consumer and industrial products to energy and pharmaceuticals. It has also developed a unique innovation tools platform to guide individuals and companies through its Discovery, Incubation, and Acceleration (D-I-A) methodology. The company's clients are Fortune 1000 and other more established companies headquartered in the United States, Canada, Denmark, Germany, and the Netherlands. Joanne speaks regularly on topics related to innovation and corporate entrepreneurship and is or has been a member of the faculty in executive education programs at Babson College, the Danish Business Institute, the Danish Technical University (DTU), Massachusetts Institute of Technology (MIT), Rensselaer Polytechnic Institute (RPI), the Industrial Research Institute, and the Tata Management Training Center in India. In the fourth quarter of 2013, the rInnovation Group will be introducing a unique innovation tools platform based on its Discovery, Incubation, and Acceleration (D-I-A) methodology.

At Nortel Networks, Joanne and her team founded its internal venturing program, a multimillion-dollar investment fund that resulted in 12 business startups, one of which, Bill Me Later, reached close to a billion-dollar exit in October 2008, when it was bought by eBay/PayPal. The Corporate Strategy Board, RPI, *Fast Company* magazine, and others have highlighted this leading-edge innovation program in reports, academic research, case studies, and numerous articles.

Joanne is a featured executive in the book *Radical Innovation: How Mature Companies Can Outsmart Upstarts* (Harvard Business School Press, 2000) and wrote a chapter in 2001 about "Using VC Experience to Create Business Value" in *From the Trenches—Strategies from Industry Leaders on the New e-Conomy* (John Wiley & Sons, 2001) based on her experiences at Nortel. She is coauthor of the chapter "Bringing Radical and Other Major Innovations Successfully to Market: Bridging the Transition from R&D to Operations" in the 2004 version of *The PDMA Toolbook 2 for New Product Development* of the Product Development Management Association (PDMA). In 2012, Joanne wrote an article entitled "What's Next—Strategic Innovation" for the International Society for Professional Innovation Management (ISPIM) Innovation Watch series (March 2012) and the *TMTC Journal of Management* (July 2012).

Joanne has held a variety of corporate and startup board roles. She graduated from Concordia University in Montreal, Canada, in 1982, with a bachelor of commerce (marketing major), and received the Marketing Medal for her academic accomplishments.

ABOUT THE ACADEMIC CONTRIBUTING AUTHORS

PROFESSOR GINA O'CONNOR

Dr. O'Connor is the Associate Dean, Academic Director for the Radical Innovation Research Project, Director of the Severino Center for Technological Entrepreneurship, and a professor in the Lally School of Management and Technology at Rensselaer Polytechnic Institute (RPI) in Troy, New York. She is also a founding partner of the rInnovation Group. Gina is a well-recognized thought leader in the field of innovation, having been widely quoted in *The Economist* and *Fast Company*, among other publications. Her fields of interest include new product development, radical innovation, technology commercialization, and strategic marketing management in high-technology arenas. The majority of her research efforts focus on how firms link advanced technology development to market opportunities.

Her articles have been published in *Organization Science*, the *Journal of Product Innovation Management*, *California Management Review*, *Academy of Management Executive*, and the *Journal of Strategic Marketing*, to name a few, and she is coauthor of the book *Radical Innovation: How Mature Firms Can Outsmart Upstarts* (Harvard Business School Press, 2000). Gina is coauthor of the chapter "Bringing Radical and Other Major Innovations Successfully to Market: Bridging the Transition from R&D to Operations" in the 2004 version of *The PDMA Toolbook 2 for New Product Development* of the Product Development Management Association (PDMA). Her executive education experience includes programs with companies such as General Motors, IBM, and Albany International, and she is consulting with others to help them develop, embed, and sustain radical innovation management capabilities. Prior to joining RPI in 1988, Dr. O'Connor earned her PhD in marketing and corporate strategy at New York University, and before that worked at McDonnell Douglas and Monsanto Chemical.

In 2008, the book *Grabbing Lightning: Building a Capability for Breakthrough Innovation* (Jossey-Bass) was released based on the insights from the second phase of RPI's research. This book won the *Strategy + Business* magazine Innovation Award as one of four most influential books for 2008, along with *Innovation Nation*, *Wikinomics*, and *Patent Failure*.

PROFESSOR LOIS PETERS

Dr. Peters is Associate Professor, Lally School of Management and Technology, Rensselaer Polytechnic Institute (RPI), New York; Area Coordinator for the Enterprise, Management, and Organization Group at Lally; and Director of the Technology Commercialization and Entrepreneurship Masters Program. As a board member of the IEEE Engineering Management Society, she organized three IEEE international conferences related to the management of technology and innovation. She was an invited visiting professor at the Max-Planck-Institute für Gesellschaftsforschung and has been an invited speaker in Japan, the Organization for Economic Cooperation and Development (OECD), European Community (EC), Latin America, India, China, and Thailand, among other places. In 2000 she received an IEEE Millennium Medal. She is also past board member of the International Trade and Finance Association, a past Principal Investigator of the RPI National Science Foundation (NSF)-sponsored Nanoscale Engineering Research Center, and a past director of the Lally School PhD program. In January 2010, the first Annual Global Conference on Entrepreneurship and Technology Innovation (AGCETI) was organized by Professor Peters and B. V. Phani of the Indian Institutes of Technology (IIT)–Kanpur, in India. She is a founding member of the Asian Entrepreneurship Association (AEA) and currently a member of the governing council of AEA. She continues to be an organizer of the AGCETI conference, the most recent one having been in December 2012.

Dr. Peters has conducted extensive research on technological innovation and entrepreneurship; on R&D globalization technological networks, including public-private partnerships; and on commercialization of emerging technologies. Her 1982 study, *Current U.S. University/Industry Research Connections*, sponsored and published by the U.S. National Science Foundation (NSF), marked the beginning of a research stream and consultancy on the role of the university in industrial innovation. Since 1995 she has been studying breakthrough innovation and is coauthor of *Radical Innovation: How Mature Companies Can Outsmart Upstarts* (Harvard Business School Press, 2000) and *Grabbing Lightning: Building Capability for Breakthrough Innovation* (Jossey-Bass, 2008). Current work on innovation includes institutionalizing breakthrough innovation through people. A recent stream of research in the latter area involves the role of emotions in the opportunity recognition process. Dr. Peters's work on breakthrough innovation provides a foundation for her research on decision making under uncertainty in the international context. She is part of a team of six (two of the collaborators are professors at the IIT-Kanpur in India) who built the Strategic Innovation Game

(SIG), an interactive digital workbook that is employed for education and research on entrepreneurship and innovation. Goals of this research stream are to investigate decision making under uncertainty, cognitive biases, and team behavior, especially international teams' behavior.

Dr. Peters teaches courses in business implications of emerging technologies, commercializing advanced technology, technological entrepreneurship, invention, innovation and entrepreneurship, corporate entrepreneurship, policy issues in energy and environment, and technological change and international competition. She has a PhD in biology and environmental health science from New York University.

ABOUT THE COMPANION WEBSITES

This book includes two companion websites, which can be found at www.innovation2pivot.com for the corporate entrepreneur and www.thepivotstartup.com for the entrepreneur.

The Innovation2Pivot is an opportunity concept development platform for corporate entrepreneurs, strategic coaches, innovation orchestrators, and the extended innovation community. It includes Discovery tools to transform your idea into a compelling opportunity concept to Plant your business vision; Incubation tools to guide testing of your assumptions in the market to Pivot to your concept proposal; and Acceleration tools to integrate this concept with your product development process and Propel your growth.

The Pivot Startup is a knowledge-building project management platform for entrepreneurs, consultants, business owners, coaches, and startups. The platform enables the startup to develop its business model, track assumptions and experiments, define market segments, and store startup knowledge and market interactions. It is a collaborative platform that allows the team to work together on the startup. It offers multiple reports that keep investors, advisers, and board members updated.

To receive these free benefits, visit the companion site that best matches you and your objectives.

INDEX